Carrickfergus Castle
COUNTY ANTRIM

View of Carrickfergus, *c* 1560 (BL Cotton Augustus I ii 42)

DEPARTMENT OF THE ENVIRONMENT FOR
NORTHERN IRELAND

Carrickfergus Castle

COUNTY ANTRIM

T E McNEILL

Lecturer in Mediaeval Archaeology
The Queen's University of Belfast

NORTHERN IRELAND
ARCHAEOLOGICAL MONOGRAPHS: No 1

General Editor

ANN HAMLIN

BELFAST: HER MAJESTY'S STATIONERY OFFICE

© Crown copyright 1981
First Published 1981

ISBN 0 337 08164 6

Contents

Foreword		*page* v
Preface		vii
List of Illustrations		
Figures		ix
Plates		x
Introduction		1
Chapter 1	The evidence of the documents	
	The Mediaeval Castle	3
	The Castle under the Tudors and Stuarts	8
	The Georgian and Victorian Castle	15
Chapter 2	The physical evidence	
	The Inner Ward	19
	The Keep	22
	The Middle Ward	27
	The Outer Ward	31
	The Gatehouse	34
	The Structures in front of the Gatehouse	38
	Summary of 1955 and 1962 Excavation Results	39
Chapter 3	The development of the castle	
	Periods I to X and their dating	41
Chapter 4	Discussion	53

Appendix 1	Excavations in the castle in 1955 and 1962	
	1955 excavation: stratigraphy	page 61
	1962 excavation: stratigraphy	68
	The finds from the 1955 and 1962 excavations	70
Appendix 2	List of 16th- and 17th-century maps and plans	85
Bibliography		86

Foreword

by David Mitchell
Parliamentary Under Secretary of State

During the 1950s the Ministry of Finance, in whom responsibility for monuments then rested, published a series of Archaeological Research Publications describing the results of important research projects. The present volume is the first in a new series of archaeological monographs produced by Her Majesty's Stationery Office for the Department of the Environment for Northern Ireland, which has been responsible for historic monuments work since 1976. The series is designed to present the results of substantial research projects, and the Department is greatly indebted to Dr T E McNeill for his important interdisciplinary study of Northern Ireland's greatest castle. It is, surprisingly perhaps, the first detailed investigation of the monument, and it is appropriate that the publication should appear at the time when the Borough of Carrickfergus has been celebrating 800 years of the castle's and town's history. I greatly welcome this volume and the start of the new monograph series.

Preface

My initial involvement with Carrickfergus castle arose from a study of Anglo-Norman Ulster, for its position in the Earldom was always as the dominant centre of politics and administration. I have received and depended on help from a large number of people over the years, which it is my pleasure to acknowledge here. First I would like to thank my wife for her support and tolerance. I have been able to discuss many general points over the years with Mr T G Delaney (whose recent death greatly impoverished the study of Carrickfergus) and Mr R H D Dixon. More specifically, I am grateful to Mr B C S Wilson and Mr S G Rees-Jones for making over to me their excavation notes and material; Mr Wilson had also gathered together more general notes on the castle. The history of the castle under the Tudors and Stuarts is based on work carried out for me by Miss Elizabeth Mullett, supported by grants from the Royal Irish Academy and the Department of the Environment, Northern Ireland. Mr Barrie Hartwell took most of the photographs used in this report, and many others besides, making a basic record of the castle for the first time. The account of the gatehouse is based on an undergraduate project by Mr C MacFarlane; Miss P Yee prepared a photogrammetric elevation of part of the inner ward as another undergraduate project; the general survey depended on Mr N McCarley at the other end of the tape. Mr P Bryan advised me on the building stones used in the castle. The section on the pottery found in both 1955 and 1962 could only be done after Miss S E Pollard had washed, marked and restored the potsherds and done much of the preliminary sorting and identification. I am grateful to the libraries and institutions indicated in the list of plates for permission to reproduce maps from their collections. Last but not least, I should like to thank Mr F Carlisle, the castle's custodian, for his many acts of courtesy and help throughout the last ten years.

This account is in four sections. The first two deal with the documentary and physical evidence (including a summary of excavations in the castle); the third seeks to establish the sequence of the development of the castle by period, and the fourth discusses the contribution of these periods to the use of the castle. The details of the excavations are to be found in an Appendix.

List of Illustrations

FIGURES

1	Carrickfergus: location map	*page* 2
2	Conventions used for periods in the plans	19
3	General plan of the castle at ground floor level (folded inside back cover)	
4	General plan of the castle at first floor level (folded inside back cover)	
5	Elevations of the probable former entrance to the inner ward	21
6	Plan and elevations of a gunport inserted into the west wall of the inner ward	21
7	Floor plans of the keep	23
8	Section through the keep, inner ward and east tower looking south	28
9	Details of the east tower basement	30
10	Floor plans of the gatehouse and sections through the gate passage looking west, north and east	35
11	North loop in the second floor of the west tower of the gatehouse	36
12	East window of the second floor of the east tower of the gatehouse	36
13	McSkimin's view of a triple arched opening 'over the castle entrance'	43
14	Reconstruction of the castle as it might have appeared in 1200	54
15	Reconstruction of the castle as it might have appeared in 1225	55
16	Reconstruction of the castle as it might have appeared in 1250	57
17	Reconstruction of the original exterior elevation of the gatehouse	58
18	Key to conventions used in the excavation sections	61
19	1955 excavations: general plan of the trenches	62
20	1955 excavations: section of trenches W8 and W9	63

21	1955 excavations: section of trench B1	page 64
22	1955 excavations: section of trench B5	65
23	1955 excavations: section of trench B2	66
24	1955 excavations: sections of trenches W2 and W5	67
25	1962 excavations: plan, sections and interior elevation of the postern gate	69
26	1955 and 1962 excavations: pots, nos 1–25 (x¼)	74
27	1955 and 1962 excavations: pots, nos 26–86 (x¼)	77
28	1955 and 1962 excavations: pots, nos 87–145 (x¼)	79
29	1955 and 1962 excavations: pots, nos 146–188 and clay pipe bowl, no 195 (x¼)	82
30	1955 and 1962 excavations: large pots (x⅛), tiles, metal and leather objects (x¼)	84

PLATES

Frontispiece View of Carrickfergus, *c* 1560 (BL Cotton Augustus I ii 42)

1 Plan and view of Carrickfergus by Thomas Phillips, 1677–85 (NLI ms 2557)

2 The castle from the south-west

3 The castle from the south-east, at high tide

4 The castle from the south, at low tide

5 The castle from the north-east, at low tide

6 The keep, inner and middle wards, from the north

7 The inner curtain from the south-west, showing the change of stone in the quoins and the original windows cut by gunports

8 The castle from the north-west

9 The south-west angle of the keep, showing its junction with the inner and middle wards

10 The keep and inner ward from the north-east

11 The keep from the south-east

12 The east side of the inner ward, showing the site of the first hall and of the original entrance

13 The east flank of the inner curtain

14 The third floor of the keep, looking north-west (Photo: B C S Wilson)

15 The north-west angle of the middle curtain showing infilled rock-cut ditch

16 The battlements of the keep looking south

17 The forework of the keep

18 The east tower at low tide

19 The west tower and gun platform

20 The outer ward and the gatehouse from the south

21 The gatehouse from the north-east

22 The east tower of the gatehouse from the grand battery

23 General view of the 1955 excavations (Photo: B C S Wilson)

24 1955 excavations: the junction of the broad and narrow sections of the middle curtain (Photo: B C S Wilson)

25 1955 excavations: wall 1 crossing the middle curtain and the outer curtain butted against it. Junction of outer and middle curtains marked by ranging rod (Photo: B C S Wilson)

26 1955 excavations: tower trenches, showing walls 1, 2 and 3 (Photo: B C S Wilson)

27 Decorated sgraffito sherds from the 1955 excavations

28 Seal-box lid from the 1955 excavations; lower face to the left, upper face to the right

29 Plan of the castle in 1811 (PRO WO 78/1158)

Introduction

Carrickfergus castle is a very complex building. It has been occupied continuously from its construction in the 12th century to its being given to the government of Northern Ireland as a historic monument in 1928. Few other castles in Ireland can show such continuity and yet have so much of the original fabric still visible. This preservation has not been a conscious act of policy: all the major military crises of Ulster's history down to, and including, the First World War, have left their mark on the castle. Given this complexity it is perhaps not surprising that although the castle has always been famous and is noticed in all general accounts of the antiquities of Ulster, it has never been even nearly completely described before. The only general description available until now was the brief and overtly preliminary Official Guide written by E M Jope in 1962. Of the three excavations conducted in the castle since 1950 only those carried out by D M Waterman in front of the gatehouse in 1950 have been published.

Carrickfergus is on the north shore of Belfast Lough, some ten miles north-east of Belfast (Fig 1). The Co Antrim shore of the Lough consists of a two mile wide strip of land of good quality, between the sea and a line of hills which rise to heights of 750 feet in places. These hills prevent easy communication by land from the Lough to the rest of Co Antrim except by the coast road to Larne or over the Carnmoney gap (between Belfast and Carrickfergus) which leads north-west to the valley of the Six Mile Water river and so to the Lough Neagh basin. The Lagan valley, the main route inland from Belfast Lough, was probably blocked by forest until the 17th century; only after it was cleared could the full potential of the site of Belfast be realised. Apart from its Gaelic name there is no evidence that Carrickfergus was occupied before the arrival of John de Courcy in Ulster in 1177. He conquered parts of the kingdom of Uladh, taking over north and east Down and south Antrim. He kept in touch with Dublin, Chester and his wife's father in the Isle of Man, by sea. The Irish royal site of Downpatrick was remote from his main centre of settlement around Belfast Lough, and it was dominated by the church. The site of Carrickfergus offered him the strategic base of a harbour close to the routes from the coast into the rest of Ulster.

This harbour was protected by a dolerite dyke running out from the shore into the Lough. This dyke provided the site for his castle (Pls 2–5), a platform of rock about 150 m long and 50 m wide, with most of it standing some 7 m above the level of high tide. To the east is an area of rock and sand exposed at low tide, but to the west was deeper, sheltered water. From at least the 16th century this has been the site of the harbour, but is now largely filled in for a car park. The rock is still exposed below the castle walls along the west and south sides; along the east it is mostly covered by a 19th-century granite plinth. The northern end of the rock where it joins the shore has been obscured by successive works culminating in the 1960s in the building of a wide road along the shore, the Marine Highway, cutting the castle off from the town. The surface of the rock does not seem to have been uniformly level originally. As will be discussed later, the eastern side of the southern half seems to have been some 3 m lower than the rest.

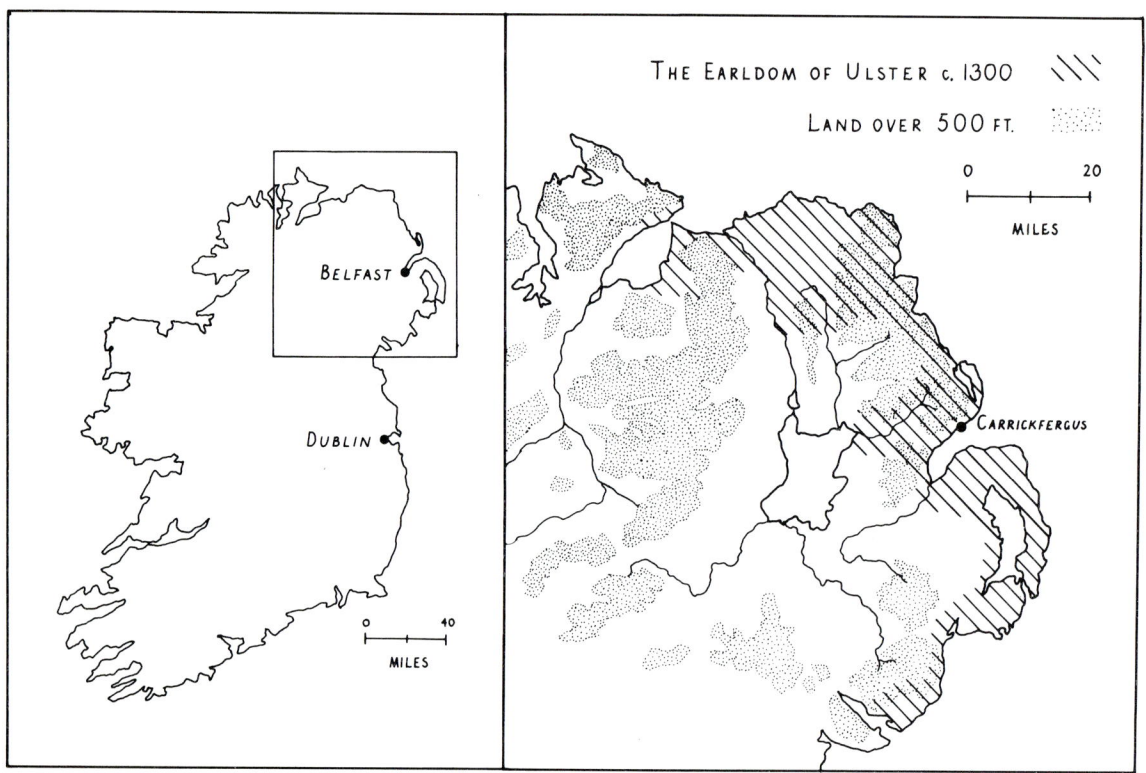

Fig 1 Carrickfergus: location map

CHAPTER 1

The evidence of the documents

The Mediaeval Castle

John de Courcy invaded Ulster early in the year 1177, going in the first instance to the centre of Uladh royal power at Downpatrick (for a general history, see McNeill 1980). In this and the following years, to consolidate the base he had won in east Down and south Antrim, he attacked the neighbouring Irish kingdoms. In 1177 and 1178 the *Annals of Ulster* record his raids into the country of Uí Tuirtre and Fir Lí, now mid and north Antrim (on the first raid he reached Armoy); in the first he was successful but he was defeated in 1178. Giraldus Cambrensis talks of his five battles, in the third of which, at some time after July 1178, he was beaten in Fir Lí. In this battle he lost all but eleven or so of his knights (he had twenty-two at Down in 1177). 'He and this tiny number of followers fought their way through to his castle, despite the fact that they had to cover a distance of thirty miles over which they continually had to defend themselves against a large force of their enemy, without their horses, which had all been lost, wearing their armour, on foot, and having had nothing to eat for two days and nights' (*Expugnatio*, ed. Scott and Martin, *179*). The site of his castle has been taken to be Downpatrick but the distance, which matches well with the time stated to make the march, is against this. Thirty miles from Fir Lí (north Antrim) would not come near Downpatrick (some fifty miles from Ballymena), but would fit very well with Carrickfergus. John de Courcy was expelled from Ulster by Hugh de Lacy in 1203-5; the fighting seems to have taken place around Downpatrick and Dundrum castle, rather than Carrickfergus. We know very little of either the course of events or the background to them and so cannot tell whether this apparent lack of reference to Carrickfergus is significant (Orpen, Normans, II, *136-42*).

Hugh de Lacy did not enjoy his earldom peacefully. He, with his Meath relations, fell foul of King John and an attack on Hugh was one of the objectives of the King's expedition to Ireland in 1210. John led his army into Ulster and spent from 19 to 28 July at Carrickfergus. The *Annals of the Four Masters* (1209) say that he besieged the castle which may explain why he made payments on the 25th to carpenters, masons and miners (Hardy 1844, *206*) along with the regular payments to his knights and others. In the following years twenty knights are recorded as captured at Carrickfergus, presumably when the castle surrendered: many have names who appear as barons of Hugh de Lacy. He certainly caused money, twenty marks, to be spent on repairing the storehouses in the castle (*ibid, 213*) during the following August. The length of his stay at Carrickfergus was only exceeded in Ireland by the length of his stay at Dublin; these two were the only places where he spent more than two or three days. John kept the earldom of Ulster and Carrickfergus in his hands having expelled de Lacy, so that it figures in the royal documents during the next fifteen years. In the Pipe Roll of 14 John (1211-12) £5-15-6 are recorded as spent on a new granary and on repairs to the kitchen and the windows of the chamber in the castle, while £5-0-0 were received from the sale of wine from the stores there (Davies and Quinn 1941, *53* and *55*). Later in the roll (*ibid, 61*) the stores at Carrickfergus castle are recorded as receiving one thousand coombs of flour, nearly half the total for Ulster and four times that allocated to Dundrum, the next largest. The next item relates to a garrison of a castle (to judge by the doorkeepers and chaplain) which is not named but it presumably follows the previous item and refers to Carrickfergus. From 25 July 1211 this garrison consisted of 10 knights, 16 men at arms, 5 cross-bowmen, 1 chaplain, 4 watchmen and 4 doorkeepers until 25 March 1212, when 4 knights, a man-at-arms and a cross-bowman left, perhaps to join in the attacks on the Irish during that summer. This garrison again is the largest in Ulster, especially in the number of knights: other castles only have one or two. The constable who received the flour was William de Serlande, who figures as constable intermittently for the following decade. He had succeeded Geoffrey de Serlande who, as constable, had sent King John messages in June and July 1211 (Cole 1844, *233-4*), and hawks in October (*ibid, 244*). By 3 and 12 February 1212 William is sending messengers as constable, and receiving four marks from the king *via* William Marshal (*ibid*, *253*, *257* and *265*). In October he was to come to England with the Justiciar, leaving the castle in safe custody (CDI, I, *445*).

The castle as we see it here in the years from 1210 to 1212 is clearly well-equipped and important, almost certainly the most important in Ulster. In 1213 we find lands attached to it: Robert fitz Serlon's land in Island Magee is to be returned to him after confiscation if the castle can do without it; if not the Justiciar is to make an exchange (CDI, I, *467*). In 1215, 1221 and 1224 there are routine records of changes among royal officials, either the Justiciar or the seneschal of Ulster and Carrickfergus castle is specified on each occasion as part of the charge the retiring official is to hand over to his successor (CDI, I, nos 611, 1015, 1158 and 1167). During this time there was royal concern about the defences of Carrickfergus. In January 1216 William de Serlande as constable was instructed to admit Geoffrey de Mariscis, the royal Justiciar, and any men he brought to help fortify the castle (CDI, I, no 674). Later in the year Carrickfergus was to be well fortified and an outer ward to be taken in to do it. In the next year William was granted £100 per year for the custody of Carrickfergus, an exceptional sum which must indicate exceptional expenditure; again he is instructed to consult the Justiciar, and put a garrison in if need be. The money must mean that the instructions about taking in an outer ward were being translated into building works.

In 1223 there came a threat to this security from Hugh de Lacy who returned to Ireland to try and reclaim his Earldom, by force if necessary. To meet this threat in June 1223 William de Serlande was made constable of Carrickfergus (we do not know when he had ceased to be so since 1216) and sent to defend it with men and provisions provided by the Justiciar (CDI, I, nos 1110 and 1111). He did not stay long however, for in March 1224 Roger Waspail was appointed seneschal of Ulster and given the custody of the castles of Carrickfergus and Dundrum (CDI, I, no 1167). For this custody of two castles he was given £20 per annum: the contrast with the £100 of 1217 is clear and must indicate that the building of the new outer ward was over. Later, in the summer of 1224, Hugh de Lacy did besiege the castle as the government had anticipated. The abbot of St Mary's Abbey beside the town of Carrickfergus sent stores into the castle and saw his abbey despoiled by Hugh's troops for his action (CDI, I, no 1225). The seige was lifted by a force sent from Leinster by William Marshal the Justiciar, under the command of his cousin William le Gras. The latter reached the castle by sea with twenty knights and twenty other soldiers, in spite of Hugh's forces who had eight boats on their side (CDI, I, no 1203; Orpen, *Normans*, III, *43*). The size of the forces involved in this action, both William le Gras's forty men and Hugh de Lacy's eight boats, which must have been very small not to stop them, is noteworthy. They link well with the size of the castle garrisons in 1212 when Carrickfergus was quite clearly the largest in Ulster with a maximum of thirty-one fighting men and nine others from which men could be detached for war. In this context £10 a year, together with lands attached to the castle, could clearly support a reasonable force.

In spite of the royal success in this siege Hugh de Lacy, with the help of the O'Neills, was able to regain his Earldom in 1227 after a short interim period when it was in the custody of his brother Walter. In these negotiations, again, the castle of Carrickfergus is named as part of the Earldom (CDI, I, nos 1371-4, 1385-6 1498). We can also see that William de Serlande, the former constable and seneschal of Ulster, has settled in Ulster: in these transactions the lands that he was granted as tenant-in-chief by King John are excluded. An indirect result of this restoration of the Earldom is that we lose the royal documentation for the castle for as part of Hugh de Lacy's Liberty, it no longer figures. When Hugh died in 1242-3, his Earldom, and with it Carrickfergus castle, reverted to the crown. In 1245 Hugh Tyrel, the seneschal of Ulster, was instructed to keep it in repair (CDI, I, no 2779) but this is all we hear of it. In 1253, when Ulster was assigned to Queen Eleanor as part of her dowry, Carrickfergus is the only castle named, and in the following year both were transferred to the future Edward I as Lord of Ireland (CDI, II, no 255). The castle played no part in the wars of the 1250s when the Justiciar and Brian O'Neill of Cenél Eógain were attacking each other: the action took place in counties Down, Armagh and Tyrone, culminating in the battle of Downpatrick in 1260. There might be enough documentation for this period in Ulster for the silence over Carrickfergus to be considered significant, suggesting that the castle was in good repair and functioning but not the scene of any notable activity. In 1264 Lord Edward conferred the Earldom of Ulster on Walter de Burgh who became the head of the dynasty of the last effective Earls of Ulster. He seems to have treated the castle as different from his others in Ulster: after his death in 1272 it was alleged that he had weakened the defences of the Earldom by leaving his wife in charge of five castles in Ulster, retaining only Carrickfergus for himself.

Under his son Richard who succeeded him as Earl there is less equivocal evidence of the high standing of the castle in Ulster. Between 1299 and 1308, various cases reached the royal courts in Dublin, on appeal from the Earl's court, held at Carrickfergus, presumably in the castle (Justiciary Rolls, Ireland, I, *214*; II, *11*; III, *50* and *56*). We would not expect many references to the castle during this period. From the time of Hugh de Lacy until the early 14th century the Earldom held the initiative in the politics of the north of Ireland, and so Carrickfergus was in a safe position in the heart of the Anglo-Norman settlement. Indeed an army was

The evidence of the documents

collected there for service in Leinster in 1311 (Tresham 1828, *19*). During this period the town was prospering as well, the most important in Ulster. This stability was however challenged by the Scottish wars of independence and their offshoot, the invasion of Ireland, *via* Ulster, by Edward Bruce. Carrickfergus had been a base for the English in Ireland: John Byset who commanded a fleet against Robert Bruce in 1307 was paid there (CDI, V, nos 610 and 627). Edward Bruce landed near Carrickfergus on 26 May 1315 and was to stay in Ireland for three years. The first attack on him, by the Earl of Ulster and the Justiciar, resulted in Bruce's victory at Connor, Co Antrim on 10 September (Laud ms Annals, *346*); the Anglo-Normans fled to Carrickfergus castle which Bruce promptly besieged. Efforts had been made to provision the castle with corn from Dublin but some at least of this corn never reached the castle, for John fitz Philip of Carrick who took charge of it for the Earl of Ulster went to Carlisle and sold the corn there. He claimed that he was blown off course and that the corn was about to spoil and had to be sold (Gilbert 1870, *334-5, 340-3* and *347-8*).

The garrison held out in spite of this, and it is doubtful, given Edward Bruce's campaigns elsewhere in Ireland during the next months, whether the siege was pressed very vigorously. In February 1316 the bishop of Connor was able to take refuge in the castle after laying an interdict on his diocese (Laud ms Annals, *349*). In April 1316 there was a serious attempt at the relief of the castle. Thomas de Mandeville, the most experienced soldier in the Earldom of Ulster, collected a force at Drogheda, supplied in part at least by the mayor and bailiff there, at the cost of £15-11-8, £6 of which were spent on wine for the expedition. All the supplies and equipment were not gathered so regularly for de Mandeville's men were accused of seizing boats and other goods on their way (Gilbert 1870, *350-1, 378*). Given the record of other de Mandevilles in Ulster in the past, the accusation seems entirely credible. Thomas arrived in Carrickfergus on 8 April and had an immediate success, killing thirty Scots. On 10 April, however, he led another sally and was killed himself in the resulting street fighting. His body was taken back to Drogheda and buried there, not at the Franciscan Friary in Carrickfergus as he had wished (Cal Papal Registers, II, *171*). The position of the garrison steadily became more precarious and negotiations began in June for their surrender. During these, they captured thirty Scots in spite of the truce, sent into the castle to carry out the negotiations (Laud ms Annals, *350*). In July eight boatloads of corn were collected in Drogheda for sending to the castle but the Earl of Ulster diverted them in order to secure the release from Scotland of his cousin William de Burgh, captured at the battle of Connor (*ibid, 296*). In September the garrison surrendered, in return for life and limb after a siege of twelve months. The castle had not been stormed but the besieged had been reduced to eating hides and, it was said in Dublin, eight Scots prisoners (*ibid, 297* and *352*).

Carrickfergus now became the Bruces' base in Ireland until Edward's death at Faughart in October 1318. After its recapture, however, the castle does not seem to have been given back to the Earl of Ulster who was held by Dublin opinion not to have prosecuted the war against Bruce to great effect. John de Athy, the King's Admiral in Ireland, was made constable after its recovery from the Scots: five ships were sent to him from Devon as well (Patent Rolls, England, 1319, *311* and *313*). John remained constable until 1326 or 1327 just before the castle was given to William de Burgh when he took up his Earldom of Ulster (*ibid, 1339, 331*). How Richard de Burgh managed without the *caput* of his earldom, we do not know. In 1322 Athy bought provisions to the value of £23-7-4 but this is the only item to appear in the audit of the Irish accounts between 1321 and 1324 as spent on the castle (Exchequer Memoranda Rolls, 1326-7, *308*). In 1326 he was sent fifty marks for six months' fees and a further hundred to meet indentures issued (Tresham 1828, *34B* and *35*). The castle was used as a safe prison for prisoners from Dublin and for two O'Neills (*ibid, 30B* and *36*). In 1327 Carrickfergus was involved in the truce between Robert Bruce and Henry de Mandeville, seneschal of Ulster. In a memorandum attached to the copy of the treaty in the British Library (ADD mss, V, 25459) the political problems of Ulster are discussed. The most important of these is stated to be the appointment of a constable to the castle: the appointment of the most capable local man, John de Coupland, would cause local jealousies. In the following year, 1328, William de Burgh was given control of his Earldom of Ulster which presumably took the problem out of royal hands and there is no reason to think that the crown retained the castle. William and Robert Bruce tried to arrange for peace negotiations between the Scots and English in Ireland. The Scottish commissioners came to Carrickfergus but the Justiciar of Ireland refused to meet them (Laud ms Annals, *367*). William de Burgh was not Earl of Ulster for long: on 6 June 1333 he was killed by his barons, probably at Belfast. To avenge the murder the Justiciar took his army by sea to Carrickfergus and then on, as planned, to Scotland after defeating the murderers (*ibid, 378*).

After William de Burgh's death, the Earldom, and with it Carrickfergus castle, went to his daughter Elizabeth, and through her to her husband the Duke of Clarence. Their heiress, Philippa, brought it into the possession of the Mortimer Earls of March, from whom it descended to the Duke of York and so to his son King Edward IV. It has remained in the crown's possession since then. Clarence and Mortimer were briefly the King's Lieutenants in Ireland but otherwise the Earl of Ulster was always in England: even when these men were Lieutenants they did not come to Ulster. As a result Carrickfergus and the Earldom were administered from 1333 effectively as part of crown possessions in Ireland. The Earldom did not, in fact, collapse as a result of William de Burgh's death but it did change. There was never again a resident Earl to control policy, and the Irish were able to make serious inroads into Anglo-Norman lands and their environs in the last third of the 14th century. Until then, from 1333 to the 1380s, we hear little of Carrickfergus in the documents. Ronald of Richmond was appointed constable on 1 October 1333 (Patent Rolls, England, *472*): he received a fee six months later (Close Rolls, England, 1334, *216*). In December 1334, no doubt to the relief of the garrison, the king's butler was ordered to send the old wine in Carrickfergus to Carlisle and replace it with 1334 vintage (*ibid, 1334, 287*).

As a result of some now forgotten bureaucratic muddle and court intrigue the position of constable see-sawed between Thomas de Menill and Ronald of Richmond. The muddle seems to have been caused by the memory that the castle had been in the king's hands for the ten years before 1328 and that it did not therefore have the same status as the rest of the Earldom, in wardship for William de Burgh's little daughter, Elizabeth. That there were two court factions involved seems clear from the references made to advice given to the king at court. In March 1337 Ronald was ordered to surrender the castle to Thomas de Menill, but in June this was cancelled; the king had forgotten the original terms. In November, however, Thomas was re-granted the custody, for the king found out that the status of the castle had been hidden from him in favour of Ronald, but in December he was persuaded by men of his council that Ronald was a good constable and should keep the office (Patent Rolls, England, 1337, *404, 458, 547* and *560*). Ronald of Richmond did continue as constable and was appointed for twelve years in 1338 (Close Rolls, England, *365*): he was rewarded in 1338 for arresting men trading with the Scots by being allowed to keep the goods he seized, to the value of £50 (Patent Rolls, England, 1338, *52*). In the next year three men, including Henry Savage, seneschal of Ulster, were appointed to investigate the sale of the king's wine from Carrickfergus castle to the Scots (*ibid, 1339, 403*). In 1340 Richmond was again rewarded for arresting traders with Scotland (they were taking beans and flour over) by being granted up to £50-worth of the goods seized (Close Rolls, England, *396*). In 1343-4 he was allowed £40 a year from the income of Ulster, more than twice the stipend of the treasurer of Ulster (Tresham 1828, *44B*). In 1346 felons were again to be imprisoned in the castle (*ibid, 53B*). The lack of references from 1350 to 1380 is in contrast to a steady trickle of Ulster material in the Close and Patent Rolls of England and Ireland.

In the 1380s and after, as a result of renewed royal interest in Ireland and the increasing Irish threat to the English position in Ulster, there is a flurry of interest in Carrickfergus. In 1381-2 the treasurer of the Liberty was sent masons, carpenters and provisions: he was to repair the great tower of the castle and other lower houses in it, that is the keep and buildings probably in the outer ward (Tresham 1828, *115* and *118*). A sign of the new powers came in 1384 when Niall O'Neill burned Carrickfergus, but probably not the castle (*Annals of Ulster*). In 1384-5 Thomas Mercameston was appointed constable to succeed John Yevele (Tresham 1828, *119*) and William de Aghton was appointed in 1386-7 (*ibid, 132*). William may have died in office for the next we hear is in 1388 of the new seneschal of Ulster, Edmund Savage, holding the custody of the castle but being instructed to deliver it to Thomas Mercameston again (Patent Rolls, England, *438*). He held it only briefly for William Merser was soon appointed, to be succeeded within the space of two or three years by Gilbert de Halsall and Robert Lang (Tresham 1828, *138, 144B* and *146B*). In 1391 we hear of the Ulster exchequer working at Carrickfergus and in the same year, possibly in spite of the work of 1381-2, the castle was to be put into a state of defence, because of the wasting of Ulster by the Irish (Patent Rolls, England, 1391, *392* and *405*). Under Henry IV the same pattern of frequent appointments to the constableship is followed: we find John de Stanlowe in 1399-1400 and Peter Dobyn, as constable, licensed to bring corn for the castle from Drogheda in 1402-3 (Tresham 1828, *160* and *162B*). In the next year the town of Carrickfergus was attacked and pleaded to be remitted £5 from the annual Customs but there is no indication that the castle was attacked or damaged; indeed in the same year the west mill by St Nicholas's church was leased (*ibid, 170B* and *172B*). The office continued to change regularly: in 1407-8 Wilfrid Bentley was appointed with a stipend of £40 a year, in 1409-10 Nicholas Orell was appointed with powers of treating with rebels and Scots and seizing ships, and in 1411-12 Richard Stoute was constable (*ibid, 185B, 190, 193, 193B* and *200B*).

During the next century there appears to be a different policy of appointing constables, keeping the one man in the office for much longer than the earlier two or three years. By the second quarter of the 15th century Carrickfergus was isolated, between the O'Neills of Clandeboy and the MacDonnells of the Glens, from the nearest area (Lecale and the southern Ards) which claimed to be English. The situation was for a long time stable: the English had no power even to contemplate regaining the lands held by the Earl of Ulster in the 13th century, while the Irish needed such ports as Carrickfergus for the trade which only the English had the ships and the contacts to carry out. Incidents might occur like the killing of Brian O'Neill of Clandeboy by the castle garrison in 1425 (*Annals of Ulster*) but we should not over-emphasise them. The constable soon after this, in 1428, was James White, presumably the same man as was seneschal of Ulster in 1426 (Patent Rolls, England, *383*); his predecessor, Janico Dartas, had been constable of Greencastle. In 1428 he was petitioning for £10 a year, complaining that he only had ten marks' income which was insufficient even to provision the castle, and that he was being attacked by Scots (Tresham 1828, *246*). In 1430 Thomas Benson of York was appointed constable (Patent Rolls, England, *100*) but his tenure does not seem to have been totally happy, perhaps because of local animosity. In 1434 the Archbishop of Armagh wrote to John Fossard, Bishop of Connor, who had joined in a conspiracy taking over the castle and preventing Benson from getting into it; he should stop this behaviour and make the others stop it (Chart 1935, *150*). By 1450 James White, perhaps a son of the earlier one, is petitioning for more money: he has £40 a year (an improvement on his predecessor's ten marks!) but says he needs £80 and requests that £20 be sent at once. White's probable successor was James Dokray but before that there was a short interlude when Carrickfergus castle was used in Anglo-Scottish politics. On 8 December 1463 the Earl of Douglas was appointed constable (Patent Rolls, England, *62*). He did not mean to take the post seriously but the manoeuvre is explained by the terms of the Anglo-Scottish truce of 9 December: one clause bound each side to disown the rebels of the other (Dunlop 1950, *239*). It was imperative that the Earl of Douglas disappear from the English court for a while and Carrickfergus was an ideal spot to stay, administratively remote from London, so that he might be disowned and yet close to his own lands in south-west Scotland.

In February 1467 James Dokray was appointed constable. He was described earlier as a merchant of Drogheda and keeper of Customs at Dundalk, Ardglass and Carrickfergus and he was to exploit his commercial knowledge as far as he could (Patent Rolls, England, 1467, *161*; Berry 1914, *97* and *569*). He repeated the pleas of James White for more money from the Dublin government with greater frequency. The terms of his appointment, which was for life, were that he was to maintain ten soldiers and pay them fourpence a day. To pay for this he was to draw forty marks a year from the Customs of Carrickfergus and Ardglass and from the manor of 'Ardmullghan'. In addition he was granted for life forty marks a year from the Drogheda Customs and up to five marks from the profits of the watermill by Carrickfergus castle. His own expenses seem to have absorbed all the resources of the castle itself, which, the documents allege, had once allowed the constable to maintain twenty-four soldiers in the castle. This income, he continued to petition, was inadequate and needed support from other sources. In 1474 he claimed before Parliament that he was owed four years' fees and had had to repair the castle from his own pocket: he was granted lands in Oriel for life (Morrissey 1939, *243*). In February 1477 he received £20 a year for five years from the fee farm of Drogheda, in order to meet the expenses of repairing the castle. This £20 does not seem to have reached him for in July the grant is repeated with more detail. The money is needed to repair the outer 'mantlet' (curtain wall), part of which has fallen, and 'half a tower' one hundred feet long and forty feet high which threatens to fall along with other items. This tower by its measurements hardly seems to be what we would call a tower: it looks like a building along one of the two long sides of the outer curtain, perhaps unsafe because it was behind the fallen stretch. It must have been two or three storeys high. The provisioning of the castle seems also to have posed problems. In April and October 1476 Richard Heron of London and Westminster, merchant of the Calais staple, was given a life grant to be captain, lieutenant and victualler of the castle with safe conduct there (Patent Rolls, England, 1476, *583* and *597*). This is not a period when Dokray was not constable: he was confirmed in office in the Parliament of 1476-7 (Morrissey 1939, *565*). This must be another symptom of the lack of resources attached to the castle. In 1479 the life grant to Dokray was repeated on the same terms as 1467 except that the Carrickfergus and Dundalk Customs were only to produce twenty not forty marks a year for him; he was however still to keep ten men at fourpence a day (Patent Rolls, England, 1479, *160-1*). He was still constable and collector of Dundalk and Carrickfergus Customs in 1481 (Morrissey 1939, *887*).

In November 1482 William Fauconberg was appointed constable to succeed Dokray, who had been in office now for just over fifteen years. The terms of his appointment repeat those of Dokray's in 1479 (Patent Rolls, England, *339*). In 1486 London merchants gave a bond to supply the castle (Close Rolls, England, *19*). In 1491 Sir Gilbert Debenham was made constable, combining the office with that of the Lordship of Carlingford and Cooley as well as the manor of Ardmolghan, like Dokray before him (*ibid*, 1491, *334*). By now Henry VII was King of England and his attempts under Poynings to assert his authority in Ireland affected Carrickfergus. This was not so much by law, although the castle was one of the six which were to have English constables: after all, Carrickfergus castle had never had an Irish constable, unless one counts the Anglo-Irish like White or Dokray. The conditions of the castle changed a little, if only in that there are accounts showing money actually paid to the garrison rather than grants in order that it might be, a distinction that Dokray would have appreciated. Between October 1494 and August 1495, Henry Wright was constable for six weeks: he received £14-0-0. William Chetwyn as constable from 26 April to 21 August 1495 received £44-16-0 for wages, himself at one shilling a day and fourteen archers at six pence (Conway 1932, *168*). Between Wright and Chetwyn, Pryngent Menou was appointed in March 1495 (Patent Rolls, England, *44*). Chetwyn and six men formed the garrison from December 1495 to the end of March 1496, but he was reinforced by Sir Richard Salkeld with twelve men for March and April 1496 (Conway 1932, *195*). Salkeld was the constable of Carlisle at the time and his journey to Carrickfergus (costing eight shillings) can be seen as a part of Henry's efforts to bring Ireland under English control. Like the rest, however, it did not last: the Earl of Kildare was re-appointed Lord Deputy in September 1496 to control Ireland without incurring the great expenditure on garrisons involved in a policy of direct rule.

Kildare's main aim was to prevent any threat to the Pale, not to reconquer Ulster for the Crown. The same isolation that had affected the fifteenth-century garrison continued to exist. In October 1496 Sir Ralph Verney reported nervously that Sir John Mor MacDonnell of the Isles was in the country near Carrickfergus with one thousand Scots and kerns (Conway 1932, *233*). Faced with forces like this a garrison of six men could hardly take the initiative. In 1506 Kildare was granted the custody of Greencastle and Carlingford castles and the Lordship of Cooley and the Mournes but not Carrickfergus (Patent Rolls, England, *443*). In 1507 the people of Carrickfergus captured Niall O'Neill of Clandeboy; he was released in exchange for sixteen hostages but returned and captured the mayor and the castle (*Annals of Ulster*). In an expedition to the North in 1523, Kildare found a Breton ship at Carrickfergus trading in Gascon wine. As he was not Lord Deputy he could not challenge it, but he did capture a Scottish ship in Belfast Lough and arrested the mayor of Carrickfergus and four others for trading with the enemy (Letters and Papers, Henry VIII, II, *99*).

The position of Carrickfergus castle between the 1380s and the 1520s seems to change little. The area of English authority steadily diminished so that both the resources and the importance of the castle as an administrative centre declined. By the later 15th century the income of the constable was clearly insufficient to support his charge. Whether he had ever actually maintained a garrison of twenty-four, it is clear that the numbers he could now employ decreased from twelve to six. To judge from the pleas of Dokray in 1477 it may well be that the last serious maintenance was done in 1381-2 or 1391. It is quite clear that it is most unlikely that any building other than routine maintenance would have taken place in the period. At the other extreme, it is equally clear that the castle was always garrisoned throughout the same period: the 1440s appear to be the only decade when there is no reference made to the castle. The castle that William de Burgh knew in 1330 seems to have substantially been the one which Henry VIII owned. The use however was to vary. From 1534 Henry and his Tudor successors were to increase the pressure on the Irish to submit to English authority and society. In Ireland it was the North which was the furthest from this English authority and in the North he had inherited the claims of the Earl of Ulster to an overall supremacy. The clearest relic of the Earldom was the castle at Carrickfergus and this castle would be one of the key bases for the Tudor expansion in Ulster.

The Castle under the Tudors and Stuarts

It was to be some time before the increasing pressure of Tudor policy actually affected Carrickfergus Castle. It took its place among the castles in Ulster (counted as part of Co Louth) which should be guarded in 1537 (Letters and Papers, Henry VIII, XII(2), no 1097). The constable in 1539, Thomas Wusle or Vusley, faced with a threat from Scotland, wrote to his counterpart at Ardglass to ask for two guns and some powder, the first mention of guns at Carrickfergus (*ibid*, XIV(1), no 1027). The castle was described as large and defensible in 1540 (PRO, SC 11/934), but it does not seem to have received attention until 1546-7 when Walter Floddy, the constable, received £19-4-6 for repairs (PRO, SP 65/5/4). The castle was used as a base for an expedition by the Lord of the Isles against Huntly and Argyll in 1545 and also for an expedition to Scotland by Ormonde (CSPI, 1509-73, *72*). In 1551 the Lord Deputy met Irish chiefs at the castle during his expedition against the Scots of Antrim (CSPI, 1509-73, *111* and *116*). He must have asked for money to fortify it for the Privy Council wrote to him in 1552, emphasising the importance of Carrickfergus and the new Olderfleet castle, of which they had a 'platte by Rogers' (SP 61/4/48); they could send no money, however, and there is no evidence of activity for some years. In 1553 Walter Floddy was removed as constable and succeeded by Edward Larkyn (CSPI 1509-73, *133*; Patent and Close Rolls Ireland, I, *313*). Floddy left to become involved with the young Lord of the Isles in 1555.

In that year the energetic and vociferous William Peers (or Pers) was appointed as constable, initially jointly with one Michael Bethel, to remain so for the next twenty years. The garrison at the time of this appointment comprised one warden, 12 arquebuses and 12 bombardiers, all at 8d per day and 5 archers at 6d; the bombardiers foreshadow the question of ordnance in the castle (Patent and Close Rolls Ireland, I, *354*). Between 1556 and 1559 Peers was paid £193-14-4 for repairs to the castle and had 48 men there for a year (De L'Isle and Dudley mss, I, *376*), the largest single payment for building works recorded in Sir Henry Sidney's accounts in these years which also saw work proceeding at Dublin castle, and Daingean and Leix forts. The work was probably only partial for in 1559 Peers complained that the castle was 'so fare in decaye' and requested money 'towards ye building, renewing

The evidence of the documents

and fortifieing ye sayd castell' (PRO, SP 63/1/43). His plea was successful: Lord Justice Fitzwilliam wrote to Cecil in May 1561 to report that he had sent money to Peers 'for the mounting of the ordnance according to his request'. Fitzwilliam also gives a glimpse of Peers' methods for he says that Peers was likely to have approached the Queen direct (PRO, SP 63/3/64). In 1565 Peers could still describe the castle as 'a great parte fallen downe' and Sidney also requested that the Queen spend £4,000 on fortifying Carrickfergus (including the town) and allow Peers 100 men for the work (PRO, SP 63/9/83; SP 63/16/35). Elizabeth characteristically baulked at the £4,000 ('there be . . . in the writing some mistaking') but allowed the 100 men (PRO, SP 63/17/8). Sidney sent lead for roofing the castle at once (PRO, SP 63/17/8). In the face of Shane O'Neill's pressure, in April 1565 the Queen allowed Peers £6,000 but warned that it must only be used in an emergency (PRO, SP 63/17/20). In 1567 she agreed to fortify Carrickfergus, with Derry and Armagh, against him but not yet, for there was no money (PRO, SP 63/21/48), and Shane O'Neill was killed in June by the MacDonnells and his head sent to Peers. Nevertheless work was going on by April 1567 when labourers, 3 carpenters and a mason were sent to Carrickfergus and in October Terence Danyell, Dean of Armagh reported that Sidney had 'built' the castle (PRO, SP 63/20/70; SP 63/22/1). Between April and November 1568 Peers built a new kitchen in the castle courtyard at the cost of £53-3-2 (De L'Isle and Dudley mss I, *408-9*). Some of this work was in brick: in 1567 Brian O'Neill of Clandeboy agreed to supply wood from Belfast for firing brick at Carrickfergus (Benn 1877, *19*).

McSkimin (1909, *220*) quotes a description of the castle by one George Clarkson which he dates to 1567 but unfortunately gives no reference for it. 'The buildings of the said castle on the south part is three towers, viz. the gatehouse, a tower in the middle thereof, which is the entry at a drawbridge over a dry moat; and in said tower is a prison and porter lodge and over the same a fair lodging called the constable's lodging; and in the courtain between the gatehouse and the west tower in the corner, being of divers squares called Cradyfergus is a fair and comely building, a chapel and divers houses of office on the ground, and above the great chamber and the lord's lodging all of which is now in great decaie as well in the couverture being lead also in timber and glass, and without help and reparation it will soon come to utter ruin'. The meaning of this description is not completely clear. The second part probably describes a first floor hall in the outer ward (that is, between the gatehouse and the keep – the 'west tower in the corner'). The main question is as to the meaning of the first part. At first sight this looks like a description of the original north section of the middle curtain and middle tower, but what we know of its plan would preclude any such elaborate structure, with prison and porter's lodge on the ground floor and a constable's lodging above. It may be better explained as 'the said tower' referring to the twin towered gatehouse with a building between the towers: a porter's lodge in one tower and a prison in the other. The drawbridge over a moat in front of the gate tower is echoed in Dobbs's description of 1683 and in the complaint that a ditch between the town and the castle was filled in 1591 (below, p 46).

The garrison also rose between 1560 and 1567. Between 1560 and 1565 it consisted of 10 arquebuses (at 8d a day) and 10 archers (at 6d), but from March to May 1565 all 20 men were arquebuses. From July 1566 to May 1567 Peers had a 'peticaptain', 4 officers and 80 arquebuses under him (Longfield 1960, *51, 56, 68, 73, 77, 85-6, 105*; De L'Isle and Dudley mss, I, *393-4*; PRO, SP 63/9/83). The reference to the entrenching of the former friary in 1566 (PRO, SP 63/19/29) brings a new factor into the history of the castle. Increasingly the government was to view the town and the castle as a single unit in military affairs, and especially to value the former friary, converted to a fortified depot known as the 'palace'. Garrisons now had to be much larger to form an effective force against men like Shane O'Neill. A bakehouse, a brewhouse and other houses for victualling the garrison were repaired, with two mills, in 1567 at the cost of £266-13-4 (De L'Isle and Dudley mss, I, *402*). In that year food for 1,000 men for six months was sent from Liverpool to Carrickfergus and Captain Cheston's band ordered to be disbanded so the men could be distributed to fill up the numbers of the bands at Carrickfergus (CSPI, 1509-73, *332, 353*). In 1568 the warden of the 'palace', Thomas Sackford, was paid £50 for fortifications (De L'Isle and Dudley mss, I, *408-9*); the bakehouse, brewhouse and mills were altered or repaired in 1569-71 (PRO, AO 1/2513/537). Work on projects in the town included Peers' repairing the pier in 1564 (PRONI, Fitzwilliam Papers D 1854/3/6) and Sidney's paving of the town and repair of St Nicholas's church in 1568 (PRO, SP 63/26/21); he bought a Bible for the latter for £1-2-0 in 1566-8 (De L'Isle and Dudley mss, I, *407*). Obviously the town wall was considered at the same time. Peers proposed one in 1564 as did Sidney in the next year, but the Queen thought the town should pay (PRO, SP 63/9/83, 63/15/4 and 5). Sidney entrenched the town (PRO, SP 63/22/1) and Elizabeth offered half the town Customs revenue for seven years in 1570 to pay for the wall, but the next year Peers still asked for £1,000 for it and a pier (PRO, SP 63/33/1).

It would seem clear from all this activity that by 1568 the castle must have been considered adequately fortified, at least as far as it could be without major expenditure. The building of a kitchen and the increasing effort spent on the town from 1567-8 on certainly imply this, and it is likely that we should attribute some of the pleas of ruin to the need to make a good case to a parsimonious bureaucracy. From 1571 the trend was to run against expenditure on the castle. In that year the Queen granted much of eastern Ulster to Sir Thomas Smyth but this alienated Sir Brian McPhelim O'Neill of Clandeboy so that on 2 June 1573 he burned much of the town. In that year Elizabeth granted Clandeboy to the Earl of Essex who openly preferred Belfast to Carrickfergus as a centre for fortification and administration (State Papers, Carew, 1515-74, *446*). Some reconstruction was done after the destruction of 1573: a 'vamour [rampart] of sods' was hastily put up in 1574 and Sidney ordered a new wall in 1575, part of which Peers built by 1579; money was spent on and wood given to the church in 1577 and 1578 (PRONI, Dobbs records, *7, 12, 15–18*); storehouses were repaired (PRO, SP 63/53/9) and Peers paid for building work in stone in 1575-6 (PRO, SP 63/55/37 III). The Queen disapproved of expenditure in Ireland in these years: in 1575 Essex's troops were cut in numbers, although Carrickfergus was still to be guarded, and Sidney was charged in 1578 with extravagance on Carrickfergus (State Papers, Carew, 1575-88, *3, 151, 342*). By 1579 William Peers was no longer constable, becoming mayor of the town by 1582 (CSPI 1574-85, *167, 418*).

These trends which militated against expenditure on the castle continued even more strongly until the early years of the 17th century. As the Irish wars escalated in general and the problem of Tyrone in particular worsened, garrisons far larger than the castle could accommodate were stationed in Carrickfergus. The numbers concerned, apart from the castle and 'palace' establishments, are mostly clearly shown in a table:

	Horse	Foot	References
July 1583	50	200	CSPI 1574-85, *457*
May 1586	50	200	CSPI 1586-8, *70*
1595		210	State Papers Carew, III, *128*
July 1598	100	200	CSPI 1598-9, *216*
June 1601	125	750	State Papers Carew, IV, *93*
August 1601	125	800	State Papers Carew, IV, *135*
November 1608		150	CSPI 1608-10, *96-7*

In addition to this information, we have other pieces: in August 1586 150 men were withdrawn from the garrison (CSPI 1586-8, *131*), while in 1594 the numbers were reinforced again, with 50 men sent in April and 2,000 men were victualled through Carrickfergus for two months during the year (CSPI 1592-6, *232, 287*). Not unreasonably we find references to problems of supply. The stores at Carrickfergus were the depot for garrisons in the Clandeboy region as well as the town's garrison. This is noted in 1586 and 1597, in both cases because it caused trouble, either by attracting raids or by leaving too little food for the garrison (CSPI 1586-8, *208-9*; 1596-7, *268*). Unlike the other forts of Ireland Carrickfergus had no demesne attached to it for its supply (CSPI 1586-8, *434*; 1588-92, *423*). Shortages occurred intermittently: in January 1586 and February 1598 there was no food and in March 1598 captured wine was sold to pay the troops (CSPI 1586-8, *4*; 1598-9, *70, 485–6*).

A symptom of this situation was the increasing importance of the warden or constable of the storehouse at the 'palace' as opposed to the constable of the castle. William Peers as constable had been seneschal of Clandeboy from 1570 to 1574 and captain of the cavalry in the town in 1577 (CSPI 1574-85, *31*; State Papers, Carew, II, *86*). His successor was Charles Egerton who held the post for some twenty years and so was presumably a relatively junior officer. Thomas Sackford had been constable of the 'palace' since 1568, a decade before Egerton's appointment and so it is perhaps no surprise that he took over the problem of victualling the men working on the town wall in 1581 (PRO, SP 63/84/49i). Sackford's successors at the 'palace', Captain Nicholas Dawtry, Captain Christopher Carlisle and Sir Edward Yorke, are all described as seneschals of Clandeboy. When Yorke was appointed it was in spite of a request for the position from Egerton (CSPI 1586-8, *251*; 1592-6, *267, 275*), who had been constable of both castle and 'palace' briefly in 1589 (State Papers Carew, II, *484*). Egerton was replaced as constable of the castle and Governor of Carrickfergus (because of personal spite, he said) by Sir John Chichester in 1596 but was reappointed the next year after Chichester's death at Altfrackyn (CSPI 1592-6, *524*; 1596-7, *326, 396-7, 444*). By 1599 Sir Arthur Chichester was governor and constable, in spite of a brief interlude in that year when William Warren was appointed by the Earl of Essex. Chichester was to dominate the town and Ulster for twenty years, prosecuting the war with Tyrone from Carrickfergus and Clandeboy under Mountjoy's direction and playing a major part in the Ulster Plantation.

The references we have to works during this period from 1580 to 1603 do not include the castle. The only mention we have of it is in 1591 when some of the townsmen complain that Egerton had filled in the ditch between the castle and the town with rubbish and had encouraged other townsmen to build over it; an extension of this work had partly blocked access to the quay (McSkimin 1909, *382-3*). These new buildings were presumably below the present road, the Marine Highway, and perhaps on the ground known as the castle green, which gave access to the quay along the west side of the castle. The defensive measures were designed to protect the whole town and stores: the town wall was still incomplete and the 'palace' was outside its line (CSPI 1586-8, *209*). We have noted Sackford provisioning men working on the wall in 1581 and in 1586 the Lord Deputy was ordered to finish it (PRO, SP 63/126/93). The corporation appealed to the government for it to be completed in 1594 and a raid by O'Neill of Clandeboy to Kilroot and Island Magee caused the government to try to get the mayor to finish it in 1596 (CSPI 1592-6, *257, 506*). In that year Egerton reported that he had built a corner flanker to the walls in stone, called Mount Russell, ironically probably after the man whom he blamed for his dismissal later in the year (CSPI 1596-7, *72, 326*). In 1601 the storehouses of Carrickfergus were described as much decayed and in need of £200 of repairs and rebuilding (CSPI 1600-1, *143*). Egerton himself had problems with arrears of food and money: he was owed £500 in 1584, five years' pay in 1596 and two years' pay and seven months' provisions in 1597 (CSPI 1586-8, *41*, 1596-7, *171, 268*). While he might have spent money of his own on the castle, it would seem most unlikely that, after Peers' term of office until the end of the century, any work was done to the castle other than the most basic of repairs.

The ending of the Nine Years' War obviously had an impact on the military life of Carrickfergus and thus of its castle. The most immediate consequences was the winding-up of the depot at the 'palace'. In 1605 its ward was reduced from twenty to five men and a constable, John Dalway who had been appointed in 1597 (PRO, SP 63/218/73). In 1607 Dalway received £80 for repairs (probably already expended) but in the same year the five wardens were discharged and it was proposed to let the palace to one George Wood but Dalway was still the constable in 1610 (CSPI 1606-8, *87, 91, 282*; 1608-10, *80, 508*). In this last year McSkimin records (1909, *154*) that Sir Arthur Chichester began his massive Jacobean mansion, Joymount, on its site. At the same time as the 'palace' ward was reduced from twenty to five, the castle ward was also reduced, but only to fifteen. In 1606 Sir Faithfull Fortescue was appointed constable, a position he was to hold until 1662, except for a Parliamentary interlude. The ward of the castle had been reduced to 10 by 1623, but from 1611 there was also a gunner and a clerk. The cost of the castle in 1611 was only £182-10-0 out of a total Irish Ordnance establishment of £2,382-7-11 (State Papers Carew, IV, *217*; PRO, AO 11/8, 11/13).

After the war it is not surprising to find only limited commitment to fortification. One long-standing project, the town wall, was finally finished under Chichester. In 1611 half the 200 foot soldiers in the town were working on the wall, while in 1615 their work seems to have finished, for provision was made for their dispersal (State Papers Carew, IV, *218*; CSPI, 1615-25, *25*). Originally while 50 of them were to be sent elsewhere, 50 were to have been used for repairs to the castle; in spite of protests (CSPI 1615-25, *38*) they were also to be sent off to serve in Sir Christopher Wilmot's company. As a result we find Carrickfergus listed as in need of repairs in 1623 and 1639. Sir Faithfull Fortescue also claimed £1,111 arrears in 1639 but while the King was prepared to consider the repairs, he was told to wait for his arrears (PRO, SP 63/237/49; SP DOM SO 3/251-2). In 1626 one of the Carrickfergus companies mutinied, often a sign of serious arrears of pay (CSPI 1625-32, *163*). The castle's condition is unlikely to have been good and it is a great pity Sir Josias Bodley's report on Ulster fortifications and the repairs needed does not include Carrickfergus, especially as we know he visited it (BL Lansdowne 156 fols 335-6; PRO, SP 63/217/79). On the other hand it was in commission, fit for use as Con O'Neill's prison in 1603, perhaps in the east tower (McSkimin 1909, *33, 226*). It had guns in 1611 (a brass saker, three falcons and a falconette: State Papers Carew, IV, *95*) and 25 barrels of powder and 4,815 pounds of lead in 1625 (CSPI 1625-32, *28*) but the effectiveness of the castle as a fighting force may be judged by an incident in 1633. On that occasion a pirate was able to capture two Dutch ships in the bay (either Belfast Lough or the harbour) in spite of fire from the castle's guns (CSPI 1633-47, *127*).

In 1641 Carrickfergus was one of the key places of Protestant refuge during the rebellion, and indeed in January 1642 a base for the counter-massacre of Catholics on Island Magee. In April of that year General Robert Munro took over the town and castle for the Scots, using it as his chief base at least until his capture of Belfast from the royalists in 1644, and twice as a prison for the Earl of Antrim, who escaped both times, in 1642 and 1643. As a base the castle was not apparently very strongly armed. A report in 1644 lists only four or five 12 pounder cannon and six or seven little pieces, apart from the field pieces of Munro's regiments; there were however 62 barrels of powder and 80 3 cwt lead pigs (Laing mss, I, *216*). The castle changed hands three times in 1648-9, from Munro to Monk (for Parliament) and then to the royalists, but finally back to Venables and Coote for Parliament in August 1649, serving as a base for them from then until the Restoration. On each occasion it was betrayed rather than captured (McSkimin 1909, *39-58*). In 1659 it was not rated as the most important fort in Ulster: it had a garrison of 60 men as opposed to 100 at Charlemont, Enniskillen and Londonderry (CSPI 1647-66, *687*). After the Restoration Sir Faithfull Fortescue was reinstated as constable, to be succeeded by his son, Sir Thomas in 1661, but the post was not without its problems. In 1660 Sir George Rawdon reacted to his appointment to it, on a temporary basis: 'I know he intends it as a favour but truly I feare it will be a trouble' (PRO, SP 63/306/31).

In 1661 the Lords Justices gave £250 for repairing breaches in the castle but the whole question of Irish fortification was reorganised in the next year. Internal excise revenue succeeded feudal dues as the principal source of regular income and the Board of Ordnance was set up to supervise the army supply and fortification. A survey in 1662 described the castle as 'of three wards' but that the store rooms had been neglected and 'had been suffered to fall into ruine'; there were 57 guns of all sorts, but most were unmounted; a carpenter and mason had viewed and costed repairs (PRO, WO 54/197). Perhaps as a result of this report the Board spent £680 at Carrickfergus in 1665 on the storehouses, gun carriages and platforms, a reasonable proportion possibly of the £4,840 spent on general repairs on Irish forts that year (in 1659 there were 57 of these: PRO, SP 63/319/272). There was not enough money for the Irish administration in these years; the Lord Lieutenant wrote to Secretary Arlington in 1666 that there was enough to pay either the men or to finance the fortifications (CSP DOM Additions to 1679, *112*). The result at Carrickfergus was a serious mutiny of the garrison for a week in May 1666 over pay; the soldiers demanded nine months' arrears and were reported to be starving as they had run out of credit to buy food in the town. Ormond as Lord Lieutenant was worried in case the townspeople and Scots might become involved, and brought four companies of Guards by sea from Dublin who forced the mutineers into the castle where they quickly surrendered. Several were killed in the fighting and ten subsequently hanged. In 1670 the army pay was £142,000 in arrears, about one year's pay to the whole force (Moody *et al* 1976, *440*).

In 1676 concern about Irish fortifications, and in particular the rising costs of Charles Fort, Kinsale, led to the Ordnance Establishment Estimates for that year containing a comprehensive survey of forts and garrisons (PRO, WO 54/197). They recommended no change in the Ulster garrisons and in the case of Carrickfergus simply reproduced the survey of 1662, but the review prompted further enquiry. Officers of the Irish Ordnance, together with an English Ordnance Officer, Thomas Phillips, were ordered to inspect the fortifications of Ireland in 1677 and report on their recommended priorities for rebuilding and repair, which they did in 1685 (NLI ms no 3137). Carrickfergus was not on the list of six key places which lay (except for Dublin) on the west or south coasts, but the area of Belfast Lough was reviewed in detail. Phillips produced a plan for a pentagonal bastioned fort alongside and over the site of Carrickfergus castle to defend the harbour, at a projected cost of £14,703. His heart was not in it, however, for he considered that the best approach was to repair the castle for the time being, for use as a barrack, while building a large new fort to command the harbour at Belfast at the cost of £42,054. He had a poor opinion of Carrickfergus, which 'as doth appear, by its situation, to have no command of the channel or river of Belfast', while 'it is not capable of having vessels of any considerable burthen come up close to it, besides they lie dry six or eight hours at every tide'. In this analysis he is confirmed by the record of the rising Customs receipts of Belfast through the second half of the century (Benn 1877, chap. XV). As students of antiquity, however, we should be glad that the government could not find the money for either new fort; the one at Carrickfergus necessarily would have destroyed the castle, while 'if that [the Belfast project] goes on, this castle ought to be demolished and the materials go towards the other work'. As part of their work the Phillips investigators produced several variations of a plan and view of the castle and town (below, p 13 and Pl 1).

As a result of this interest in fortification, work was carried out in Carrickfergus castle. Twenty cannon were ordered in 1674 (McSkimin 1909, *224*) and William Robinson, the surveyor, visited it in or soon after 1677 (PRO, SP 63/361/137). By May of that year Sir George Rawdon reported that guns were being mounted and repairs made to walls that had 'slipped down in several places'; Robinson was paid £186-0-0 in 1679 for this work with £25-12-0 to be spent on two new field gun carriages (CSP DOM 1678 and ADD 1674-9, *164*). In 1679 any surplus in Irish revenue was to be devoted to financing public works (PRO, T14/2) but this did not result in more work on Carrickfergus. Major projects such as the fort at Duncannon built to protect Kinsale harbour took most of the available money: £11,557-1-1 had been spent there by March 1680, while £2,642 worth of work was still to be done and work was still proceeding there in 1687-8 (PRO, T14/2, *41*; T14/5, *72*). In 1685 the permanent garrison of Carrickfergus castle, a storekeeper, a gunner and a matross (gunner's mate), cost £71-18-9. The lowness of the priority given to it may be judged by the money devoted to other garrisons for wages: £3,553-7-6 for Dublin or £277-5-0 for Kinsale establishments. The lowest figure was for Waterford with a single storekeeper at £10-0-0. The castle is briefly noticed in Dobbs's description of Co Antrim in 1683, which refers to several 'arched vaults' within the castle and notes that there are two strong gates with a drawbridge between them, with a platform over the inner of these, which overlooks the town, apparently the present gatehouse (Hill 1873, *386*). The list of ordnance in Irish forts in 1684 shows Carrickfergus in commission like the rest with a variety of brass and iron pieces with powder and shot for them; the numbers are in line with other places but most of the guns are unmounted (Ormonde mss (1), I, *395*).

The town, and with it the castle, was held in 1688 for King James by its garrison in spite of the Williamite sympathies of the population of both the town and region, particularly Belfast. In August 1689 Schomberg captured it after a siege of a week. The fighting, however, centred on the town and its walls not on the castle, which figures only as a storehouse for the Jacobite garrison and whose roofs were used as a source of lead by them (Story 1691, *9*). In 1689-90 minor repairs, costing £9-19-0, were done to the magazine and £160 spent on repairing breaches in the town wall and castle, probably mainly the former (PRO, T37/4). Although William III landed at Carrickfergus, both for Schomberg's campaign of 1689 and William's of 1690, Belfast was the main supply base. In 1691 Lord Talbot put forward a scheme for repairs at the castle costed at £12,000 but it can hardly have been taken seriously as he admits that Carrickfergus harbour could not accommodate ships of heavy burden (PRO, SP 8/11/11). The 1690s saw major works on Irish fortifications but mainly in the South and West of the country again, to counter the threat of French invasion, while Carrickfergus was neglected. There were no officers there in 1690-1 and it was not included in the list of garrisons in 1692 (PRO, T14/6; T37/1). This was purely an economy measure and in 1693 the case for its reinstatement was argued: this rested on its closeness to Scotland and the fact that it was the only garrison place and depot in eastern Ulster; by an adroit use of pension funds for French officers the expense of its maintenance could be met (PRO, SP 63/355/271). By 1698 a storekeeper was the only man on the establishment there (paid £36-16-5) but in 1704 it had achieved the 1685 manning of storekeeper (at £40) gunner and matross (PRO, T14/7, *178*; T14/9). In 1696 a surveyor was at the castle and in 1704 minor repairs there and at other castles cost £170-13-11 (CSP William and Mary 1696, *199*; PRO, T14/8, *190*). Estimates for the construction of gun platforms and carriages were prepared in 1705 (with two costings, of £193-10-5 – TCD, ms no 1180 f187 and £185-16-7 – TCD, ms no 1181 f203), but the work was probably not carried out until 1706, when payment for it was probably included in the £500 given to Thomas Burgh (Ormonde mss (2), VIII, *174*; PRO, T14/8, *215*). In 1711 30 guns were mounted at the castle (McSkimin 1909, *224*), and in 1715 infantry barracks were built there (PRO, T14/9, *238*). These cost £13,336-10-0 which puts the other expenditure quoted above into perspective. Clearly any idea of closing the castle had been abandoned but the castle was not seen as a major fortress, rather as an infantry barrack and depot, on the lines of the 1693 memorandum, or even the arguments of Thomas Phillips in 1684. The government owned the castle and needed an army base in the area.

During this period, as well as the documentary evidence outlined above, we must also consider the information provided about the castle by a number of contemporary plans and views (listed in Appendix 2). The earliest surviving is probably the one now in the British Library (ms Cotton Augustus I ii 42), but like most of the others it is undated (*frontispiece*). The evidence for dating it comes in part from the castle keep where the inserted windows which have brick rear jambs are shown in the south wall while the great arch over the third floor is also shown, although aligned east-west not north-south. The town of Carrickfergus, curiously distorted in the perspective chosen, has a slight bank and ditch around it; outside this at the north-east angle are the buildings of 'the Freres', the friary converted to the 'palace' stores and fortified in 1566. The plan thus pre-dates that year but, to judge from its portrayal of cannon in the castle and the keep modifications, which make use of brick (not building material used in pre-Elizabethan Ulster), not long before. The view centres on the castle and appears to have been drawn in order to illustrate conditions in it rather than in the town. It is probably to be associated with Peers' refurbishing of the castle in about 1560.

The next illustration is one of a pair preserved in Trinity College Dublin, mss 1209.26 and 1209.27. The first (no 26) shows the 'Palace, late a friar's house' defended by a bank and ditch, and the town defended by a wall on the west but only a bank and ditch on the north and east. The second (no 27) shows the town completely walled (including a wall linking the towerhouses along the south side of the present High Street), but with fewer internal details; the castle is shown only in ground plan. These should be associated with the visit of the surveyor, Robert Lythe, to Carrickfergus. On 25 September of that year Thomas Jenison wrote to Cecil: 'Your servant Robert Lythe arrived here six days since and hath, by my Lord Deputy's order drawn two platts of this town . . . the one as it is now, the other as his lordship is minded to fortify the same' (Dunlop 1905, *326* and *331*). No 26 is a plan of the town as it was, no 27 the proposed fortifications. It is to be noted that, in accordance with the policy noted above, by 1567 the emphasis of the drawings is on the town, not the castle. One of these mss, no 27, also forms the model for a poor copy, by John Dunstall, dated 1612, now in the British Library, Cotton Augustus I ii 41. A third plan, attributed by Dunlop (1905, *89*) to Lythe c 1569, is a plan of the area of Belfast Lough, in the Public Record Office, London, SP 64/1/0 or MPF 77. This includes a view of the castle and town but it is less than an inch square and so of little use. The list of 16th-century plans is concluded by another in the Public Record Office, London, SP 64/1/31 or MPF 98. This shows the town wall as built only on the west side, as in TCD 1209.26, but the bank and ditch along the north as more complete and better integrated with the 'palace' defences; St Nicholas's church lies roofless. This view probably relates to the raid of 1573 and the hasty construction of defences in 1574; it may perhaps be dated 1575-6 (the church was repaired in 1577).

The 17th-century plans are mainly those drawn to accompany Thomas Phillips's report of 1685, begun in 1676. Several versions of this exist, in the British Library and in the National Library of Ireland. These are plans of the castle and town, often showing the site and design of the new fort proposed in his report; there are also a number of views of the castle and town from a position about a hundred yards out from the shore, a little to the east of the town. Three, the two in Dublin (NLI mss 2577 and 3137) and British Library K TOP 51-42 are very similar, plans of the town and proposed fort with views at the foot of the sheet; of these NLI no

3137 is less elaborate and has the dimensions of the fort drawn in, while NLI 2557 (Pl 1) is from the Ormonde Papers, along with a copy of Phillips's report. British Library K TOP 51-44 and 45 are very similar, copies of the plans of the existing town and castle, simplified versions of the first three except that the gardens of Joymount are shown either in greater detail or with more imagination. BL K TOP 51-46 is also a plan alone; it has a version of Joymount's gardens perhaps taken from no 44 or 45, but also shows the proposed fort. Curiously it is annotated in French; the caption and scale are in English written with the south at the bottom of the page whilst the annotations are written with the north at the bottom. BL K TOP 51-47 is a very small plan, only 4¾ by 3½ in, and clearly simplified for this reduction. It was probably made for the sheet of Irish towns, copied from Phillips's reports, BL ms 10920(i), made for 'Mr. Tindal's continuation of Mr. Rapin's history' according to a caption at the bottom of the drawing. A second edition of this, the continuation of M Rapin de Thoyras' *History of England from the Revolution to the accession of King George II*, was published in 1751. The last in this series is BL K TOP 51-48, a fanciful version of the views of Carrickfergus of the two NLI mss and K TOP 51-42. Finally, preserved in the National Library of Ireland is ms 2742, identified as a survey of the town and castle possibly by Goubet in 1690-95 on a Sotheby's sale catalogue entry attached to the manuscript. It is rather careless in details and looks like the result of working up field notes some time after they were made.

The evidence about the castle given by these plans is best considered ward by ward in the castle; all agree in showing three wards. The inner ward is entered, on all maps, by a gate in the east curtain, half way along it, or a little to the south. All show the keep at the north-west angle: BL Cott Aug I ii 42 shows big two-light 'Tudor' windows (placed in the middle of the wall) on two floors and the arch over the third floor; TCD 1209.27 shows the dividing wall of the keep with the wall; it, PRO MPF 98 and the Phillips mss show the keep door on the east side. TCD 1209.26 alone shows a building at the south-west angle of the ward, built against the west wall. The Phillips maps (except NLI 3137) show either the north or south wall of a building against the east curtain; presumably it was ruined. The middle curtain, as already noted, is complete in all maps and the east and south-east towers are likewise shown in all. Only TCD 1209.26 omits the middle tower (it would be hidden behind the keep in BL Cott Aug I ii 42). TCD 1209.27 alone has the gate to the middle ward through the middle tower while the others have it beside the tower to the west; Goubet's plan has a twin-towered gate. All the Phillips drawings show, with more or less detail, a dog-legged line across the middle ward south of the entrance to the inner ward. This is presumably a light wall but may be a step down to the postern gate, which is not shown. BL Cott Aug I ii 42 is unique in marking a low shed against the middle curtain between the east and middle towers; it also has this section of curtain as convex to the field unlike the other plans which show it (correctly) as concave.

There is rather more disagreement and complexity with the outer ward. The west side has a platform against the west curtain wall and a building against the platform south of the west tower in BL Cott Aug I ii 42. The building, but not the platform, is present in TCD 1209.26 and PRO MPF 98; the Phillips maps have a building against the curtain south of the west tower with a platform against the wall between the west tower and the gatehouse; Goubet's map appears to agree with Phillips. Except for PRO MPF 98, all the plans show a large building against the east curtain, with its north wall a little south of the gatehouse and its south wall at or near where the east curtain bends to the south-west, a position now occupied by a row of storehouses. This building is clearly ruined in BL Cott Aug I ii 42; the Phillips views show three large windows or embrasures in the curtain wall at that point, featureless except for the fanciful K TOP 51-48 where they are shown with fine tracery. To the south of this building, between it and the east tower, BL Cott Aug I ii 42 shows a raised platform, carrying guns, while TCD 1209.26 shows a scarp down to a lower area between the building and the middle curtain. The Phillips maps and Goubet show a wall parallel to the curtain, some twenty feet within it, perhaps retaining a platform. The gatehouse is shown with round towers in all views (although very sketchily in TCD 1209.26 and PRO MPF 98). In BL Cott Aug I ii 42 they lack parapets and roofs and the upper parts are ruinous at the rear. The Phillips views show the east tower more ruined in its upper parts than the western one; they also indicate the east window of the east tower at second floor level. As to the area just outside the gatehouse, there is no information in BL Cott Aug I ii 42 or TCD 1209.26 for the area is hidden by the gatehouse. TCD 1209.27 rather hesitantly adds 'Capt. Peers' house' to the north-east of the gate; it is shown clearly in PRO MPF 98, with a strong wall around its back plot running apparently right up to the east tower or the gatehouse. It seems to have been removed by the time of the Phillips plans: they show two long walls flanking the present line of approach with the only building a small one at the north end of the west wall.

Examination of these plans and views emphasises that information derived from them must be used as evidence with care. Several factors clearly affect their accuracy. First, the intention of the artist is important. Jenison's letter of 1567, for example, shows that Lythe was briefed to produce TCD 1209.26 to illustrate primarily the town of Carrickfergus, not its castle, some details of which are very sketchy in his plan, for example the gatehouse. Certain details could have been por-

The evidence of the documents

trayed as a form of shorthand rather than exactly. For example in BL Cott Aug I ii 42 the large keep windows are shown in the centre of the wall, while only three storeys are shown. What is being conveyed here surely is not exactly what the artist saw but simply that 'there are large windows in the keep'. Then there is also the problem of whether the work depicted actually was carrried out or if the drawing includes an element of forward planning or wishful thinking.

The Georgian and Victorian Castle

The earlier 18th century was not a period noted for its enthusiasm for the army and expenditure on its barracks. The castle remained in military occupation as a magazine or depot and as a barracks, normally used for regular troops; during the crisis of 1745, however, it was garrisoned by militia and by a Volunteer company from Belfast. That the whole castle was not well maintained would seem to be shown by the tradition, recorded by McSkimin (1823, *164*), that a length of about fifty feet of the outer curtain fell down. The location of this stretch of wall is confused by his description of it as being 'on the south', yet the curtain wall on the south appears to be intact, and it is difficult to find any section of the wall there of anything like that length. From the way this breach was considered a real weakness in the castle's defences, too, in 1760, it seems unlikely that it was on the south side, relatively inaccessible until the building of the present pier in 1885. The southern half of the outer ward may be what is meant here. The castle was not entirely neglected however at this time for it is also recorded that in 1754-5 the keep was re-roofed in lead. This lead roof apparently replaced an earlier one of Co Down slates, which was used to block the spiral stair from the third floor to the battlements; this was found in the mid 19th century (Swanston 1898, *3*). In 1769 the Board of Ordnance reported that the 'large and square tower which is used as a magazine and ordnance store house, is in good repair' (McSkimin 1823, *164*). In addition, although perhaps not Ordnance responsibility, were the barracks built in 1715, presumably the ones built over the vaulted storehouses and demolished in 1802. Probably the castle consisted, in the eyes of the military, largely of these barracks and the keep which could be used as a magazine; the rest of the building was not of much importance. In 1760 the garrison was drawn from General Strode's regiment, the 62nd of foot, about one hundred and eighty men, mostly recruits in training, and guarding some French prisoners of war. On 21 February, however, about eight hundred French, under Commodore Thurot and General Clobert, landed near Kilroot and attacked the town. The garrison defended the town walls between Joymount and the north gate as long as their ammunition lasted, and then retreated to the castle. The French followed up and attacked the main gate of the castle, breaking through it once but being expelled at bayonet point. The garrison had no ammunition left and the castle, largely because of the fifty foot breach from 1754, still unrepaired, was thought to be indefensible and so it surrendered, but one of the conditions of surrender was that no damage should be done to the castle (Strode's report, 23 February 1760, in McSkimin 1811, *138-43*). Thurot re-embarked his men on 26 February, only for his ships to be intercepted by the Royal Navy off the Isle of Man, and sunk or captured. By 1761 some urgent repairs to the castle had been made. The guns, spiked by the French, were restored and a wall between the castle and the High Street, which had given shelter to the attackers, demolished. The parapet of the gatehouse was repaired 'which had been suffered to fall down and go to ruins; in so much as in the last attack . . . the garrison had no place to fire from but through the wicket gate, which for that purpose they threw down' (*Belfast News Letter*, 20 February 1761). The castle was in use as a prison for captured French in 1760 and in 1771 it served the same purpose for men arrested in the Hearts of Steel disturbances.

In 1811 McSkimin (p *55*) describes the castle as 'in a very ruinous condition' before 1793. The French wars and the United Irishmen tension, culminating in the 1798 rebellion, impelled the authorities to overhaul the castle for use as an infantry barracks. In 1797 dissident soldiers planned to seize it for the rebels, but in 1799 it was again used to house prisoners after the rebellion, being thought more secure than the county Gaol. In 1793 the keep had been converted for use as a barrack, in spite of a remarkable protest from the mayor and corporation of Carrickfergus who objected to the defacing of their famous antiquity, but as so often with such things in later times, their efforts to save the castle for use went unheeded. During this work the lintel of the third floor fireplace was replaced. The outer wall was also repaired in that year (McSkimin 1823, *165*), a reference either to a repair of the wall collapsed in 1754 (it seems unlikely that it remained open for over thirty years after it had been instrumental in causing the castle's surrender), or, more probably, equipping the battlements with musket-loops or making the present grand battery. In 1802 new officers' quarters replaced the barracks over the vaulted storehouses on the east side of the outer ward. At the same time a barrack and guard room were built opposite, the latter presumably beside the gatehouse (*ibid*, *157*) where it was in 1923. In 1814 a small square tower 'on the south' was taken down and rebuilt (*ibid*, *165*). Later, we will see that the east tower appears from the fabric to have had its first floor and battlements rebuilt at the same time as musket-loops were built along the other parapets. There was also a tower near the postern at the south-east of the castle to which McSkimin refers elsewhere (p *158*) and it is not clear which of the two towers is referred to here. In the next year, 1815, the keep was again re-roofed: the lead was taken off and replaced by two brick vaults, resting on the inserted arch dividing the third and fourth floors. These vaults together with six 600 gallon water tanks were removed in the winter of 1930-1; they had gone a long way towards breaking the arch. McSkimin records that the new roof also 'rent the north wall' of the keep (1823, *165*). During this time ('a few years since' in 1823, *158*) a 'small magazine' was built in the inner ward; this may be identified as the storehouse built against the east curtain. McSkimin also illustrates a triple arrow-slit (1823, *158*) 'over the entrance to the castle', which will be discussed later under the work of period II (below, p 43).

A plan of the castle (at a scale of 1in to 25ft) was prepared in 1811, to accompany the inspection return for March 1811 (PRO WO 78/1158; MPH 205 (3)) (Pl 29). A second plan at the same scale (MPH 205 (1)) was made in 1822 to accompany General Fyers' report of 15 February, concerned with purchasing land just outside the castle gate. Both are ground plans except for the keep (shown at entry floor level) and the gatehouse (shown at second floor level). The later plan differs little from the earlier, and both show that the castle at the beginning of the 19th century was, except for its eastern flank, very similar to the building of today. The inner ward was entered through a gate mid-way along the east wall; north of the gate was a 'storehouse' against the curtain. The curtain had musket loops on the west and south. The southern end of the curtain was taken up with an 'expence magazine', marked by very thick walls, and with a flight of steps against the west wall; a 'store house' and an 'engine house' were built against the magazine's north wall. The entry floor of the keep appears to have been identical to its present state. The north part of the middle curtain was, as now, demolished; between the east tower and the postern there were three gunports in the east curtain similar to those along the west. The south-east latrine tower was cut down as at present but there was a tower over the postern, with musket loops on the north, east and south. The east tower was much as it is now, with a flight of steps built against the curtain south of it and leading from the courtyard to a platform on its west side at first floor level; from this platform a second flight led to the battlements. Against the west side of the tower was also built a narrow 'armourer's workshop', from the line of the middle curtain on the north and half way along the steps to the south; there is no indication of any room below either flight of steps.

The outer ward had 'officers' barracks, Royal Artillery' at first floor level against the east curtain, part of which is now the castle custodian's house; they are those of 1802 referred to by McSkimin. The curtain itself had the six gunports of the present grand battery. South of this, between these quarters and the east tower, the curtain was built in more sections than at present and had four gunports instead of the present two; behind it in the ward was a shot furnace, noted by McSkimin. On the west side the curtain had musket loops along the battlements; then as now the wall walk was carried over the west tower by an arch. Behind the curtain from the gatehouse to the west tower was a platform at first floor as at present and against this was built a guard room and artillery barracks, presumably also those referred to by McSkimin as built in 1802. There was a well some 10 feet in from the curtain and half way between the west tower and the stump of the middle curtain. The gatehouse was largely as it is now with a 'mess kitchen' built against the south wall of the west tower. The battlements are equipped with gunports and musket loops as they are now. The south wall of the east tower is shown without the windows and towers it now has. The approach to the castle was along a passage between two long curving walls, mostly reduced now to foundations. The wall on the south and west side was equipped with musket loops. The north wall was partly so equipped and outside it was a further wall enclosing the 'lower battery'.

Changes between 1811 and 1822 as shown on the second plan are, as already noted, few. In the inner ward, a building was erected on the triangular space north of the store against the east curtain which was given musket loops. In the outer ward the barracks on the west side were extended south, nearly to the line of the destroyed middle curtain. The main details are outside the castle between it and Castle Street, where the land intended for purchase lay. To the north and east of the entrance passage lay an 'exercise ground, Lyndon's garden, rented by the Ordnance'; two small pieces were detached from this, the castle storekeeper's stable yard and land 'rented to Mr. Craig'. South and west of the entrance lay a parade ground bounded by a wall joined to the castle at the south end of the west tower; in the angle of this wall and Castle Street, separated by a road to the harbour from the Customs house, was a non-conformist 'chapel'. This chapel and the land beside it was the area to be purchased in 1822.

When the Napoleonic war was over, the castle clearly declined in importance. The Ordnance Survey Memoirs (Antrim, Box 7) record that it was changed from an infantry barracks back to a magazine in 1816. In 1834 the ammunition was taken to Charlemont and the garrison reduced to twelve men and a sergeant. In 1839 even these were withdrawn to Belfast and, of the thirty-one guns, thirty were dismounted. The garrison was left as two invalid gunners and a master gunner. The town was alarmed at this, however, for it left the gunpowder, the property of the private suppliers of the area, which was stored there, virtually unguarded. As a result in September 1839 a detachment of thirty men and a subaltern were sent from Belfast to guard it

The evidence of the documents

(Boyle's Memoir, vol II, *114*). In 1855 the castle was brought back into more active use, as the artillery headquarters for the North of Ireland (McSkimin 1909, *226*). In 1857 six 24-pound guns were placed on the grand battery and apart from these there were then six 64-pounders, seven 32-pounders (probably the ones now on the grand battery) and a mortar. In 1889 there was a remarkable addition to the castle in the shape of a tramway from the quay through a tunnel in the rock to the inner ward and the rest of the castle.

From the later 19th century to the years after the First World War the castle increasingly reverted to a role of Ordnance Depot and general Army stores. The position at the end of this last seventy years of military use is summed up in a survey of 1923. In addition to the buildings of 1811 and 1822 which have been noted, others had been built and other changes made. The inner ward was entered, as it is now, by a gate beside the keep and the east gate was blocked. A light wagon shed (perhaps wooden and of 20th-century date) was built by the west curtain. The storehouse against the east was now the RAOD 'long store', of two storeys, connected to the entrance of the keep by a bridge at first floor level. Access between all keep floors was by an inserted wooden stair built against the south wall except between the first and second floors, where it was built against a partition just north of the entrance door. A hoist was mounted on the north wall and doors cut through it at each floor. The whole of the area between the west side of the keep and the middle curtain was blocked, providing a boilerhouse against the keep wall at second floor level, reached by stairs to the north.

There was a small stone building, more square than the armourer's shop of 1811, against the east tower, which was used at first floor level to provide lavatories for men and NCOs whilst the officers' lavatory was carried on an arch between the tower and outer curtain. At the first floor level on the platform just north of the west tower there was another small store, perhaps the one implied by the wall bonded to the 16th-century wall thickening at this point. Between the two early 19th-century ranges in the middle of the outer ward were two light Ordnance depot stores with a filter tank below. The main garrison hutments (for eighty-eight men) were outside the gatehouse to the north and along the shoreline to the north-west. The stabling, for thirty horses, was in the area known as the castle green west of the gatehouse. Many of these buildings were cleared either in the decade after 1929, when the keep was re-roofed, for example, and the huts and stables taken away from outside the gatehouse, or in the fifteen years after 1950. This could be drastic, as seen by a photograph (Chart 1939) of the clearance north of the gatehouse, where most of the soil seems to have been removed and what appears to be the outer end of the opening of the bridge-pit water outlet exposed.

This is not meant to be a complete account of the castle during this period but an outline of some of the events which help to explain the appearance of the castle as it now stands. There is a need for a proper account of the measures taken in the 18th and 19th centuries to fortify Ireland against rebellion and invasion. The fortification of Carrickfergus will take its place in this account.

CHAPTER 2

The physical evidence

The Inner Ward
(Figs 3-4 folded inside back cover)
The inner curtain wall encloses a polygonal enclosure some 47 m long by 27 wide at the southern end of the rock (Pl 2). The curtain wall, normally 1.80-1.90 m thick, and *c* 9 m high to the wall-walk, is of coursed basalt and dolerite rubble, apparently (from the rounded edges of the blocks) not quarried but collected from the shore, with small pinnings. The exterior quoins at the junctions between the straight sections of the wall are of red sandstone for the lower 2.50-3 m and creamy-yellow Cultra stone for the upper 6 m (Preston, quoted in Jope 1962, *21*). The curtain wall at the north, where the keep occupies about one third of the courtyard, will be described with the keep, of which it forms part. The north-eastern section of the curtain wall contains the present entrance to the inner ward, a 19th-century structure, with a segmental arch of thick bricks carried on splayed jambs of hammer-dressed granite. This arch is aligned on the north-west jamb with the wall above the topmost of two irregular offsets on the inner side; the upper part of this wall appears to have been refaced on the inside at the time when the present entrance was built. The lower part of the wall, however, which is up to 50 cm wider, is of one build with both the keep and with red sandstone dressings cut by the north jamb of the present entrance arch. The inner face to the south of the gateway is also much patched and in its present condition at least the upper half (which contains much brick) appears to be contemporary with the gate. Approximately half way along this stretch there is a blocked opening *c* 80 cm wide and 60 cm high with jambs of Cultra stone: the walling here is clearly disturbed, probably by the robbing of some of the dressings and by its blocking. This opening can be seen more clearly on the exterior of the wall. To judge from the coursing which continues unbroken above it the opening cannot have been higher than about 50 cm above the present ground level, which, according to the excavations of 1955, is itself within a metre of the surface of the rock. The use of this opening is unknown.

The outer face of this part of the curtain seems less patched than the inner (Pl 10). Some 3 m above the present ground level there is a chamfered offset of sandstone, continuing round from the north wall of the keep. At the angle close to the keep a further 2.50 m higher, a second chamfered offset in sandstone continues round from the keep about 2 m along the cur-

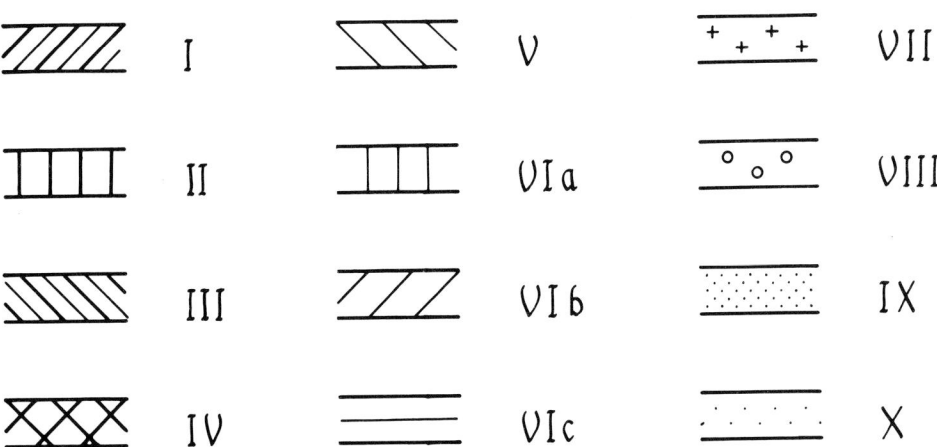

Fig 2 Conventions used for periods in the plans

tain. The quoins of the angle are also in sandstone and continue up in this stone 2 m above the upper offset. At the southern angle the quoin is built in Cultra stone from one course above the offset. There seems to be a change of walling continuing the line of the upper offset nearly as far as the quoins at the southern end of the section: below this line the wall is of larger, more regularly coursed blocks. Around the end of the upper offset and the top of the sandstone quoins is a rectangular setting of Cultra stone flush with the face of the wall below the offset and the wall to the south where there is no offset. The wall face above the second offset and of one build with the sandstone quoins is thus recessed within this setting. It does not run through the wall to the inner face, and has no sill nor a north jamb, so it does not seem to be an opening of any sort. Its sole use appears to be to link the two faces of the wall tidily. It would seem that there was a break in the building of the wall at the point when it had been built up to the course above the lower offset for the whole of this north-east section. At the northern end the wall had been carried up to above a second offset, to a point marked by a levelling course in the north wall of the keep. This height had only been achieved at the angle; for much of the length of the wall it had reached the course below the second offset, but was awaiting the quoins between it and the eastern section of the curtain wall. When building was resumed, dressings were in Cultra stone, not sandstone, and the upper offset was abandoned. To bring the wall-faces flush a setting of Cultra stone was contrived. The battlements, which butt against the keep, for most of the length of this section have been rebuilt with musket loops angled to command the outer ward.

The eastern section of the inner curtain is also complex in its fabric. On the outer face the lower chamfered offset continues in sandstone from the north-east section for 11.50 m (Pl 13). The chamfer of the offset is stopped and seems to be returned to the vertical in the last stone of the course, which has, however, suffered badly from erosion. Within half a metre of this end of the offset there is one course of sandstone blocks above the offset. Stones of this last course form the sills and the lowest jambstone of the north jamb of the more northerly of two fine windows (Pl 12). The exterior openings are 1.20 by 0.30 m, with chamfered sills, jambs and heads. The head of the northern window is round, that of the southern bluntly pointed and in sandstone unlike the rest of the dressings beside the southern window which are in Cultra stone. The rear arches of these windows are large, 2.60 m high and 1.80 m wide, and round-headed; their sills are at low first-floor level, 2.30 m above the present ground level. Part of a window seat is preserved in the northern window and enough survives to show that there were seats c 50 m high down both sides of the recess. The southern recess is less well preserved and has been partially blocked to raise the sill 30 cm. Over the windows on the inner face of the wall are preserved three transverse gables in thin[1] handmade brick, very dark red in colour.

At the southern end of these gables is a succession of openings through the curtain wall, which fortunately match on both sides (Fig 5). At first floor level is a door of hammer-dressed granite, flat-lintelled on the outside but with a shallow rear arch of thick bricks. This door is cut by an arch, also of thick bricks, 2.80 m wide and 3.60 m high, which also truncates the wall running out from the inner side of the curtain which is of one build with the jambs of this door. The arch is itself blocked, at the outer side, by the southern gun emplacement of the east battery; the wall is brought flush with bricks identical to those used in the arch. Built against the inner jamb of the arch, presumably at a similar time to the gun emplacement, is the south wall of the building known in 1923 as the 'long store'; it partially covers the north jamb of the arch. This sequence is straightforward, but the stonework of the first floor doorway is curious. It might be expected to make only a minor disturbance of the curtain wall for the insertion of its jambs, but the area of walling associated with it is both unexpectedly large and asymmetrical. It carries on above and to the south of the door more than to the north, yet on the north is the junction with the wall on the inside of the curtain. Above the door on the outside the walling seems to be filling an arch, while to the south there is a line of Cultra stone on the inner side. It will be argued later that these are the remains of a mediaeval window destroyed by the door. Although the bricks of the two structures are different, it is tempting to associate the three gables to the north, the end of which aligns with the first floor door, with it and its wall off to the east. This was succeeded by the brick arch through the curtain, and then by the 'long store'.

South of this late archway the curtain wall continues without any original features to its southern end: clearance of the last 13 m in the 1962 excavations exposed its full height on the outside of 13 m above the rock. On the inner side both jambs of the archway cut sandstone dressings at the first metre of the wall's height. These seem to be in bond with the wall on either side and are possibly original. Sandstone dressings are re-used at the southern jamb of the 19th-century arch below the Cultra stone just noted to align it with the inner wall face to the south above two successive, irregular offsets. The wall above the upper of these offsets appears to have been refaced at the same time as the building of the arch: it contains much quarried dolerite rubble with sharper angles than elsewhere, laid in less regular courses. Against this wall, and filling the whole of the southern end of the ward, was built a thick-walled

---

[1] All bricks in the castle are about 23 cm (9 ins) long and 11–12 cm (4½ ins) wide. 'Thin' bricks are 5.0–6.5 cm (2–2½ ins), 'thick' bricks 7.5–8.0 cm (3 ins) thick.

The physical evidence

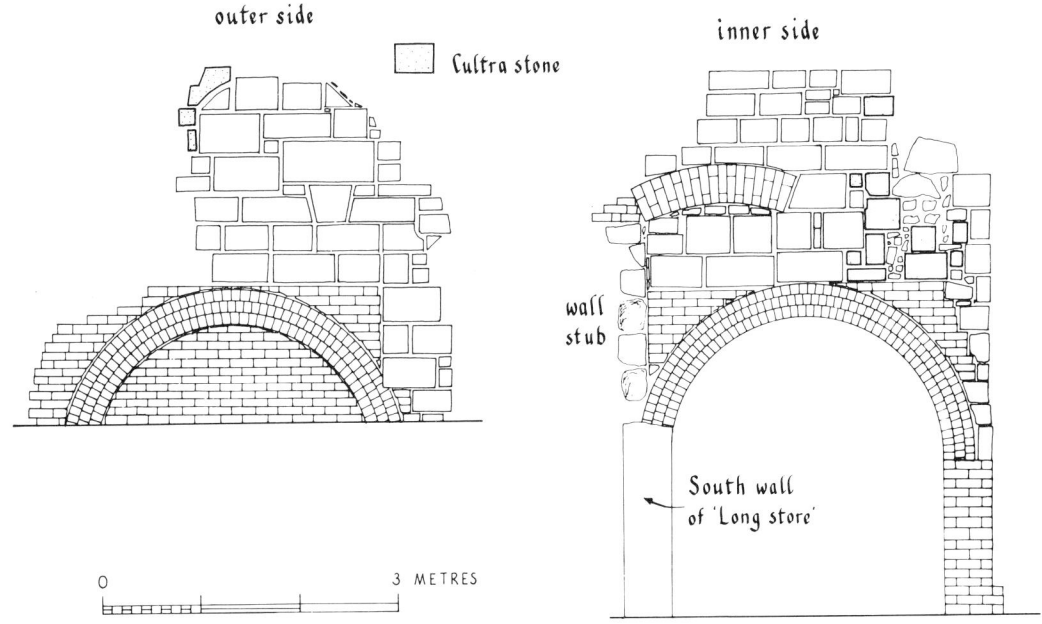

Fig 5   Elevations of the probable former entrance to the inner ward

chamber of brick with its wall face to the ward of hammer-dressed granite. It has two entrances, one angled in from the south-west angle of the inner ward and one from the former yard over the postern gate of the middle ward. This last has a dog-leg in the passage while the ventilation shafts of the room within are screened in brick on the inner side. The room itself is a plain brick-lined chamber with a brick barrel vault. It had a one-storey building built on to its north wall and against the inner face of the inner curtain. Its wall-plate was taken right through the latter but the roof-scar looks as though it was added and it would thus seem to be later than the brick archway in the eastern section of the inner curtain. These buildings are those marked on the plan of 1811. Above, and reached by a long stair in the south-west corner of the ward, are two semicircular gun emplacements of hammer-dressed granite. The inner room, a magazine, can be seen on the outside of the southern sections of the curtain to have blocked two gunports of thin, handmade bricks of the type best seen along the west side of the castle, and a third was blocked by the staircase to the gun emplacements above. The two westerly gunports can also be seen to have cut semicircular-headed single-light windows of Cultra stone on the exterior (Pl 7). The one opposite the staircase has preserved the top two courses of the jambs; of the other only the window-head is left. Near the top of the stairway on the interior face of the curtain can be seen the upper part of the rear arch of that window, built into the new facing of the curtain for the stair and magazine. It is also of Cultra stone and, although no part of either jamb is left so its dimensions cannot be measured, it would seem comparable, certainly in workmanship and probably in size, to those in the east section of the curtain.

The curtain wall on the west side of the inner ward has few features. Clearly cut through at courtyard level are three gunports of thin bricks, the southern two still open (Fig 6). They are very similar to those extant

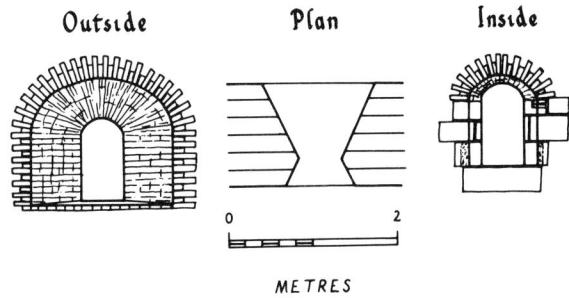

Fig 6   Plan and elevations of a gunport inserted into the west wall of the inner ward

along the western side of the middle and outer wards at first floor level. The actual embrasure, segmentally-arched, is about 1 m high and 35-40 cm wide, and 35-40 cm in from the inner face of the wall. The embrasures splay to c 80 cm wide and 1.30 m high on the inner wall-face and to 1.30-1.70 m wide and about 1.50 m high on the outer face, where again the embrasures have segmental arches. Against the inner angle of the curtain and the keep, and arching over the northern blocked one of the three gunports, in a very similar manner to two late arches in the outer ward, was built a thick, battered wall supporting a stair, with hammer-dressed dolerite dressings, leading to the battlements. This northern gunport itself destroyed an earlier round-headed arch of red sandstone voussoirs and jambs. The north jamb has been demolished as has most of the southern by the gunport but enough is left to show that it was about 1.50 m wide and more than that high. The gunport has removed any traces of it on the outside of the wall, and so it cannot even be said whether this arch belonged to a door, a window or a recess. North of this, the junction of the inner face of the curtain and the keep is obscured by the stair but the outer face can be seen to be of one build with the keep wall. The battlements are tied in to the keep and the Cultra stone dressings of the angle buttress start from the first merlon. Below this is a line of sandstone dressings acting as stops to the two chamfered offsets of the keep wall. Like those of the north-eastern section the battlements have been rebuilt with musket loops south of the junction with the keep.

The Keep (Figs 7-8, Pls 10-11)

As already noted, the north and west walls of the keep are part of the inner curtain. On the exterior of these walls there are two chamfered offsets, 2.60 and 5.40 m above the present ground level respectively. Above these, clearly visible on the north wall, but hardly so on the west, is a levelling course at 7.40 m above the present ground (Pl 6). At this level the dressings of the quoins are built in Cultra stone but below it the quoins and offsets are of sandstone. The chamfered offsets terminate at the south-west angle of the keep at a vertical line of sandstone dressings which rises to the level of the inner curtain battlements (Pl 9). At the north-east, the lower offset continues around the inner curtain, as already described, while the upper one ends at the rectangular Cultra stone setting which we have already noted as bringing the upper parts of the curtain flush with the rest over the upper offset at the height of the levelling course. The outer north-east angle of the inner curtain is 80 cm west of the point at which the outer wall of the keep joins the inner curtain. In the angle thus created there are large projecting stones most reasonably interpreted as being left for the later attachment of the keep. This attachment, which links well with the position of the angle in the curtain wall, would indicate that at the time when the builders decided to change to using Cultra stone for the dressings, they also decided to build the keep a little smaller. It may not be a coincidence that there is a curious buttress projection of 75 cm at the west end of the south wall. Work on the keep may in fact have started at the masons' benches when this decision was taken, for the bottom eight courses of the south-west angle quoins and many of the quoins of the forebuilding projection are of hard chalk (Pl 17). The keep as built was not square: the two northern angles are very nearly right angles but the southern wall is decidedly off line. As a result the exterior walls are all slightly different lengths: the north wall is 17.00 metres long, the west 17.40, the east 17.70, and the south 17.80. The north and west walls, as befits their position facing the field, are considerably thicker than the other two. The two southern angles have buttresses. The eastern projects 97 cm from the east wall above the level of the forebuilding and dies into the upper wall in two weathered offsets at fourth floor and battlement level. The south-western angle has projections on both sides. To the south a buttress projects 75 cm from the inner curtain wall-walk level as already noted and dies into the south wall in a weathered offset at fourth floor level. To the east spring corbels resting on the upper chamfered offset of the west wall, supporting a projection which contains the latrine chutes, and continues unbroken to the top of the turret over the battlements. The keep is approximately 25 m high, from the top of the turrets to ground level. A feature of the north wall is the 19th-century hoist at battlement level, with resulting openings at the first, second and fourth floors below it. These have now been blocked but the patching is quite visible externally (Pl 6).

The Ground Floor

There are few original features of note at this level. The west wall, 3.70 m thick, has nothing to note internally and only the lower chamfered offset externally. During the 19th century a chamber 2.90 by 1.75 m was hollowed out in the thickness, 3.70 m, of the western half of the north wall, and lined with thick bricks. It had a door through to the outside which has now been blocked although the scars of the patching remain visible. A building has been added to the south wall, 3.00 by 8.90 m internally. It is of granite, massively built for a one-storey room of its size (the south wall is 1.45 m thick), and the door in the south wall is covered by a thick masonry arch. The south side at least appears to have been designed to resist blast although the windows and door in the west and east walls are open. This room connects with the inside of the keep through an inserted door and another door, markedly irregular on the inner side, has been inserted south of this added room to connect the inner ward and the keep interior. The east wall has a small slit near the northern end, its outer side enlarged and replaced by a grille. On the inside it splays to a round-headed rear arch of Cultra stone, 1.50 m wide and 1.70 m high; the splays were carried on plank centering. At the south end there is a

The physical evidence

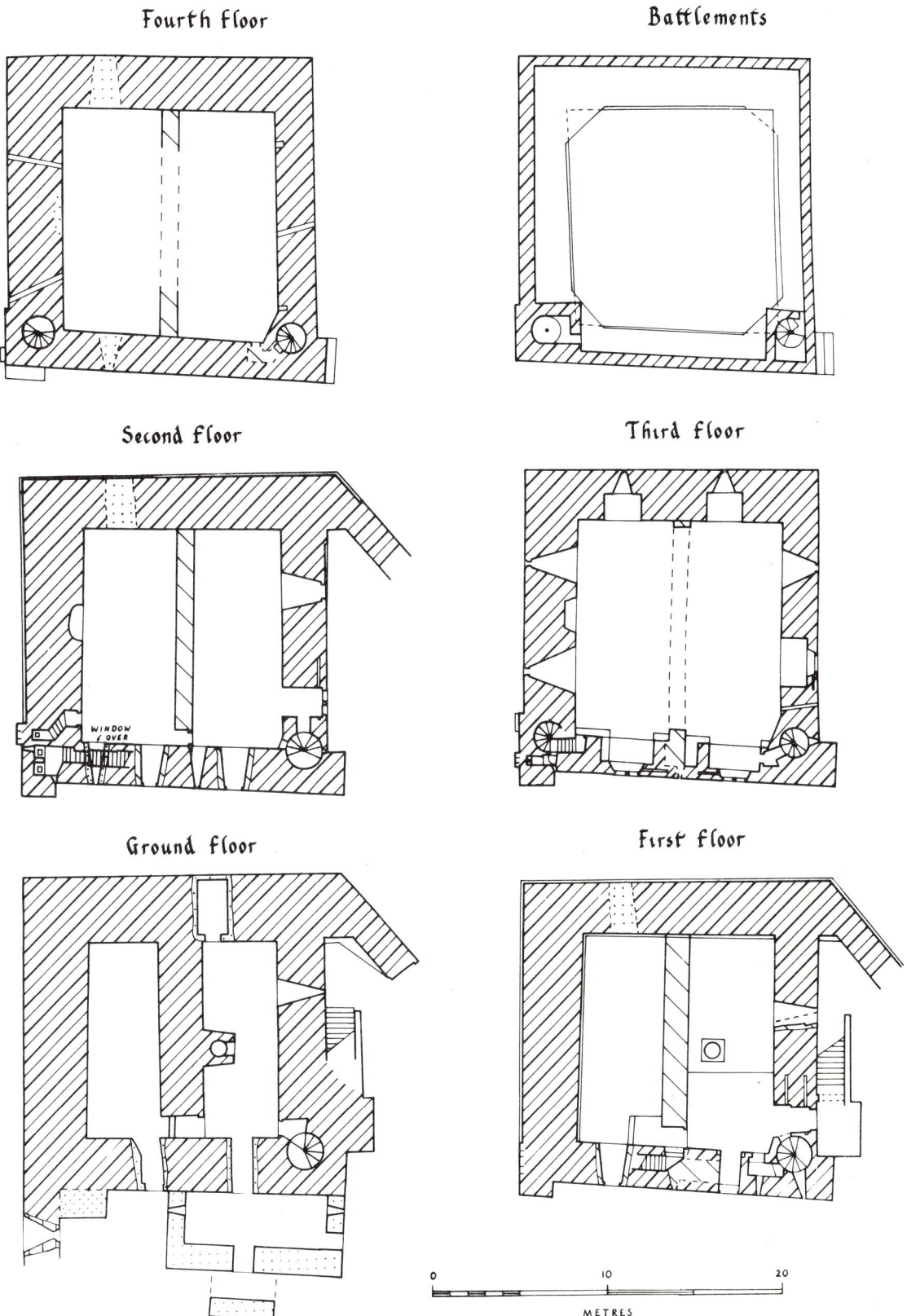

Fig 7 Floor plans of the keep

door in Cultra stone, rebated on the side to the stair, which leads, through a chamber big enough to accommodate the opening door, to the spiral staircase. This would, of course, have been the only original access to the ground floor. The ground floor is divided into two chambers, both vaulted, by a thick wall running north-south down the middle. It appears to be bonded in at the north end, but a better argument in favour of its being original would be that its dressings are of Cultra stone, and that the projection from it housing the well-shaft is certainly bonded. The well-shaft continues to the first floor, with an arch at ground floor level for access to it. At the south there is a doorway, rebated unexpectedly to the west in Cultra stone, which originally gave access between the two chambers; its head and the vault of the passage between the chambers have been rebuilt in thin bricks. This passage has recently been blocked. The segmental barrel vaults are not original for they are broken to accommodate the window and, door in the east chamber.

The First Floor

The original entrance to the keep was in the east wall, now reached by a flight of modern granite steps. The retaining wall of these steps looks much patched: it contains two probable voussoirs of Cultra stone loosely built into it. The steps lead to a rectangular platform outside the door of the keep. The walls of it seem less patched and the south-east quoins are largely of red sandstone (Pl 17). That there was a forebuilding here originally is shown by the jamb of an arch projecting from the keep wall and of one build with it, of Cultra stone but now broken off at the springing. The east wall of the present platform would have to have extended further to the north to support the other jamb. It is now cut down flush with the flags of the platform but in 1923 a bridge connected it and the first floor of the RAOD 'long store' to the east. The actual details of any forebuilding, such as whether there was a pit, lie beneath the flagstones of the present arrangement. The door itself is round-headed, 1.10 m wide and 2.20 m high; its jambs and voussoirs are rounded on the external arris but otherwise the opening is plain. Within there were two doors, marked by rebates and higher arches (2.90 m in the case of the innermost). There are two drawbar holes to close the inner door, but only one for the outer, 1.70 m long, in the north wall. The socket for the drawbar of the outer door survives in the south wall but the two for the inner door have been destroyed on the south side, along with part of the jamb beside them, by a door driven through the wall of the entrance doorway. This door, with irregular corbelled lintels contrived from the ashlar blocks of the entrance doorway wall, leads to the spiral stair in the south-east angle of the keep. It is clearly a later insertion replacing the more complex original arrangements. In these, access was gained to the stair from a door in the south wall. This door, rebated on the south side, led to a small passage, lit by a narrow loop in the south wall (now blocked by the roof of the 19th-century building against the keep), and the passage gave on to the staircase. Thanks to changes in the floor levels within the keep, the sill of the door to this chamber is now down a 35 cm high step; once it was probably (if there was a step at the keep door) only half that; likewise a step has been inserted by the staircase. This last, 1.80 m in diameter, spirals clockwise upwards, and is lit by a loop in the south wall. The east wall is angled at the south to accommodate the staircase.

Apart from the entrance and the staircase, the east wall also has a window to the north. This was originally an externally chamfered, round-headed loop in Cultra stone, c 10 cm wide and c 1.70 m high, splaying to a rear arch c 1.10 m wide and 2.00 m high; the arch of the splay was plank-centred. This was later widened on the south to make a window 37 cm wide; the rear arch was also widened, to 1.44 m, and the new south jamb contains thin brick. Internally the north and west walls have an irregular offset some 20 cm wide, at 1.60 m above the level of the doorway; it does not continue around the south and east walls. This is about 2.75 m below the levelling course visible on the exterior and can have nothing to do with any change of plan associated with it. It might, however, indicate that at a time when the keep had just been started its first floor was intended to be at this level, some 5 m above ground level. Externally both walls have the upper chamfered offset half way up this floor, and there is a blocked 19th-century opening below the hoist in the north wall.

The south wall is on this, as on the other floors, the most complex. At the west end is a round-headed window with external jambs much restored in the 1930s, 75 cm wide and 2.00 m high. Its recess splays slightly to a segmental rear arch, 1.63 m wide and 2.15 m high. It appears contemporary with another window beside the original door to the staircase, with a segmental rear arch, 1.00 m wide and 2.63 m high, carried on jambs made largely of thin bricks. The recess of this window is straight sided, 2.30 m deep, leading to a round-headed window, 2.05 m high but partly obscured by the roof of the 19th-century building attached outside. The inner jambs of this window fill up rebates of an arch of Cultra stone, 1.48 m wide and probably some 2.30 m high. The later recess can be seen to have cut through a barrel vaulted passage or chamber, 1.25 m wide in the thickness of the wall; the east end of this passage or chamber was used as the east side of the later window recess, while it clearly extended to the west but was blocked. In the centre of the south wall of the keep there is a third round-headed opening. The upper part of this and the eastern jamb have been blocked by an inserted cross-wall but it can be seen to have been

1.37 m wide and at least 2.10 m high. On the outside a loop can be seen partly blocked by the 19th-century building. Within the archway there is now a round-headed door (the original opening) leading up three steps to a triangular space from which a flight of steps to the west leads up a passage in the thickness of the keep wall. The diagonal wall of this space is clearly inserted to block the passage which formerly extended to the east as well. This blocking is of one build with that of the original arch in the wall, put in to support the cross-wall of the keep. Before this cross-wall and the eastern window in the south wall were built, it would seem that there were two arches in this wall, which led to a wall chamber some 1.25 m wide and 4.40 m long, lit by a loop in the south wall at the west and possibly one at the east. From it a mural staircase 85 cm wide and c 2.50 m high roofed with stepped lintels led up to the west as it still does by twenty-one steps to a latrine chamber at second floor level. The north (inner) wall of this stair-passage has been straightened by means of a 15 cm rebate 3.25 m along; at 5.70 m along it is rebated on both sides for a door. At the top of the stair the passage widens into a chamber, 1.30 m long and 2.65 m wide, roofed with corbels. The west wall has two latrine recesses, separated by a short wall and arched with shouldered lintels. It is lit by a loop in the north latrine recess and one in the south wall of the chamber, in the angle between the south wall of the keep proper and the south buttress. The chutes of the latrines, as already noted, are corbelled out from the upper chamfered offset of the west wall. This complex arrangement of the first floor latrines at second floor level may have been contrived because the west wall had been already built: the latrine chamber floor is at the same level as the levelling course visible on the exterior of the north and west walls.

The interior of this floor is now divided by the cross-wall, 1.40-1.50 m thick, already referred to as partly blocking the original central arch. It does not block this archway completely because at the south end there is a segmental arched doorway through it, 1.13 m wide and 1.95 m high, rebated for a door to the west. It is the south jamb alone which blocks the archway, leaving room for the door to the latrine stairs. Within the eastern room, near the cross-wall is the well-head, now covered in a recent wooden box for protection and display. There is also a step across the floor of this eastern room which preserves the line of a 19th-century partition, but the two steps in the western room do not seem to have such an easy explanation. In the north-west angle a wide wooden stair has been built recently for the convenience of visitors.

The Second Floor

As with the lower floors, there are signs of changes of plan on the exterior of this floor. On the north and west walls at 11.60 m above ground level there is a projecting string-course, chamfered below. This ends neatly enough against the latrine buttress at the south end of the west wall but turns around the north-east angle only to end against nothing some 2 m along the east wall. About a metre further along the wall there is a vertical setting of thirteen Cultra stones projecting from the line of the rest of the east wall although flush with the part to the north. At the top of this setting the projecting part simply tails off and above it the wall aligns with the rest. The quoins at the north-east angle of the keep reflect this change, stepping in c 10 cm at this point. It looks as though the builders contemplated building a wide shallow pilaster from this point, perhaps to set off the turret above. If so, they had the idea, and abandoned it, after giving up the idea of a string course as well.

The north wall has no features other than the string course and the blocking of the 19th-century hoist opening, visible on the outside. The exterior of the west wall is much disturbed by later flue openings: there was a boiler-house outside it at this level in 1923, reached from a stair to the middle curtain wall-walk. In the interior at the centre of the west wall is a fireplace, 2.00 m wide; the jambs have heavy three-quarter roll mouldings, and the lintel is a single stone. At the south end of the wall a doorway with chamfered jambs, lintel and sill, which is now 75 cm above the floor-level, leads to a latrine chamber. The floor-level is unlikely to have changed however since this door was built, to judge by the levels of the sill of the door to the stair at the south-east angle or the fireplace. The doorway is rebated for a door on the west and opens onto a small space just large enough for the door to open into. From this space an angled passage leads to the south-east up five steps to the latrine chamber itself, 80 cm long and 55 wide. There is probably a blocked slit above the seat in the south wall of the chamber best seen outside. The single shaft discharges down a chute corbelled out for it from the south buttress.

The east wall of the keep has two windows. The northern one is a single opening, round-headed (restored in the 1930s), 78 cm, wide and 2.25 m high, with chamfered Cultra stone jambs and sill; it splays to a round-headed rear arch of Cultra stone, 2.10 m wide and 2.80 m high. In spite of its size which might seem inappropriate in a keep there seems no reason to doubt that it is original. To the south there is a large rectangular recess, 1.60 m wide and 2.10 m deep, with a round-headed rear arch 3.70 m high. On the outer side of this within an inner arch are two windows, each 50 cm wide and 1.32 m high, separated by a pillar 22 cm wide; the pillar is of red sandstone but the heads of both windows are made from a single block of Cultra stone. Both windows seem to have been closed by a single shutter, secured by a drawbar in a hole 1.70 m long in the north wall, and a socket in the south. In the south side of this recess, beside the inner arch, is a door leading down a short passage to the stair. The door is 72 cm wide but its lintel has now been lost and the passage is corbelled. The stair is lit by a loop in the east wall, in the angle of the buttress. There is also a window looking into the staircase in that part of the east wall angled to accommodate the stair.

The south wall has four windows. At the west end, high up in the wall to avoid the stairs of the first floor latrine, is a small window of dark red, thin brick. This is flat-headed on the outside, c 40 cm wide and c 80 cm high, splaying internally to a segmental rear arch c 90 cm wide and c 1.80 m high. Possibly related to this, in level at least, is a blocked opening in the west wall, above the fireplace, some 2 m wide and apparently quite low. This may be a new fireplace for a floor above the present one. Either because of the position of the latrine stairs, or because of an internal partition (see page 42), the other three windows are displaced towards the east. On either side there are two with round-headed window openings and segmental rear arches, the latter chamfered on the arch and jambs, the chamfer being neatly stopped before the sill. The eastern one of these two seems to have been lengthened downwards, for the chamfer now stops about 70 cm above the sill, which is itself irregular. Between these is a narrow loop with an external round-headed opening of chamfered Cultra stone, 15 cm wide and 1.60 m high. This can be seen to have splayed to a round-headed rear arch, 90 cm wide and 2.20 m high, in spite of the partial blocking of its western side by the later, inserted cross-wall. This wall is carried straight up on the east face from the first floor but a 50 cm offset in the west face reduces its width at second floor level to just one metre. That this offset is not evenly taken out of both sides would seem to be because of the position of the more northerly of the two large segmental-headed windows. It would have been encroached on by the wall if it came 25 cm closer, while it could not be moved to the west because of the first floor latrine stair-passage. As at first floor level there is a segmental-headed door at the south end of the cross-wall, linking the two rooms, 60 cm wide and also rebated for a door on the west.

The Third Floor (Pl 14)

This is very clearly the most elaborate floor of the keep with two windows in each wall. Because of an offset in all four walls it is also larger than the floors below. The windows in the north wall are not central but offset to the west. Each window has a round-headed loop, externally chamfered in Cultra stone, 15 cm wide and 1.80 m high. These open off rectangular recesses in the wall, 2 m wide and 1.40 m deep, with rear arches of Cultra stone 2.90 m high. The west loop was widened out in the 19th century and restored in the 1930s. There is a central fireplace in the west wall, 2.00 m wide and spanned by a flat stone lintel. On either side are two more windows, of differing sizes. The northern is the smaller, a loop 15 cm wide and 1.78 m high, splaying to a round-headed rear arch 2.07 m wide and 2 m high. The southern light is 40 cm wide and 1.55 m high, with a rear arch 2.70 wide and 3.10 m high. The internal and external dressings are of Cultra stone and the external ones are both chamfered. The north window in the east wall is comparable to those in the west wall, a single light, chamfered externally, 35 cm wide and 1.75 m high, splaying to a round-headed rear arch 2.12 wide and 2.75 high. The southern one has a wider light, 90 cm wide and 1.32 high, round-headed and chamfered externally but much restored. This opens off a rectangular recess, 2.73 m wide and 1.50 m deep with a rear arch 3.35 high. In the south splay of the opening into it is a drawbar hole, 80 cm long at least, with a socket in the north splay. This is to secure a shutter, and shows that the jambs (and so the window) are original. Beside this, about 2 m above floor level, is a small opening about 27 cm square running indirectly through the wall (no light is visible but a draught can be felt); its purpose is unknown. Again, the east wall is angled at the south end to allow for the staircase.

The south wall is complicated by the addition of a skin to the wall, the thickness of the floor offset, about 40 cm. This is quite low, especially in the centre of the wall where it is only 12 cm above the present floor level, but at the east side, against the angled east wall, it is 2 m high. Its purpose is unknown but it is of one build with the blocking of the central window, part of the support for the dividing arch. The wall is dominated by two similar, double-light windows. These, as now restored, are 55 cm wide and 1.62 m high and have shouldered lintels, carried on a central pier 20 cm square, with an external relieving arch above. They open off rectangular recesses, 2.90 m wide and 1.40 deep from the original wall face; the rear arches are 3.70 m high. Both have drawbar holes in the splays of the windows, running into the centre of the wall. The western recess was blocked to about 50 cm high on the west side at the time the skin was added to the wall-face, possibly for a window seat. In the east side of the east recess is a doorway with a shouldered lintel, to give access to the staircase. It is rebated for a door on the east and leads into a passage slightly widened on the south side to allow the door to open freely. The stair, which narrows to 1.60 m in diameter at a corbel between the third and second floors, has a light in the east wall in the angle of the buttress. Between the two double windows is a smaller one, now blocked for the dividing arch support. On the outside the window-head of the narrow loop can be seen but the jambs and sill have been removed and the coursing continued, apparently unbroken, across the gap, a salutary lesson in the

The physical evidence

difficulty of detecting changes in rubble masonry. Internally a rectangular recess off which the loop presumably opened, has been partially unblocked in the 1930s restoration; it is 1.90 m wide and 1.30 m deep, with a round-headed rear arch 3.05 m high.

At the west end of the wall is a door with shouldered lintels, rebated for a door to the south. This leads to a short mural stair to the west, 75 cm wide, with six steps. At the top of these a door in the south wall opens into a narrow passage, 55 cm wide, with two more steps (the lower canted to allow the door to open) up to a single latrine, in a chamber 50 cm wide and 95 cm long. This discharges through a chute corbelled out from the latrine buttress, over the chutes of the first floor double latrine. Also reached from the stair passage is a spiral stair, 1.40 m in diameter, mounting to the south-west turret. It is lit by a slit in the south wall and is now broken at fourth floor level. The third floor is now divided by a high arch corresponding to the dividing walls of the first and second floors, which also, as already noted, blocks the central window in the south wall. It is carried ultimately on heavy corbels springing at a height of 1.70 m in the north and south walls. It is not quite a semi-circle, being about 5 m high at the crown but 11.40 m in diameter.

The Fourth Floor
The best evidence that there was a floor at this level where there is now none, some 4 m above the third floor, is to be found in the staircase at the south-east angle. Here, one full turn of the stair above the door to the third floor is another, blocked, doorway. It has well-dressed jambs and gives every appearance of being original. In the south wall, over the east side of the eastern window of the third floor, the shadow of a doorway can just be made out beneath the plaster and whitewash, which looks like the other end of a passage from the stair. On the east wall, at about 4.5 m above the present fourth floor, there are three large square holes in the wall. The two at the north and south are reflected by ones in the west wall, but in the middle the wall has been patched. The holes in the west wall and the central one in the east wall ran through the full width of the wall (but are now blocked except for the central east one, reused for a down spout); this, together with their size, should argue against their being later insertions. If these holes supported the ends of floor beams, they would have been destroyed when the existing arch across the third floor was inserted. At that time the fourth floor must have been removed and the third floor extended, as it does now, to the roof level. The problem in this is that the holes are not opposed, but the fact remains that they match the level of the blocked door. In the 19th century the floor was restored, although not the access to the south-east staircase, for a new stair was inserted against the south wall at the east end. At this time a brick round-arched window, now blocked, was inserted in the south wall at the west end; an opening, also blocked, in the north wall was linked to the hoist above. The stair at the south-west angle did not communicate with this floor.

The Roof Level
The history of this level is clearly not straightforward. In the north and west walls at the top of the fourth floor, below the present wall-walk level, there are what appear to be six blocked weepholes of Cultra stone (they have lintels and so are not blocked battlements) (Pl 10). In the south wall there is one at the same level at the west end, but at a slightly lower level, some 3 m above the heads of the large double windows on the third floor, are two others, one central and one at the west end. Half way between the windows and these possible weepholes several courses of the wall are largely composed of Cultra stone (Pl 11). A similar situation is to be found on the outer face of the east wall: a smaller, blocked weephole at the north end (like the six in the north wall) and a larger central hole above. The present light roof is quite recent. The inner wall-lines appear to continue up from the fourth floor to an offset, varying in width from 15 to 30 cm, some 70 cm below the wall-walk. From this offset spring three squinches at the angles; the remains of the fourth at the north-east are clear. The south pair (Pl 16) now carry the inner angles of two small corner turrets which rise some 3.75 m above the wall-walk; the top 50 cm or so were rebuilt with hammer-dressed basalt in the 19th century. These turrets contain the heads of the two staircases. The east turret has a door facing the east wall-walk; the west turret has one facing the south walk. That there were two northern turrets originally is shown by the squinches at the angles and the wider, higher merlons at the corners. The battlements between the turrets had on each wall four embrasures, 1.15 m above the wall-walk and 60 cm wide with wide merlons between, now rather ruined but originally at least 2 m above the wall-walk.

The Middle Ward (Figs 3-4)
Any account of this area of the castle must anticipate the account of the excavations carried out in 1955 and 1962, which will be found later. This is not only because these uncovered much of the middle curtain and its associated structures but also because they gave us some insight into the contours and levels of the southern end of the rock on which the castle was built. On the west the rock falls steeply from the keep and inner curtain, originally to the quay and harbour, now-

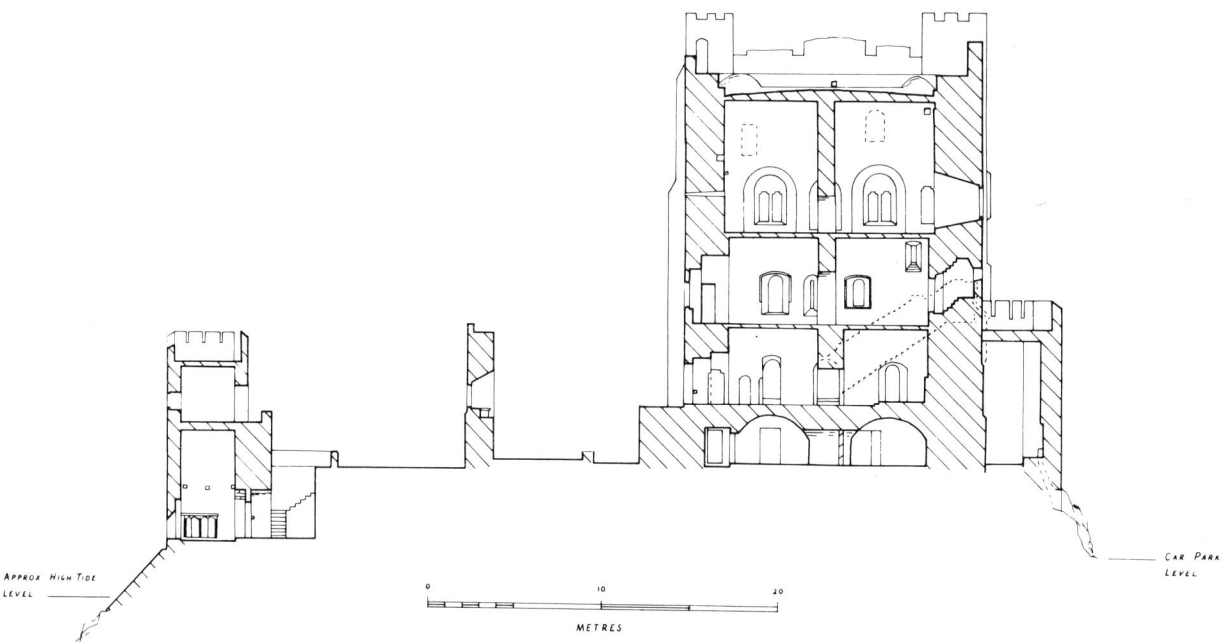

Fig 8   Section through the keep, inner ward and east tower looking south

adays less romantically to the carpark, so that the middle curtain was built close to the keep. To the north it would seem from the excavations of 1955, and the cut visible in the rock below the north-west angle of the middle curtain (Pl 15), that a ditch in front of the inner curtain ran across the rock some 8 m north of the keep. Along the east side of the inner ward there appears to have been a shelf of the rock above high tide level, rather wider to the north than to the south. This permitted or demanded that the builders put in basements in this east section, unlike the rest of the castle (Fig 8). It also meant that the middle ward was little more than a thin strip of land; there are not now, and probably never were, any buildings in it except the towers on the line of the middle curtain.

At the south-west end the middle curtain is clearly secondary to the keep, for it butts against the wall, oversailing the two chamfered offsets; indeed it has now come away and developed quite a gap between it and the keep, inefficiently plugged with 19th-century brick (Pl 9). From the keep it returns parallel to it after just 2 m and at the same interval turns out again to form the south wall of the south-west latrine tower. This has a sill 45 cm high from the present ground level to its floor, which is only 1.70 m square internally. In the angles between the west and the north and south walls are the supports for a latrine seat which, from its width of about 1.50 m, must have been a double one. The arch of the chute is clearly visible although patched and blocked in the outside of the wall below. The outer wall at ground level is only one metre thick but it is thickened to 1.20 m by internal corbelling 1.75 m above the floor. The tower seems always to have been open-gorged and there is no sign of a first floor in it; the present concrete platform over it at second floor level dates from the 19th-century reconstruction of the battlements. The battlements all along this western part have been rebuilt with musket loops commanding the harbour. About 10 m north of the south-west latrine tower there is an open brick-built gunport of 16th-century type at first floor level. On the inside can be seen two sockets for the floor behind it, surprisingly slight to support a gun, and very possibly dating from the 19th century. Below this gunport is a possible later doorway through the curtain. On the inside the north jamb is the clearer with two hammer-dressed dolerite stones projecting into the ward; the south jamb is hard to make out and externally all that can be seen is an area of patched walling. Some 2 m north of the gunport the curtain turns east at the north-west angle over the gap in the rock below, already mentioned (Pl 15). The quoins of this and all the other angles of the middle curtain are of Cultra stone.

The stretch of curtain along the north is entirely known from the results of the excavation in 1955. It has been cut down to ground level at the western end and finished off like a buttress in two weathered offsets of brick. The western half of the northern curtain is built in two straight sections, 10 and 8 m long and 1.20 m wide, meeting at a shallow projecting angle, and at the east end it runs into the middle tower. Only the plan and lowest three or four courses of this tower are known. It has four sides of unequal length and no right angles, giving it a shallow projection on either side beyond the middle curtain which here again alters its line. At the south-west inner angle the quoins of Cultra stone show that it was either open-gorged or else that the door to it was unrebated and either the full width of the back wall, or else built hard against the west end of it. East of the middle tower the wall has been built up along the original lines to raise it above the present ground level; the original masonry has been reburied. The wall for this section, between the middle and east towers, is of two widths, 1.20 m to the west and 90 cm to the east; the two meet at a shallow re-entrant angle (Pl 24). The narrower wall also has a very slight re-entrant angle approximately half way along its length. At this point, since 1955, the wall of a light building of late 19th-century date (wall 3 in the excavation account) has been restored to serve as the parapet of a well for stairs leading down to the basement of the east tower. At its north end the middle curtain can be seen built over in the early 19th century when a wall was built over both it and the outer curtain, which was butted against it at this point (Pl 25). Within the stair-well the middle curtain and east tower can be seen to be of one build.

The east tower (Pl 18 and Fig 8) is built out on a projecting boss of rock, some 3 m above high tide level. It is of four storeys, including the basement, and nearly square (4.25 m by 4.70 m externally). The walls, 80 cm thick, have no batter externally nor offsets for floors internally except at battlement level. It is recorded as rebuilt in 1814 (McSkimin 1823, *165*) which presumably refers to the battlements and perhaps the second floor, while a sloping granite skirt was added to the base as part of the late 19th-century artillery fortifications. The basement is now reached by three flights of steps in the well already mentioned, built since 1955; within the angle of these steps, at the base of the well, are preserved low, right-angled foundations. The date and function of these is unknown but a flight of steps would have been needed between the courtyard and the tower basement. This basement is reached by a passage 1.30 m long, at a slight angle again to the middle curtain between it and the doorway (Fig 9). This is rebated for a door to the inner side of the tower. There are two sockets on the other side, both less than 30 cm deep and so too short for drawbar holes. The door lintel alone could act as a rebate for a door but the sockets are below it, not just outside it and the door must have been on the inside. At basement level the whole of the passage is original, and for at least the lower 3 m or so the wall running south from it, the present east wall of the stair well, must be so as well; it becomes very mixed above this. Within the tower, the basement has an impressive array of loops. In the north-west wall, squeezed between the north corner and the door, there is a single loop, 10 cm wide and 70 cm high, with a rear arch 80 cm wide with a lintel supported on two hollow-moulded corbels. There are three slits in the south-west wall under a single lintel supported by two hollow-moulded corbels which project from the webs dividing the splays of the individual slits. The most westerly of the three slits was partly blocked when the granite skirt was added to the outside. The other two walls have more elaborate arrangements, with the triple slits opening from a single arched recess: the north-eastern arch is 1.80 m wide and 2.20 m high while the north-western one is 20 cm wider and 10 cm higher. The outer pair of slits in the latter are lintelled while the middle one has a round arch splay. The slits of the north-eastern recess splay to a central round-headed rear arch but the two outer ones have half-round arches. The slits themselves are of the same dimensions in all four walls. In the triple openings the slits reach down to the present floor level, itself a restoration of the floor found by excavation in 1955 when the basement was opened. The fields of all three do not quite converge to cover the entire perimeter of the tower, for an approach at 45° straight to a corner is in dead ground, but the coverage is remarkable, as is the high quality of Cultra stonework of the slits and recesses.

The ground floor of the tower was carried on three joists, the holes for which are visible, although blocked; the floor has been removed. There seems no evidence of any door to this floor from the courtyard, presumably because of the steps down to the basement. It must have been entered by an internal wooden stair or (more likely) a ladder from the floor above or below. There is a small loop in each of the north-west and north-east walls, both round-headed slits with shouldered lintels to the splays. The second floor is 6.65 m above the present basement floor and is reached from the courtyard by a stair from the south carried on the east face of the wall over the basement entrance. The south end of the stair is of hammer-dressed granite and, like the capping of the curtain wall, added to it. Under this stair there has been contrived, within the thickness of the wall, a small brick-lined room 1.85 m long and 1.10 m wide. The stair leads to a narrow platform, running between a parapet on the west and the curtain wall, from south of the tower up to the junction of the north section of the middle curtain and the east tower. The middle curtain has been rebuilt at this point but its line is preserved for the first 2 m or so, at least on the north face. There are two doors off this platform, both apparently of one build with the wall, one of thick, handmade brick to a small, brick-lined and vaulted recess (for it is hardly a room) 1.30 m by 80 cm. The northern door, with a sandstone arch, leads by way of a canted passage to the first floor chamber of the tower. This is now heavily plastered so that the only features visible are the windows in the north-west and north-east walls, widened slits with flat-lintelled, irregular

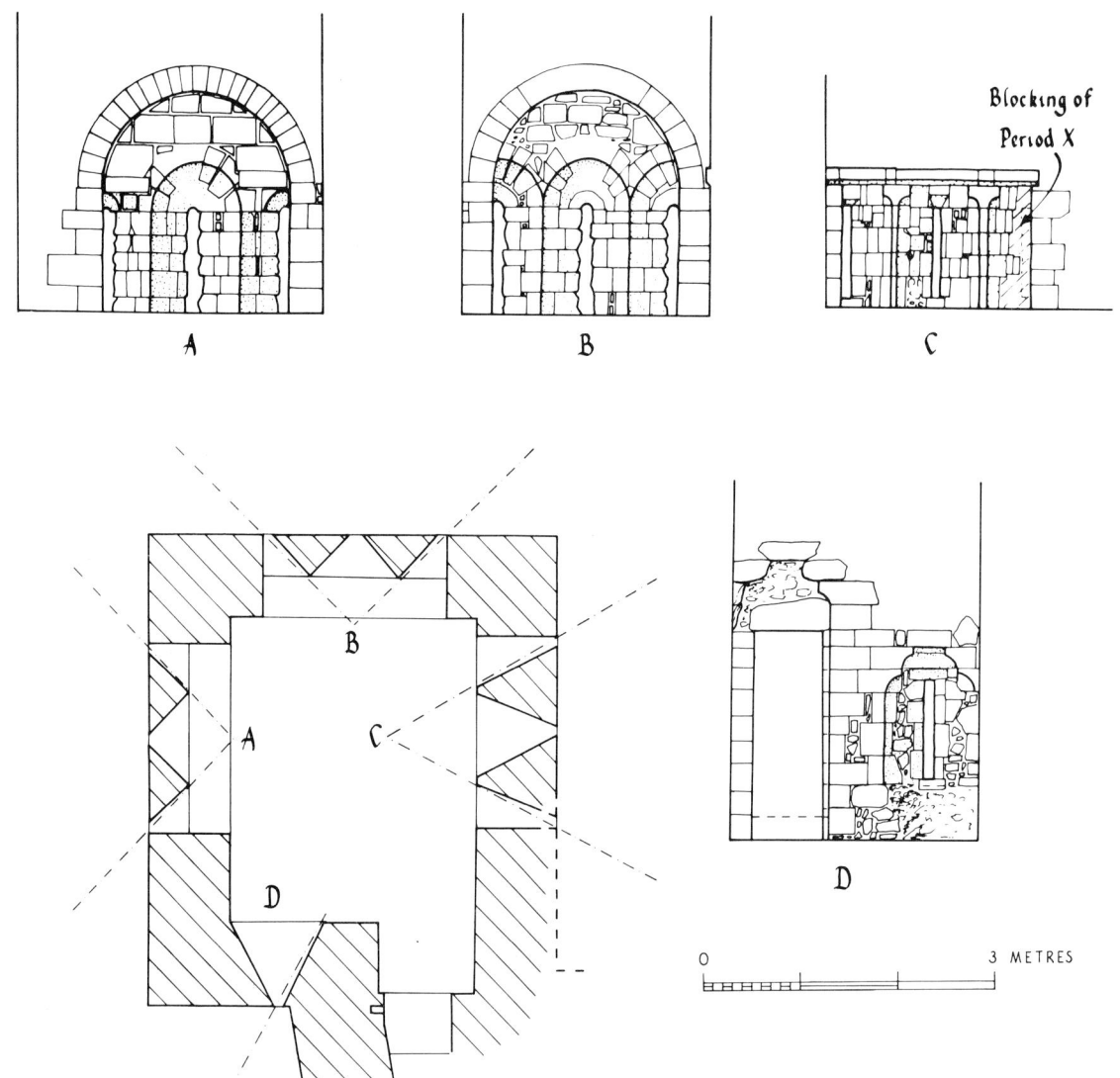

Fig 9 Details of the east tower basement

splays, and a shallow recess or cupboard in the northern angle. This floor and the battlements above evidently largely date from 1814 when the tower 'was taken down and rebuilt' (McSkimin 1823, *165*). The quoins and exterior walling generally appear unchanged, however, and the rebuilding was probably not so drastic as McSkimin implies. The battlements are reached from the first floor platform by a narrow stair set against a wall to the east for most of their length and bent in plan along with it as a result; the stairs reach the battlement level at the south corner. The battlements have musket loops in all four walls but concentrated in the north-western and the loops are angled to command the curtain to the north of the tower.

The middle curtain to the south of the east tower has been much affected by later rebuilding. The wall on the outer side of the steps to the first floor and battlements of the east tower is of hammer-dressed granite, of one build with the two large gunports in the curtain along this section. The whole upper part of the wall, at ground level, was clearly rebuilt when these were put in. Both are designed to provide wide embrasures for the present 64-pounder rifled guns, part of the east battery, turning on swivel rails. 6.5 m south of the east tower there is a clear change visible in the exterior of the wall below the internal ground level. Between here and the tower the wall is of hammer-dressed granite with some dolerite butted against the normal coursed dolerite rubble of the curtain to the south. The hammer-dressed granite is coursed with the granite and dolerite plinth which sheaths the rock between the base of the wall and high tide level, whereas elsewhere this can be

The physical evidence

seen to be added to the wall. The rock is visible to a much higher level to the south of this junction. The original middle curtain seems to have had a re-entrant angle at this point, following the line of the rock, which was filled in when this southern half of the east battery was constructed. The southern emplacement of this battery is different from the other three. Instead of an embrasure there is a wide, sloping semicircular parapet, 2.60 m wide and *c* 1.50 m high, in front of a raised platform on which the gun and its swivel rail are mounted. It is this platform which blocks the brick arch through the inner curtain wall. Below the curved parapet and the dressed granite capping of the wall top, the earlier wall of coursed dolerite rubble with Cultra stone quoins continues, in three straight lengths meeting at shallow angles, to the south-west latrine tower. The late 19th-century capping does not quite reflect the plan of the wall below: the circular parapet of the south gun emplacement stops short of the angle below it, while the projection of the latrine is stepped on the north side and not reflected on the south.

This latrine tower on the outside is 2.10 m wide and it only projects some 22 cm (Pl 3). The projection reflects in fact the actual latrine recess on the inner side, for which the chutes can be seen at its base, rather than the whole tower. This is mainly built to the inside of the middle curtain wall (Fig 25). It has in effect only two walls, the north and the east, both 75 cm thick and without surviving features except a small recess in the inner face of the north wall. The south wall is effectively completely taken up with the doorway of Cultra stone (like the tower quoins) with a shouldered lintel and internal rebates. The east wall is thinner than the curtain wall of which it is part (the angle forms the east rebate for the door) so that the chamber inside measures 2.20 m long and 1.10 m wide. In the thickest part of the east wall is a low segmental-headed recess with Cultra stone voussoirs and jambs, 1.80 m wide, 1.40 m high and 38 cm deep (the curtain wall is reduced at this point to a thickness of only 30 cm). Within this recess are the two supports for the seat, 1.25 m long, of a double latrine. This latrine tower has now been cut down to a height of about 2 m above the original ground level as revealed by excavation. South of this tower, in the re-entrant wall of the middle curtain coming to meet the inner curtain, is a postern gate (Fig 25 and Pl 3). It has Cultra stone dressings, with a plain lintel internally and a shouldered one on the outside. It is rebated for a door on the inner side and has a drawbar socket to the east and west: that on the east is 24 cm deep, twice as deep as the one on the west. It opens out onto a series of irregular steps in the natural rock which might, with difficulty, have been used for access to a boat at high tide. Above the postern, a 16th-century gunport has been inserted, its splay distorted to give a greater field of fire to the north. Below this gunport is a socket for a floor joist to support the gun and the ghost of the joist can be seen in the 19th-century walling built over it and against the middle curtain. The later granite and dolerite plinth at the base of the curtain wall ends at its south corner. The excavations of 1962 showed that the latrine tower had been blocked and this area filled up with earth to this level. The sequence would seem to have been first latrine tower and postern open and in use, then the insertion of the gunport over the postern and the filling of the area beneath the gun, followed by a lowering and thickening of the upper parts of the middle curtain to the east, associated with the east battery gun embrasures. At the same time a brick arch was built behind the 16th-century gunport which both covered the east entrance to the magazine at the south of the inner ward and supported the parapets connected with the gun emplacements over the magazine.

The Outer Ward (Figs 3-4)

This is enclosed by the outer curtain and, with the gatehouse, takes the northern half of the rock promontory into the castle perimeter (Pl 20). At its south-east end this wall butts against the middle curtain just outside the east tower. Below the stump of the truncated middle curtain wall, and the wall built diagonally across it, the junction has been preserved, visible at the north side of the stair-well down to the east tower basement. Here because of the earlier demolition of the middle curtain, the end of the outer curtain stands some 50 cm higher than it, clearly originally built against it. At basement level on the exterior, the sequence is also clear, below an arch of thick bricks, which runs between the outer curtain and the east tower at courtyard level. This arch supports a small room used in 1923 as the officers' lavatory, reached from the courtyard by a brick arch between the middle curtain and the outer curtain to the north. The outer curtain continues along nearly the same line for some 9 m northwards, at which point it divides into two parts. The lowest 2 m projects below the main line of the wall which is set back about 1 m before continuing north. The level of the rock here is similar to its level below the east tower, markedly lower than its level below the grand battery. Above this the wall is stepped inwards again to the capping of hammer-dressed granite with a little dolerite associated with the present wide gun embrasure of the east battery. The curtain at this point seems to have run originally along the line of the lowest part, to have been cut and rebuilt about a metre within this line and then the upper parts rebuilt for the east battery. The section of some 18 m from this re-entrant angle to the angle at the south end of the grand battery is of different construction to the rest of the outer curtain to north and south: better coursed basalt rubble with quite an amount of brick included. The original section of curtain to the south contains a shallow arch of

Cultra stone some 3.30 m wide, now built up (Pl 18). It looks like a relieving arch but the walling below it is different from the wall above, also containing bricks, so that it may once have been open. Whichever it was, it must be associated with the probable low level of the rock here, as far as this can be judged, obstructed as it is by the late granite and dolerite plinth at the base of the wall. The whole of the curtain wall from the east tower to the grand battery has been rebuilt in hammer-dressed granite for the two embrasures for the two northern 64-pounder guns of the east battery. On the inner side these embrasures are flanked by plinths about one metre above the courtyard, reached by four steps, which act as wall-walks and off which ammunition lockers open in the thickness of the wall.

The grand battery is at first floor level to the north, reached by steps at the north end against the gatehouse and by a ramp, itself flanked by a flight of steps, at the south end. At the top of the ramp is a four-sided platform with a gun-embrasure, similar to the others of the grand battery, in its south-east wall. This last appears to be of one build with the outer curtain below the battery, and is presumably the original curtain. Against it are butted the lower section of curtain wall to the south and the south retaining wall of the ramp to the grand battery; the hammer-dressed granite work of the east battery is butted against this latter wall in turn. From the platform at the top of the ramp, two steps lead up to the main platform of the grand battery itself. Along its curtain wall, or parapet, are spaced six similar gun-embrasures. They appear in plan to be like the 16th-century gunports of the rest of the castle, but with their inner splays widened by up to 50 cm to around 1.00 or 1.20 m in width. Except for the northernmost one they also lack any arch over them: the wall has apparently been cut down by about 3 m from its original height. This last can be judged by the sloping part left against the gatehouse at the north end. The curtain wall itself is regular along the inner side of the battery until a point some 8 m from the gatehouse. Here it changes direction and there is a projecting step in the plan on the inner side, which thickens the wall. Modern pointing has somewhat obscured this and the junction of the curtain and the gatehouse on the inside. On the exterior the two can be seen to be bonded. Apart from the battery itself about a quarter of the platform is occupied by the present custodian's house. This is built of hammer-dressed dolerite, with granite quoins and sash windows originally arched in thin bricks although now patched and there are two added porches of thick bricks.

The battery platform is supported by a range of seven barrel-vaulted rooms set against the outer curtain, for the purposes of this description numbered one to seven from the north. Numbers 3 to 7 are larger because they have their west wall parallel to the curtain; north of them it is angled to align with the entrance passage; the wall south of the angle is now covered with cement rendering. All the floors are below the courtyard level and reached by steps. There are pairs of slit windows beside the doors of numbers 3 to 7; they and the present doorframes are of brick. The doors of the other two are set within segmental arches, of Cultra stone in the case of no 1, and thin bricks in the case of no 2. There are no windows to room no 1 and only a small slit on the south side of the door to no 2. Room no 1 is a very irregular shape: only the eastern part of the north wall is straight. In the north-east corner there is a block of rock or masonry, built over by the north and east walls, about 50 cm high at its highest point in the corner. The barrel vault of the room preserves the marks of its wicker centring, whilst the floor is of earth and coal dust. Room no 2 preserves some of the arrangements of its conversion, along with nos 3, 5, 6 and 7, into an air-raid shelter in 1940. Its floor was concreted (the others already had concrete floors) and the vault and walls plastered and whitewashed; at the inner end are the brick screens for the lavatories installed then. A second exit made by enlarging the ventilation shaft to the platform above at the inner end has been reblocked and the baffle walls in front of the doors removed. In no 3 there is a large quarter-round projection into the room at the north east corner. This is now plastered over and no further details are visible but it is directly below the change in plan in the curtain wall at first floor level. The inner faces of the west walls of the largest three rooms, nos 4 to 6, have been doubled in thickness with brick piers or skins of thick brick, done since the present windows and doors were built, for the joint between the original wall and the thickening is visible in their splays and jambs. Room no 4 has a wider doorway than the rest and a small window or ventilation slit cut through the east curtain wall.

The west side of the outer ward has been affected in its fabric by the erection of buildings for the Army in the 19th century and their demolition since 1928. At the southern end the outer curtain is rather irregular, but can be clearly seen, especially on the outside, to butt against the north-west angle of the middle curtain. This section runs over a second cut in the rock (Pl 15), north of the one beneath the middle curtain already noted as an early ditch, which perhaps is the end of a new digging of that ditch after the building of the middle curtain. At the base of the wall where it crosses this northern cut in the rock is a blocked, flat-arched opening some 1.50 m wide, much disturbed by recent drains but originally with Cultra stone dressings. On the inner face this section of the wall, from about 2 m north of the middle curtain for 9 m, has been largely rebuilt in the 19th century. North of this is a confused area. The later refacing seems to end at a point south of the west tower where some hard chalk blocks seem to mark a 1 m wide first floor opening through the curtain. Against these blocks, which are of the same stone

The physical evidence

as the quoins at the west end of the rear of the gate passage, is built a patch or skin of thin bricks similar to those of the 16th-century gunports. This appears to be part of the wall running north and cut in the 19th century or later, visible at first floor level.

The outside of the curtain wall from this section to the gatehouse is fairly homogeneous and straightforward (Pl 8). There are two towers, the west tower and the north-west latrine tower. The walling is of coursed dolerite and basalt rubble like the rest of the castle and the quoins are of Cultra stone. The first of these towers presents four sides to the field at obtuse angles following the edge of the natural rock. At first floor level there is a small inserted gunport in the south wall, angled to face south-west and now blocked at the inner end. It is of brick and clearly belongs with the 16th-century series although of different design having no internal splay. An open gunport of the conventional 16th-century type (*cf* Fig 6) is inserted at the same level in the south wall. Two more can be seen in the stretch of wall between the towers, also inserted. The north-west tower is rectangular, projecting unevenly from the curtain wall because of the topography of the rock. There are signs of a window in its south wall at first floor level and at the base of the west wall is the blocked, but still clearly visible, chute of a latrine, lintelled with a relieving arch, about 1.40 m wide. Its blocking contains brick and there is some brick patching in the walls above. The wall between this tower and the gatehouse bonds with both. There is an inserted 16th-century gunport at first floor level and some disturbed walling at the base about half way along but otherwise the wall is without features. The battlements along the whole of this side of the outer curtain have loops for muskets, rendered over with cement but clearly containing much brick. The quoins of the towers and the walling between continue unbroken to them so that the walls must have always been of at least this height. The quoins of the north-west tower indeed run right to the top of the battlements which may well indicate that it was cut down when the present battlements were built.

The inner side of the curtain and the west side of the outer ward is more complex. At ground level the main feature is a long building, 18.60 m by 4.70 m internally, running parallel to the curtain wall. This building was taken down except for its west wall in the 1950s and for display purposes the east wall has now been rebuilt to about 50 cm above the courtyard level. Excavation for a new ticket office in 1979 showed that it was built directly on the rock and that there was a low wall down the centre to carry the floor joists. Buildings were added to this one at both ends. At the south rather slighter walls are butted against it: the west wall links the long building to the outer curtain at the southern corner of the west tower, while the eastern one (again a reconstruction) formerly continued to the middle curtain. It is this building which butts against the brick patching noted as added against the possible blocked opening in the curtain at the angle of the west tower, and which cuts the wall, at first floor level, against which a 19th-century arch was built. At the north, the guard-house has also been largely destroyed, except for its west wall which supports the springing of a barrel vault of thick bricks. Against this wall is built the retaining wall of a flight of steps between it and the gatehouse. These steps lead up to a platform at first floor level behind the outer curtain and retained by the line of buildings just described.

This platform and its associated buildings involve several periods and at the south end, in the west tower and behind it, most are represented (Pl 19). The original curtain wall is pierced by two 16th-century gunports, as can be seen most clearly on the outside. The open one of these, in the south-west wall of the tower, has a wide arch over it, which carries the present wall-walk across the tower. The southern abutment of this arch blocks the smaller gunport in the south wall. Less than a metre along this wall, east of the arch abutment, is a break: to the east the wall is ragged and patched, where a second wall ran off to the north but has been cut. It is this wall which links to the brick patching noted at ground floor level. On the north side of the tower the arch abuts against the north tower wall as far as the inner angle of the tower and the curtain. Here some Cultra stones can be seen in the upper part of the wall, presumably the internal quoins of the tower. The lower part is covered by an internal thickening or skin running along the curtain to the north, some 20 cm thick and of uneven height, its top not finished off but left as a ragged offset. Of one build with this skin is a wall formerly running eastwards 1.20 m north of the inner tower angle. Also of one build with the skin is the gunport north of this again, at the outer angle of tower and curtain: the bricks surrounding its inner splay are bonded to the skin, and the splay itself is of the same thickness. North of this gunport is a flight of stone steps up to the battlements, supported on an arch similar to that filling the west tower, which is built over another gunport. The inner skin also bonds with the inner splay of this gunport, and runs behind the flight of steps. The sequence of these walls is clearly first, the west tower and the outer curtain, secondly the insertion of the gunports, the thickening of the curtain on the inner side, and the building of the wall east from it and thirdly the construction of the present wall-walk, arches and steps to it.

The northern abutment for the arch supporting the steps just described cuts the lower courses of the inner skin on the line of the north wall of the north-west tower; the upper courses are at least partly bonded. This tower is blocked on the inside by the abutment. The skin or thickening resumes along the curtain wall between the north-west tower and the gatehouse, about 1.75 m high and again with no upper finishing course. It steps up over the northernmost gunport in the west curtain, and again bonds with the bricks of its inner splay. North of this it stops or, more likely, is cut by a flight of steps to the platform outside the second floor of the gatehouse; the bottom step alone is built out around it. Along the whole length of this curtain the wall-walk is of one build, as we have seen, linked to the steps and the arch in the west tower and it seems to have been made for the musket-looped battlements. At the northern end Cultra stone marks the junction of the gatehouse and battlements which here seem to be their original height.

The Gatehouse (Fig 10, Pls 8 and 21)

The twin-towered gatehouse stands across the narrow end of the rock, controlling all easy access to the castle; it is not quite at the end of it, however, for there is a small area in front of the gate before the ground falls away. Access across this area was originally impeded by a bridge-pit in front of the gate (Waterman 1952). The two towers are not quite the same size: the western has the larger diameter at 12.10 m, while the eastern one is 11.50 m (that is two feet less). In this account the two towers will be described first, followed by the gate passage and the buildings above it, ending with the battlements.

The ground floor of the west tower is now blocked behind the back wall against which a flight of steps runs to the first floor. That there is a ground floor is shown by the arrow-slit covering the entrance, which is below the first floor level. From the outside the stones filling the ground floor can be seen through the slit. The present first floor, to which the steps already noted lead at the level of the platform against the west curtain, consists of a semicircular room reached by a long passage. The wall to the east of the outer segmental sandstone arch of this passage is of random rubble, bonded with the arch and of one build with the room above it, but butted against a line of quoins on the west side of the gate passage. To the west, between the arch and the curtain wall, the wall and steps to the second floor are of hammer-dressed dolerite, clearly added to the arch. The passage itself (unrebated for a door) is paved with stone slabs and approximately two thirds of the way into the passage there are vertical cracks in the wall, perhaps marking a junction. The semicircular room within has only one feature of note, the upper part of the ground-floor arrow-slit already mentioned. The outer end of this has been opened into a small rectangular window and the segmental inner arch of the embrasure, 1.60 m high, partly blocked by the south wall and so it is most irregular in plan.

The second floor has two rooms opening off a small platform reached by the steps against the west curtain. The northern one is semicircular again, 85 cm longer from east to west than the one below, presumably because of an internal offset for the floor. There are three rectangular gunports at this level, low, segmentally-arched openings off rectangular recesses in the wall. The actual ports are framed in thin bricks internally but are largely of Cultra stone externally (Fig 11). The segmental rear arches of the recesses are 1.70 m wide and 2.40 or 2.50 m high, with jambs and arches of Cultra stone. In the outer walls of the western and north-western recesses can be seen the jambs of earlier, higher openings, presumably original arrow-slits reaching the full height of the recess, but the more symmetrical and wider splay of the north-east gunport has destroyed them. The western recess has a door in its southern wall, with a shouldered lintel, leading to a spiral stair. This is now reached by an awkwardly set step and it would appear to have been reset as a result of the building of the south wall. The stair, 1.80 m in diameter, now leads up to the battlements but presumably originally led down to the ground floor as well. The south wall can be seen at the east end to be built against the main tower wall. The room is covered with a brick vault, set (presumably on the offset which formerly supported the floor above) into the tower walls. It has a central opening to give light. In the south wall are two doorways, one at the west end by which one now enters the room and a blocked one about in the middle of the wall, both with dressings of brick. Outside the west door is the platform which is served by the stair from the first floor level. It also gives access to a smaller room built onto the southern wall of the first room, as can be seen at the north end of the west wall of the second room. This has a door in its west wall and two sash windows in the south wall. This is built over and with the south wall and arch of the first floor below, and also butts against the quoins at the western side of the gate passage.

The east tower is similar in its general arrangements. The ground floor is again blocked. The arrow-slit commanding the entrance is also divided between the floors and is actually in two parts, divided by a block of Cultra stone, but a photograph by R J Welch taken before repointing (Ulster Museum WO/31/23) shows this to be part of a later disturbance. The first floor is also reached by a flight of steps against the south wall, which lead up to the grand battery as well. At the top of these there are two steps down to the area in front of the present south wall of the tower. This area is partially enclosed to the south by a wall (on which was built the stairs to the second floor) which curves around in a quarter-circle whose inner face reflects the circle of the rest of the tower. The room now enclosed by the present south wall has two windows. One, to the west, is the continuation upwards of the ground floor slit, for the floor of the recess slopes down to meet it; the other, facing east, is similar but the opening has been changed into a small rectangular window, now blocked. The rear arches of

The physical evidence

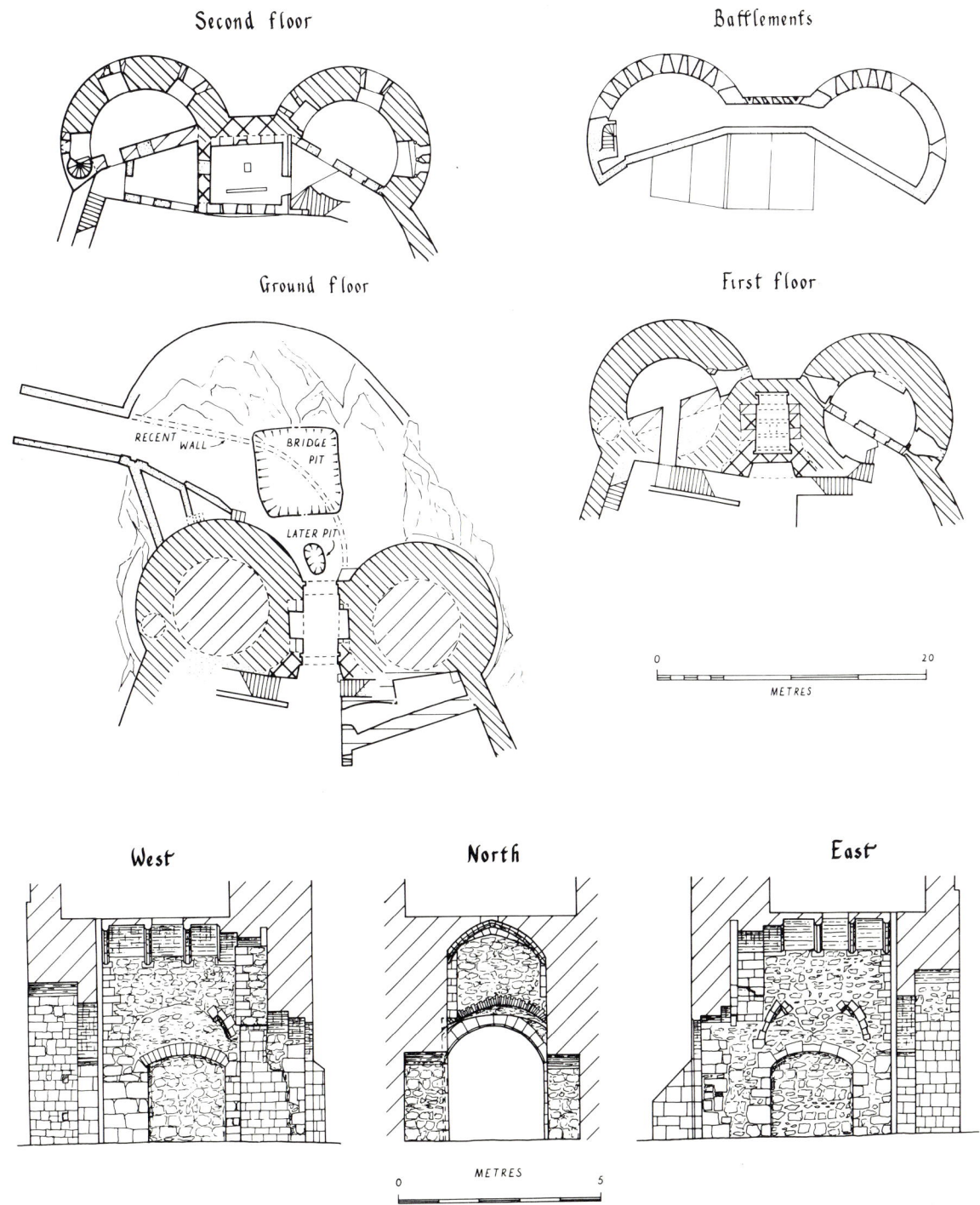

Fig 10 Floor plans of the gatehouse and sections through the gate passage looking west, north and east

both are of brick and interrupt the curve of the tower wall. Against the latter, on the north, a brick fireplace has been added. The south wall of hammer-dressed dolerite with basalt is clearly an addition and it is pierced by a door and a window.

As already noted the second floor is reached by a flight of steps at the south, which lead to a platform, carried on a flat arch of bricks between the entrance passage and the present south wall of the tower (Pl 22). From this platform open two doors, to the west into the

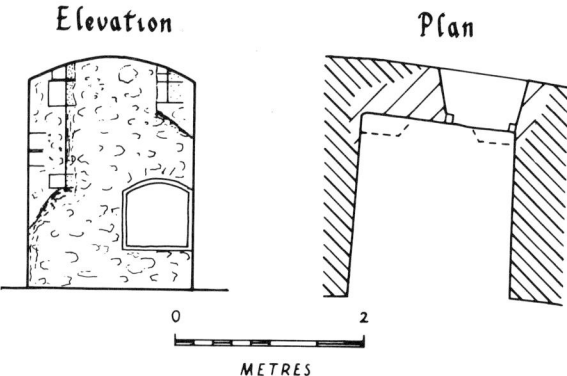

Fig 11 North loop in the second floor of the west tower of the gatehouse

room over the entrance passage and to the north into the tower. This last room is like its counterpart in the west tower, 75 cm longer from east to west than the first floor room, presumably because of a floor offset. It is dominated by a two-light window facing east (Fig 12). The two lights are round-arched, splaying mildly to round-headed rear arches, all in Cultra stone. The jambs of these rear arches are decorated with attached shafts which have triple rings half way up. The bases of the two side shafts are composed of two rings separated by a deep hollow whilst the central shaft has a base of three superimposed circles. The capitals of all three are separated from the shafts by rings and again the side ones differ from the central one. The first are simple, rather clumsy versions of volutes; the central capital has a design worked in rather low relief, a formal arrangement of foliate motifs roughly symmetrical on all three sides. The bases of these shafts do not stand on the sills of the present window, but are continued down in the rubble walling about 45 cm, and the same treatment can be seen on the outside. The window is seen in plan to be set awkwardly into a rubble-arched recess, which is 35 cm deep on the north side

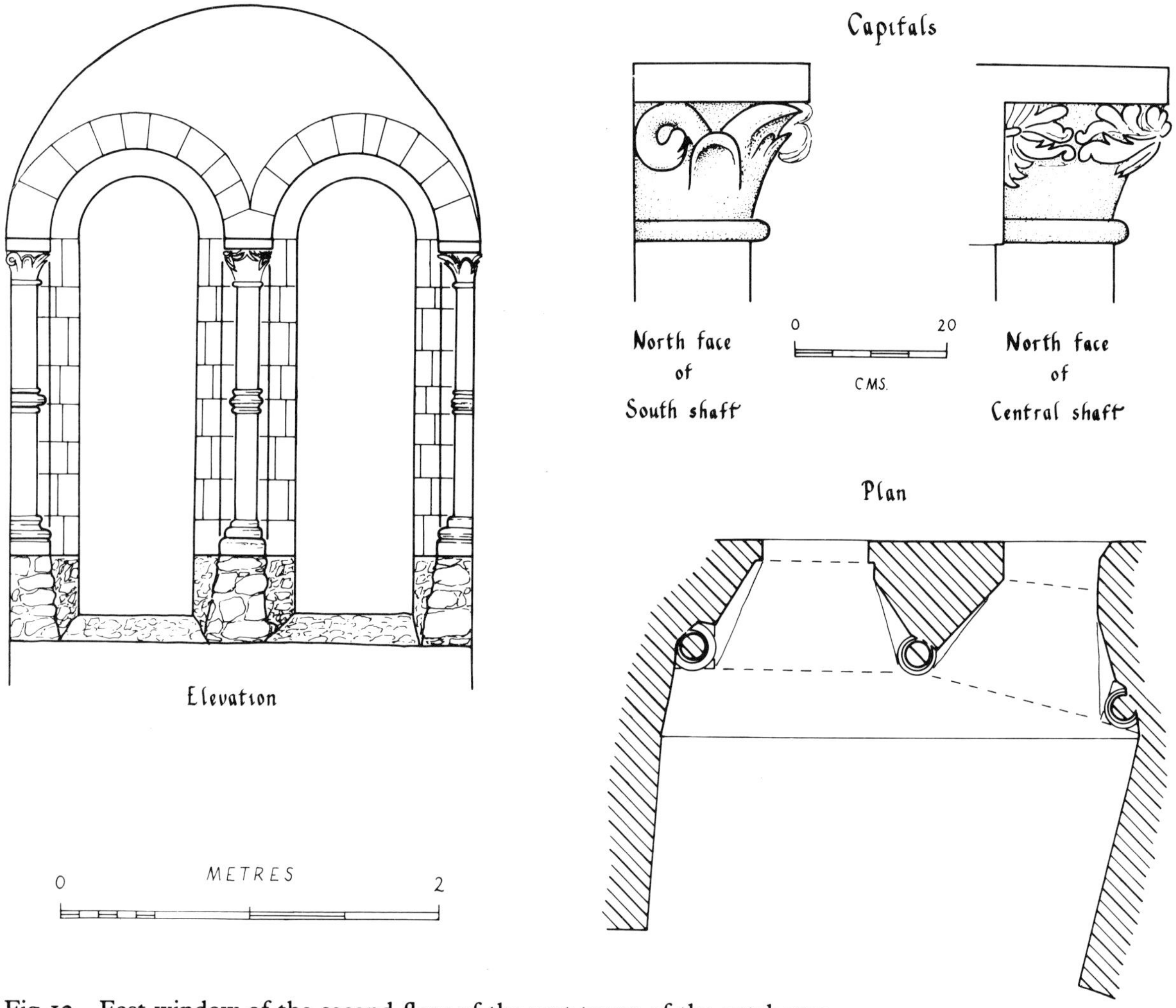

Fig 12 East window of the second floor of the east tower of the gatehouse

but hardly exists on the south. It has been suggested that the whole is a later insertion (Jope 1962, *12*) but the exterior certainly gives no support to this theory. A better explanation of its awkwardness is that it was re-set in this wall when it was built, having been taken from another building, probably one with a straight and rather thinner wall.

There are three gunports at this level as in the western tower. The eastern one is contrived in a curious way below the north light of the window just discussed; it is now blocked on the inside. Of the other two, facing north-west and north-east and opening off recesses in the walls, the north-western rear arch is 1.80 m wide and 2.21 m high and the north-eastern has been restored recently (it was once converted to a fireplace) but presumably both were like those in the west tower. The gunports also have segmentally-arched openings but the sill slab is supported by a vertical pillar between two smaller openings below. This arrangement impedes the depressing of cannon in the port and it must be a later addition, perhaps for hand-guns. The south wall of the room is not straightforward but consists of two structural elements. Springing from the second floor level is a large round arch spanning the whole width of the tower, and constructed of thin bricks. This has been filled by a wall of hammer-dressed dolerite with basalt, the present south wall of the room (Pl 22). This, which is the upper part of the first floor south wall, also has a door and a window. Removal of the pointing in 1978 showed that the wide arch was built against the east wall of the present room over the entrance passage, and had in fact covered the slates which had once covered it. Above the arch are some thick bricks patching the wall. The wall itself was very badly built of coursed rubble, with poor mortar and many gaps, as found during conservation in 1978. It includes at least one carved stone and several possible voussoirs. The second floor room is vaulted in brick, a flattened dome with a groined cell to accommodate the high, two-light window. There is no gap in it like the central eye of the one in the west tower.

The entrance passage (Fig 10) shows the remains of several periods of adaptation and rebuilding. On the outside the present round-headed arch of red sandstone can be clearly seen to be an insertion into the front wall, which, however, bonds into the towers at both sides. Above the gate is a high, single machicolation arch, with Cultra stone springings but otherwise of grey stone, apparently a rebuilding. Immediately above this run the present battlements. In the inner face of this front wall in the gate passage itself, the present gate can be seen again as an insertion into a slightly larger arch. Some 30 cm behind and above this is another roughly pointed arch of rubble, which carries the actual inner face of the wall. It might be like the original rear arch of the gateway with the door closing against a smaller arch below but it looks inserted. Behind this rear arch, on both sides of the passage, are the grooves for a portcullis slot, now blocked above the gate passage. Its rear face is formed by a segmental-headed arch, largely of Cultra stone. This arch was once presumably carried down to the ground but is now cut away about 3.75 m above this on the east by the north jamb of a sharply-pointed, externally chamfered arch in grey calcareous sandstone. This arch is one of a pair of rear arches to niches in the east wall, about 60 cm wide, separated by a pier also some 60 cm wide. The niches run back without splay about 80 cm to a wall against which they are built; they are now blocked but loosely enough for these details to be seen or felt. The niches themselves appear to be of one build with the present line of the east wall of the passage which terminates in a second, rear portcullis slot. The niches which had cut the arch behind the front portcullis are themselves cut by a 2 m wide segmentally-arched recess, which ends against the same inner wall as the niches.

The west wall of the gate passage reflects the eastern one. The arch behind the front portcullis is also cut by a niche matching the northern one in the east wall, but less of the arch has been removed, only to about 3.25 m above ground; the cutting is confused by recent brick patching. A south niche if ever present is now gone, presumably when the wide lower recess, matching that on the east, was built. The west wall also ends in a slot for the south portcullis of one build apparently with the wall associated with the niche. The wall below this niche was built out in a rebate wider than the cut-back jamb of the arch. As a result the wall could be canted at an angle to the wall at the back of the wide recess. This was also done with the wall associated with the niches in the east wall so that the line of the secondary gate passage, which has been followed since, runs somewhat more from the north-east at the outside and to the south-west on the inside than the original. The passage is now vaulted with a pointed barrel vault carried on four chamfered ribs. The front one of these butts awkwardly against the arch at the rear of the front portcullis but the rear one fits in with the front of the rear portcullis slot. Between the central pair of ribs is a rectangular murder hole from the room above the passage. The centre line of the vault (marked by the keystones of the ribs) is related to the wall built with the niches: they, the rear portcullis slot and the vault are of one period, later than the front portcullis and the arch behind it but earlier than the wide recesses at ground level.

The rear wall of the gate passage is carried on two arches. The front one is a round-headed arch of Cultra stone. Its jambs at least appear to be of one build with the rear portcullis slot although its style appears to be anachronistic. Behind this the wall is set back to a wider rear arch, a flat segmental arch similar to the rear arch of the front wall. This appears to be of one build with the rear wall of the gatehouse on the west side at least, as far as the quoins which mark its end 2 m west of the rear arch jamb. The jambs of this rear arch show no signs of drawbar holes for a rear gate, nor are the walls thick enough to contain them. These quoins of hard, grey chalk rise to the second floor of the gatehouse. Built up in the inner face of the present front wall of the gatehouse, and visible above the valley between the roofs of the second floor rooms above the gate passage and the south tower, is a second line of quoins in line with and similar in appearance to those at the south-west of the gate passage: they seem to represent the two ends of the one wall. The line of this wall is the same as the east face of the west wall of the present room over the passage. The quoins, and the south wall of the passage in general, show a break at second floor level: the quoins include sandstone blocks while the wall shows a slight offset caused by straightening a bulging wall. The wall from this level is the south wall of the room over the gate passage, now notable principally for housing the modern replica of the machinery operating the reconstructed rear portcullis. In the south wall are two square-headed windows, each originally divided by a mullion into two lights but now fitted with wooden sashes. The north or front wall of this room is the one which blocks the front portcullis slot. The present roof-line is lower than the original gable for this room, as it can be seen built up in the present front wall. It was this steeper roof that the arch in the present south wall of the east tower was built against, preserving the ends of the slates of the roof. The scar of a chimney from a fireplace in this wall can also be seen above the gable. The room is now entered by a door in the east wall while there is another blocked in the west wall. The two faces of the west wall are not parallel. The west face, as noted, is in line with the two sets of grey chalk quoins, and is itself parallel to the wall at the back of the recesses and niches in the west wall of the gate-passage. The east face is parallel to the east wall of the room and at right angles to the south wall.

The battlements are reached by means of the spiral stair in its west wall from the second floor of the west tower. This stair does not lead straight out onto the battlements but is broken off after something more than half a turn. At this point a short flight of steps leads up the west wall of the tower to a small housing of wide bricks with a slate roof. This arrangement certainly seems to be caused by the insertion of the brick vaults over the second floor. The stair formerly continued to make a complete turn which would bring it approximately to the level of the springing of the vault. As has already been pointed out, this springing seems to rest on an original floor offset. An offset seems unlikely at battlement level and so we may postulate that originally there was a third floor in the gatehouse. The vaults and battlements are both designed for the use of cannon. The area of the battlements covers that of the main room in each tower linked by a narrow space over the front wall of the gateway, widened by including the blocked machicolation. Both towers have three embrasures of thin brick for cannon symmetrically disposed towards the front. Each of the two sections of parapet between the three embrasures of the west tower has three loops for muskets, also of thin brick, but only the western section of the east tower has these loops. The forward-facing parapet, over the machicolation, has five loops, the outer pair divided to command two fields of fire, the middle three angled to the north-west to command the approach. All the loops are sloped to fire downwards. The loops and the embrasures appear to be of one build, of thin bricks, but patched and repaired with thicker ones. Some of the loops have round heads cut out of Cultra stone and look like reused mediaeval slit window-heads; whether they are is unknown.

The Structures in front of the Gatehouse
(Fig 10)

The gatehouse is not sited quite at the end of the rock promontory of the castle site: in front of it is a semi-circular area, steep to the east but not particularly steep or high elsewhere but now grassed to a fairly uniform slope. Even in the last thirty years there have been a number of changes involving the approach to the castle, and each has helped to obscure the original rock. Traces of revetment at the base of the scarp were noted by Waterman (1952, *104*, fig 1): he suggested that some of it at least was mediaeval. The centre of this forework was occupied by a roughly square bridge-pit, excavated and fully described by Waterman in 1950. To keep it clean it had access by stairs at the south and to keep it from flooding it had a water outlet to the north. The pit is not sited directly on the axis of the castle gate-passage, but canted to the west. It was clearly nearer the west tower than the east, presumably because the line of access was always more from the west where the rock step up towards the gate seems to have been less steep. There are no signs of a drawbridge in the gatehouse and nothing was found in the pit like the pivot of a turning bridge. The span of the pit with the steps on the south was at least 10 m and it must have been spanned by a bridge like a ship's gangway. While the open pit presents problems of interpretation they become no less after its abandonment. The excavation found that there was a primary fill of organic rubbish and building rubble containing a large amount of mediaeval pottery. While this cannot be more precisely dated now than when it was excavated in 1950 it seems most reasonable to conclude that this fill was put in the pit in the 14th century. It did not however completely fill up the pit: a step about 1.50 m high was left at the south side nearest the gate-passage (Waterman 1952, fig 2). This was not enough to be an obstacle to military assault, yet would have made access by carts and even horses very difficult. The filling which later levelled it up included a clay pipe of the early 17th century. Unless the upper fill was removed in the interval the gate passage was apparently in this condition for perhaps three hundred years. A still later, probably very short-lived, pit was dug just at the entrance; filled with hand-made brick, it may have been a drainage sump or else a minor emergency obstacle to a foot-rush on the gate.

These pits are now filled up and the approach to the gate follows a curved path from the north-west. The low wall revetting this on the north and east is entirely recent; the wall on the other side is not. This is in three sections, of which the western, outer one is reduced to just above ground level. Both it and the eastern section are butted against the middle part. This is of coursed rubble broken forwards at the east end. This thickening has a quoin of mixed Cultra stone, sandstone and basalt at the break but the wall is then made of thin, hand-made brick. On the north face there is a recess, 40 cm wide and about 12 cm deep, running up the height of the wall but too wide for anything like a portcullis slot. It does not widen towards the ground nor does the wall on either side appear truncated, otherwise it might be a chimney flue, perhaps for a guard chamber. This wall terminates just east of the recess but at the base of the south side is a small squinch to carry a cross wall over a gap in the rock at that point. This wall to the south, linking the wall of the approach and the west gatehouse tower, has been completely refaced if not rebuilt. The new work butts against the truncated earlier outer face and, less clearly, the inner face. At the top it contains loops for muskets commanding the approach from the harbour. Parallel to this wall is one 2.20 m to the east, bonded to the wall of the approach but now in poor condition. It ended until recently in a flight of steps leading up to the platform between the gatehouse tower and the walls just described, at the right level for a man to use the musket loops in the western wall. East of these walls and butted against the junction at the eastern end of the wall of the approach between it and the cross wall, is an irregular wall joining the approach and the gatehouse. It also ends in steps against the tower, which lead to a platform intermediate in height between the approach and the western platform.

Summary of 1955 and 1962 Excavation Results

Two excavations, details of whose stratigraphy and finds will be found in Appendix 1, were conducted within the castle: in 1955, directed by B C S Wilson, and in 1962, directed by S G Rees-Jones. Neither has been published before. The aim of the 1955 excavation was to trace the line of the middle curtain wall, visible as a truncated stump north-west of the keep (Fig 19). When this had been traced in a series of trenches the whole wall was exposed and examined further in a number of small, deep trenches cut down against its outer and inner faces. The 1962 work was more limited, aiming to expose the inner face of the blocked postern visible from outside the castle at the south end of the middle ward (Fig 25).

The most obvious result of the 1955 excavation was the exposure of the remains of the middle curtain and middle tower and the demonstration that it was of one build with the east tower and built before the outer curtain. The trenches north of the curtain wall found that it had been built at the edge of a ditch or natural cut in the rock. On the east side the rock, where it is exposed below the 19th-century granite sheathing, can be seen to drop sharply down from the salient angle of the outer curtain south of the grand battery, and to run at this lower level along to the postern gate. On the west side the middle curtain is built partially over a V-shaped cut in the rock. The bottom of this cut in the rock, as with the lower area on the east side, is a little less than 3 m below the general level of the courtyard surface. It seems clear that there was originally a natural step in the rock on the east side, south of the salient south of the grand battery. The lines of the dolerite sill run from north to south and so this step probably ran half way across the outer ward from the salient and then along towards the south. The inner ward was built on the part of the rock so defined, and a ditch cut across the narrow neck just north of the keep. The middle curtain was built at the edge of this cut except on the east side, where the east tower commanded the north and east flanks. The curtain crossed the cut at a point west of this tower: the 1955 excavations found that the rock on which its foundations were built was near the surface east of the middle tower, but was some 2 m deeper by the east tower. South of the east tower the curtain followed the edge of the lower rock shelf, some 3 m above high tide level.

The northern part of the middle curtain, as exposed in 1955, was destroyed to foundation level and as a result no sign of the entrance was visible. It had one peculiarity of construction, as noted above (p 29), being built in two widths: the excavations showed that while the foundations of the narrow wall were laid first, this was purely a constructional sequence, for the wall above was of one build. The ditch or shelf north of the middle curtain remained open until the mid 16th century, to judge by the pottery found at all levels in its fill; at the same time as it was filled the doorway to the east tower basement was blocked and the access stair well filled up. The middle curtain survived to be recorded in the late 17th-century maps of Phillips and Goubet. Near the east tower the sequence following its destruction involved the construction of three small buildings (Pl 25). The first (wall 1) was erected and demolished before the general level of cobbling (which still paves the outer ward) was laid. After the cobbling two buildings (walls 2 and 3) were constructed against the east tower, the later of which was demolished as part of the Ministry of Finance clearance of the 1930s. The earlier of these two buildings (wall 2) is probably to be identified with the 'armourer's workshop' marked on the plan of 1811 (PRO, WO 78/1158, Pl 29) whilst the later (wall 3) is shown on the plan of 1923. The pottery above the demolished curtain wall but below the cobbling formed a second large group after that of the ditch fill, of c 1700 on internal evidence.

The 1962 excavations uncovered a rather simpler sequence. The postern and the south-west latrine tower had been kept open, until the whole area was filled up to the general level of the present middle ward. The postern was walled up and the interior of the tower blocked with its paving slabs tipped on edge. The tower was cut down to the same general level, that of a floor below the gunport inserted into the wall over the postern gate. The whole operation would seem to be connected, the aim being to fill up solid the area below the floor on which the cannon would be mounted. This produced another group of pottery, broadly comparable to that from the fill in front of the middle curtain found in 1955, but associated with a potentially datable event in the castle's development, the mounting of cannon in the gunports along the curtain walls. The actual date of this will be discussed later (period VI) but it may provide a group of post-mediaeval pottery with a firm date of deposition, which may be extended to the ditch fill found in 1955. The pottery from the general level of courtyard cobbling, lying over the destroyed middle curtain, may give us another group whose deposition is also independently dated, as discussed below (period VII). As with the details of the stratigraphy full descriptions of the pottery and other objects from the excavations are to be found in Appendix 1.

CHAPTER 3

The development of the castle

Period I (Fig 14)

The inner curtain wall must be the starting point for any consideration of the castle's development. The middle curtain and all other walls which can be related to it are clearly later than it. The earliest castle consisted of this enclosure at the western side of the south end of the rock, fronted by a rock-cut ditch. This statement, however, needs definition: is this enclosure itself of one period and how do some buildings, principally the keep, relate to it? These questions were raised in 1962 when Professor Jope drew attention to the change from the builders using sandstone as the material for dressings to Cultra stone. This change he linked to the building of the keep and so concluded that the two belonged to different periods, at least implying that for a time the inner curtain existed as the castle by itself and that the keep was built significantly later, along with the middle curtain. This argument lays considerable emphasis on a change in building materials at a time when the Anglo-Normans were presumably only beginning to assess the resources of the land they had taken over. It could also be criticised for overlooking the use of hard chalk for the lower quoins of the south-east angles of the keep and the forework (Pl 17). It is from the details of the way in which the keep and inner curtain interrelate, however, that the main reasons for linking the two into one period come. Above all there is the selective heightening and thickening of those north-western sections of the curtain which were to be the north and west walls of the keep: these were taken to more than twice the height of the rest before the Cultra stone was introduced (Pl 10). The lower of the two chamfered offsets, both of which are of sandstone, is finished off at both ends, half way along the eastern and western curtains (Pls 19 and 13). On the eastern wall the last stone seems to preserve the stop of the chamfer, and on the west it ends against a break forward in the wall, outlined in sandstone and carried up to the next offset. Both these terminations coincide with arrangements of buildings within the ward, the probable hall on the east and the keep on the west. The projecting bonding stones which were not used to link the curtain and the keep at its north-east angle are again referred to by Jope as evidence that the keep is later. In fact, taken in conjunction with the position of the angle between the north and north-east sections of the curtain, the position of the break forward and the termination of the offsets, with the buttress against the south wall, at the south-west angle of the keep, they are better explained as changes in the details of the keep. The change comes in the decision to build the keep some 80 or 90 cm smaller in plan rather than in any change as to where it should be built or even whether there should be a keep at all. It seems clear that both the latter questions were resolved in the builders' minds from the start of the work, and probable that they also planned the siting of an important building against the east curtain.

There seems to have been a series of changes in plan in the whole building of this keep and inner curtain. The change to Cultra stone for the dressings seems to have been the first. It is possible that the offset visible internally on the (earlier) north and west walls above the present first floor level implies, as already suggested, that the original plans were for a keep not only a little larger than the one actually built but also with a higher first floor. The complex arrangement of the first floor latrine with its long mural stair in the south wall may also be the result of a decision to put the latrines at that corner of the keep having been taken after the rest was started. On the outside of the north and west walls the upper chamfered offset was abandoned at the corners of the keep; at the south-west this was achieved tidily by springing the corbels of the lowest latrine chutes from it, but at the north-east it simply ends. The resulting difference between the two outer faces of the wall had to be overcome by a Cultra stone setting. Higher up the same walls was a string course, also abandoned a short way along the east wall from the north-east angle (Pl 10). In the same place is the slight break forward in the east wall outlined vertically in Cultra stone, which, it has been suggested above, may have been the start of an intended shallow pilaster leading up to the angle turret. The changes of the roof implied by the blocked weep-holes in the north and west walls may not be the result of changes in plan but of repairs after some time. In all this, however, it is difficult to single out any one of these alterations as marking a new period. They are changes in the detail not in the basic planning of the castle.

The castle in period I is therefore to be considered as consisting of the keep and inner ward. Together with these go at least two other buildings. In the east curtain are two fine windows, with their outer sills resting on the lower chamfered offset, which ends just south of the southern window. It is difficult to conclude that these were not also an early part of the scheme. Certainly they were finished, with Cultra stone jamb splays and rear arches, in one build with the upper part of the curtain wall (Pls 12-13). This upper part, with Cultra stone quoins, appears to have been finished only after the second storey of the keep had been built: it butts against the keep at its north-east angle. The northern window has a damaged window seat in the splay, and it seems very likely that the southern window, more seriously mutilated by later rebuilding, also had one. The two must mean that there was an important building or room at first floor level in this part of the ward, planned from an early stage and constructed along with the curtain wall. There was a second important building at the southern end of the ward, marked by the two blocked windows in the curtain. The rear arch of the western one of these certainly seems to be that of a window similar to those on the east. The entrance to the castle certainly from the next period onwards was apparently through the east curtain, south of the two fine windows. The evidence for its existence is mainly tied up with work of period II and it will be discussed with it. It is possible that the sandstone ashlar by the west jamb of the present entrance, itself dating to the 19th century, could mark an original arch or door at this point but there is not enough evidence to tell. Likewise the arch in part preserved in the inner face of the curtain wall by the south-western corner of the keep must also be left unexplained for lack of evidence. Finally the rock on the west side and the results of the 1955 excavations indicate that this first period castle was isolated at the end of the rock by a ditch across the penisula, dry but kept clean.

The last question to be considered is the size of the keep and how it was roofed. The internal span to be crossed is 11 m at its narrowest, requiring balks of timber some 12 m long, if straightforward joists or tie-beams were used (Figs 7 and 8). The windows in the north wall of the third floor and south wall of the second floor are markedly displaced off-centre. It is possible that the rooms, above the ground floor which has a stone spine wall, were divided by a north-south timber partition or arcade carried ultimately on the ground floor wall. This would obviate the need for such massive joists, anticipating the function of the inserted Tudor wall at each level. The problem of the roof is more complex. The actual roof itself was probably carried on the internal offset below wall-walk level. This offset is blocked by the springing of the squinches which support the angle turrets. These turrets also block the continuous line of the wall-walk around the keep, which should surely have been kept free. The original roof seems to have shed water, to judge from the weepholes in all four walls, equally on all sides; that is, not to have had gables. If the wall-walk was carried around the turrets, as the squinches would seem to require, we must propose an octagonal roof structure. The angles of the five large beam holes in the west and east walls over the fourth level do not allow beams to run directly across from one to the other. They might however have been for beams running to the centre of the keep, meeting on a central arcade as proposed above and supporting a central pillar for such an octagonal frame.

There remains the question of the date of this period. If the identification of Carrickfergus with John de Courcy's castle of 1178 is right then we must push the start of the work back to either 1177 or early 1178. This first work presumably involved the construction of the lower part of the inner curtain, using the sandstone from nearby for the quoins and any dressings. The reason for starting with this was surely a simple question of security: John de Courcy must have wanted a strong base, surrounded by a wall ten feet high and enclosing the site of the later well (its shaft is lined with Cultra stone), for his conquests in Co Antrim. After this was erected, and when his political position became more secure with an alliance with Cummee O'Flynn, King of Uí Tuirtre in 1182, the work on the keep could begin. How long the whole would have taken to build we cannot tell. On the one hand, John de Courcy needed the castle as soon as possible, for he had nowhere else to use as an administrative centre, or simply to live in dignity in the area. On the other hand, he built the stone castle of Dundrum, the abbeys of Inch and Greyabbey, the cathedral of Downpatrick and probably the new parish church of St Nicholas in Carrickfergus. These were all works unprecedented in pre-Norman Ulster (the abbeys were in the new Gothic style) and must have created a considerable problem in finding masons. The Cistercian order in the north of England must have helped with Inch and Greyabbey, but we should remember that there was no local building industry to call on for this scale of work in Ireland as there was in 12th-century England, France or Germany. Balancing his needs and his resources, we might suggest at least a decade as a reasonable time to allow for the work of building period I, and that it should be dated c 1178 to 1190 or 1195.

Period II (Fig 15)

The work of this period consists largely of the middle curtain wall, butted against the inner curtain at both ends. This wall did not extend the internal area of the castle by much, a narrow strip about 7 m wide at best, but it did solve a tactical problem. The middle curtain, to judge by the levels of the postern gate and the basement of the east tower, took in a shelf of rock, some 3 m above high tide level along the east of the inner curtain. It brought the castle defences up to the inner lip of the ditch of the first period and to the southern edge of a creek or indentation in the rock on the east side. To judge by the arch on the west side below the outer curtain at the north-west the period I ditch was redug on a line further north. This can be seen, as it were in section, in the low level of the rock below the outer curtain north of the east tower and continuing as far as the southern end of the grand battery. To defend this the wall had two principal towers, the middle and east towers, the former destroyed in period VII to below ground level, but the latter with its multiple arrow-slits a very powerful defensive structure. The east tower is quite clearly designed to command all the approaches to the castle exposed at low tide. These gave access to the rock shelf just mentioned which lay in fact in dead ground from the keep, sheltered by the inner curtain itself. This contained the entrance so that a move to outflank the most powerful defensive feature of the castle in period I, the keep, led directly to the weak point of the gate (Fig 8). This the east tower blocked while the approach along the rock was reinforced partly by it but mainly by the middle tower and the keep. The distance between the middle curtain and keep is such that the curtain wall would have to have been some 10 m high to shelter men on the outer lip of the ditch in front of it from fire directed from the battlements of the keep. The two flanks each had a turret for protection, also used as a latrine tower, and again the keep would have safeguarded the western side.

This curtain contains one oddity in the section of wall between the east and middle towers where there are two wall widths and two changes of direction, one at the junction of the two widths and one in the narrower part. The width of the narrower section is dictated by the length of the wall of the east tower between the basement door and the north-west loop. The direction the wall takes is designed to align with the field of fire from this loop. The direction of the wider wall is likewise dictated by the need to command the outer face of the wall, in this case from the middle tower. In both cases it would appear that the towers were built first and only then did the builders think about the curtain wall between them. The whole of the middle curtain is roughly symmetrical about this junction between the two widths: each part has a tower, a smaller latrine tower, and the same length of curtain wall. It is tempting to deduce from these observations that the middle curtain was the work of two gangs of masons, one working from the south-east and the other from the south-west. Each built the ground floor or basement of its tower before proceeding to lay out the last section of the curtain. By this stage they were presented with a choice between nullifying the flanking fire from one of the towers and accepting that they would meet at a concave angle. The same impression of haphazardness is given by the narrowness of one part of the curtain wall, the result of the tower design. This should have been corrected by breaking the wall forward on the inside as soon as possible, when it would not have interfered with access to the east tower basement.

McSkimin (1823, *158*) gives an illustration of a triple arrow-slit which was then to be seen over the entrance to the inner ward (Fig 13). This shows a feature very

Fig 13 McSkimin's view of a triple arched opening 'over the castle entrance'

similar to the triple slits in the basement of the east tower, which was then almost certainly blocked up. Although the perspective of the engraving is most odd, it would seem that the recess behind the three loops was deeper than the 50 cm of the ones in the east tower. The outer face of the wall over the present entrance appears quite unbroken and even the chamfered offset is only cut for some 30 to 50 cm on either side of the actual opening which is itself not very high. There is not enough disturbance for a triple slit to have been sited over an entrance in that position and for both it and the original gate to have been destroyed by the present entry. Half way along the east curtain, on the other hand, is a considerable area of disturbance, where a 19th-century brick archway through the wall cuts the lower part of a first floor doorway also through it (Fig 5). It has already been noted how the surrounding inserted hammer-dressed granite associated with this door is more extensive above the door and on the south side than elsewhere. It has Cultra stone around it in places and on the outer face of the wall appears to have been inserted into a semicircular opening. The two triple slits of the east tower have rear arches 1.80-2.00 m wide and 2.20-2.30 m high. Given that the brick arch is approximately in the same position as the original entry, shown on plans from the 16th century on as in this area, and approximately the same height, it would leave room for a triple slit of this kind above it. This triple slit would just take up the space at present occupied by the first floor door and the surrounding patching associated with it. It seems too much of a coincidence for us not to conclude that this door was made not by cutting through the whole curtain but by taking out the triple slit portrayed by McSkimin. The greater depth of the illustrated recess when compared with the ones in the east tower is readily explained by the width of the walls in which they were set: the tower wall is 80 cm wide while the inner curtain at this point is about 1.90 m. After these observations it is reasonable to ask where the gate through the middle curtain was sited. The destruction of the curtain in period VII removed any sign of it. The falling away of the rock near the east tower precludes a position by that tower: the east flank is inaccessible except on foot at low tide and the west flank is unbroken. It must therefore have been sited near the middle tower, either close to its east wall or to the west, between it and the north-west angle. Of these the latter would be more protected, covered by both towers and the keep. This is the position indicated by the balance of the cartographic evidence of the 16th and 17th centuries.

The date of period II must be associated with the attention given to the castle by the crown between 1216 and 1223. In the first year William de Serlande, the constable, was instructed to take in an outer ward. He was granted £100 a year in 1217, presumably because of the work, while his successor in 1224 received only £20 a year for two castles, indicating that the work was over. A sum of £500 could cover the bulk of the cost of a keep for Henry II (Renn 1968, 21-3) and so we can reasonably conclude that this is the date of period II, 1216 to 1224. This can be further narrowed down for it is unlikely that work would have continued during 1223 when the castle was put into a state of defence against Hugh de Lacy. It is probable that the middle curtain, started in 1217 was finished by the end of 1222.

Period III (Fig 16)

The most obvious element of this period is the outer curtain, butted against the north wall of the middle curtain on the east and the west. At both sides there are arches apparently built to span the ditch across the peninsula dug in period I and remodelled on the west in period II. On the west this arch is narrow and seems to be simply a drainage outlet; it has certainly been much used for recent drains. The eastern arch would seem too wide for security if open, but if it was simply a relieving arch over the ditch there might have been problems of drainage. As noted above, the area below it has been patched so there may have been a smaller actual opening. The line of the outer curtain follows the crest of the main rock scarp very closely. On the western side this resulted in varying plans for the two towers set along the line of the curtain: the rock did not permit a full rectangular plan for the west tower so one corner was cut off. On the east side, south of the grand battery, there is a truncated stub of a wall on a line further out from the rock than the present line, which seems to mark the original wall before a collapse caused it to be built on more secure ground further in.

The outer curtain culminates in the great gatehouse at the north end of the rock. This had two completely round towers originally, as shown by the butt-jointing of the present cross-walls to the tower walls; the truncation of the latter is visible especially in the upper part of the west wall of the west tower, and the line of the east tower wall continuing for three-quarters of the circle at first floor level. This division of the towers is not the only change made in the gatehouse since it was built. The gate passage has been substantially rebuilt. The original parts seem to be the front portcullis and the arch behind it, with the wall at the back of the present niches and recesses. All other elements in the gate passage either cut or abut these three features and the first two are clearly of one build. The additions (mainly of period IV) as well as the features themselves tell us something of the original arrangements The passage was clearly about one metre wider on either side than the present passage behind the portcullis and arch, and to judge by the arch centre and the rear wall of the recesses and niches it was aligned more towards the north-west (at the outside) than the present one. If the passage was vaulted all traces were destroyed when the present vault was built but it was more likely covered with a wooden floor at the level of the present second floor. The passage was probably shorter than at present. All the rear 2 metres are of one build with the niches along the present passage walls, which cut the arch behind the portcullis, and the quoins at the west side of the rear wall imply that this projected beyond the rear walls of the towers. To summarise, the gate passage seems originally to have consisted of, successively from the outside, a gate (now replaced), a portcullis, an arch behind, a break back to a passage some

The development of the castle

2.00 m long and 4.50 m wide, with straight walls, which led into the rear walls of the towers.

Above the gate passage the gatehouse has been completely rebuilt since period III. The towers have also been rebuilt in part, as well as divided. The present first floor, which cuts the arrow-slits on either side of the entrance, was inserted presumably when the towers were divided, over the resulting rubble which was used to fill the ground floor. The present second floor, the original first floor, at the level of the vault of the gate passage, contained two fine rooms. In the western tower the remains of two high arrows-slits survive their conversion to gunports (Fig 11). In the eastern tower there is the double-light window in the east wall with the only carved stonework in the castle (Fig 12). It has been noted that this does not seem to have been designed for its present position yet seems bonded into the wall (Pl 21). The later editions of McSkimin contain references to the possibility that this room was the castle chapel but without giving any authority for it, except a rather vague description of 1567 which need not mean more than that the castle had a chapel, probably in the outer ward. The cross-wall of this tower contains a quantity of Cultra stone dressings. There are two sections of a keeled three-quarter round attached shaft and one elaborately decorated with cusped ogees. These presumably came from the rear wall of the tower when it was destroyed and were then reused. The elaborate stone seems too wide for the top of the exterior of a loop but too small for its rear arch or as part of a wider window. It could however easily have been the lintel of a statue niche or piscina. The two-light window on stylistic grounds should date to *c* 1200, too early a date for the gatehouse (the outer ward must post-date 1223 and the middle curtain). The early castle, the present inner ward, must have contained a chapel (there was a chaplain in 1211-12) but it must equally have been cramped. The curiously anachronistic and ill-fitting double-light window, which faces east, could be explained as being from a former chapel in the inner ward reset in this tower and the carved stones in the cross-wall would fit easily into this explanation. There is thus a reasonable possibility that this room was indeed a chapel. A final feature of the original gatehouse to be noted is that it was higher than at present. The existing battlements serve the platform carried on the inserted brick vault and this rests on an offset which was probably for another floor, the second floor in the original scheme. Above this again came the original battlements. Outside the gate we may assume that the bridge-pit excavated by Waterman in 1950 belongs with this gatehouse of period III.

We know less about the buildings within this outer ward, the *domi inferiores* of 1381-2, than we do about those in the inner ward for the larger area it contained tempted more thorough rebuilding in later periods. The west tower with its irregular shape would seem awkward as a room and it appears to have an internal quoin at the junction with the curtain to the north, precluding a north wall to the tower at this point. On the other hand at the south-east angle of the tower the original wall does seem to have run on to the north before it was truncated, which would argue in favour of a building along the curtain at this point. The northwest latrine tower should also have served some sort of domestic range. On the other side of the curtain, where the line of vaulted storehouses now stands, there is more evidence. It would be very difficult to find an alternative area in the castle to put the 'tower' 100 feet long referred to in 1477. The description of the castle in 1567 tells us that there was a first floor hall in the outer ward, then in poor shape. The mid 16th-century view, BL Cotton Augustus I ii 42 (*frontispiece*), shows a large roofless building in this position, against the east curtain. The north wall of storehouse no 3 is thicker than the others; it ends in a curious quarter round 'pilaster' at its junction with the curtain wall and above this point the curtain wall changes direction. The other end is more or less concealed by the ramp up to the grand battery, as are all the details of the walls of storehouses 3-7, by rendering or plaster. It seems difficult not to conclude that part of the work of this period was the erection of a large building, including a first floor hall and possibly other chambers, against this part of the outer curtain.

There are no documentary references by which we can date period III. It must clearly post-date the middle curtain and so must be after *c* 1225 at the earliest. Carrickfergus is conspicuous by its absence from the documents of the period between 1243 and 1254, when the Earldom of Ulster was in the king's hands, or from the next decade when it was in the hands of the Lord Edward. Arguments from silence are, of course, notorious but what we know of both political activity and castle building in these two decades involves the frontiers of the Earldom not its rear. The royal authorities pursued an aggressive policy towards Cenél Eógain in particular and bases were built in west Down and on the opposite bank of the Bann to Coleraine. It seems unlikely that such a large work as the outer curtain of Carrickfergus would either have been considered necessary or left no trace in the documents. This leaves us with a choice of 1226-42, under Hugh de Lacy or after 1264 under the de Burgh earls. On the grounds of the parallel at Chepstow, to be discussed in the next section, the former is preferable.

Period IV

Work of this period is confined to the gatehouse with one possible exception. The gate passage is the easiest starting point for consideration of it. Here on either side are the acutely pointed niches built against the earlier side walls of the passage and cutting the arch behind the front portcullis. The rear portcullis slot is of one build with the southern niche of the eastern pair. The vault above is carried on these niches and also abuts against the arch behind the front portcullis. The purpose of the niches is to narrow the passage to allow it to be spanned by the vault, without making it too high, and to be closed by a portcullis at the rear. The rear arch behind the present front gate and the rear arch which carries the south wall of the present room over the gate passage are similar in their shallow segmental shape and their construction in narrow rubble slabs. The southern wall of the gate passage appears to be all of one build with the side niches and rear portcullis slot. The only problem here arises over the relationship of the actual rear arch of the passage recessed within the south wall proper of the gatehouse. The jambs of this arch are in Cultra stone, unlike the rest of the work, but seem to be of one build with the rear portcullis. The Cultra stone arch itself is round-headed with simple chamfered imposts and would seem anachronistic when compared with the style of the niches and vault. It could be that it was reused from a 12th-century building but this seems much less likely than that it is later. The present front arch, also round-headed, is clearly an insertion into the wall and both may well be later 16th-century or 17th-century work. An insertion would be difficult to detect in the case of the rear arch for little of the wall above it is visible. The upper part only of the arch, not the jambs, would be affected. The rest of the rear wall of the gatehouse is not much wider than the gate passage. The original end on the west is marked by a line of hard chalk quoins which rise to the level of the present second floor, where there is a clear break in the rest of the wall, as far as the south-east quoins of the present portcullis room. Above this the wall and quoins are later but there is a second line of quoins in the front wall above the western eaves of the portcullis room (Pl 20). These align with the western face of the west wall of the portcullis room, while the eastern face is at right angles to the south wall. It seems clear that the present portcullis room is a rebuilding of an earlier building which rose to the level of the present battlements at least. This building is of one build with the changes in the gate passage already noted. A final feature in the gatehouse to be considered here is the front machicolation arch which seems to have been replaced in grey stone on the original Cultra stone springers.

This work on the gatehouse may have been accompanied by a reorganisation of the defences in front of it. At some point, datable only by the pottery evidence, in the later 13th or 14th centuries, the original pit was filled in (Waterman 1952). There is a certain amount of later information that it may have been replaced by an outer barbican, perhaps along the line of the end of the rock. In 1591 there were complaints that the ditch between the castle and the town was being filled up, and that this filling also impeded access to the quay. Dobbs's account in 1683 speaks of two strong gates with a drawbridge between, the inner one apparently being the present gatehouse. If this is so, it would confirm the interpretation of Clarkson's muddled description of 1567, that he describes a drawbridge, moat and outer gate in front of the gatehouse (page 9). The plans of the castle from the 16th and 17th centuries all show some form of outer work although the details vary. Unfortunately the archaeology of this area has been virtually destroyed by the clearance of army hutments in the 1930s and the driving through of the Marine Highway in the 1960s. Waterman noted an intermittent stone revetment in this area but could not date it. Finally, possibly to be included in the work of this period, is the blocked opening through the curtain south of the west tower, constructed of the same stone as the rear quoins of the gatehouse.

The purpose of all this work is clearly to strengthen the gatehouse, adding a second portcullis and a fireproof vault. The date of the work is unclear, the only evidence being the stylistic date of the plain chamfered vault ribs and the acutely pointed niches of the gate passage; there are no capitals. The plain forms argue for a 14th-century date or later, while the acute point should argue against a 15th-century one. One possibility, that the work was undertaken in the 1320s to repair damage inflicted in the Bruce siege, would run counter to the known low expenditure at the castle between 1321 and 1324. Likewise the work should have left some trace in the royal documents after 1333. Two alternatives remain: that the work was done for Richard de Burgh before 1315 (and that was why the castle withstood Bruce for so long) or for his grandson between 1328 and 1333 (perhaps belated repairs from 1316). Of the two, an attribution to that formidable castle builder Richard is the easier, but the evidence must be considered lacking for any firm conclusion.

Period V

Work of this period is confined to the keep. The most obvious feature is the wall built dividing the first and second floors and the great arch over the third and fourth floors (Pl 14). The reason for this must at least in part have been to make the flooring and roofing of the building easier: the main joists must now have been more than 350 years old. In view of this it seems reasonable to attribute the inserted ground floor vaults to this period (the eastern one in part blocks the rear arch of the window) although there is no direct evidence of their date. These vaults apparently raised the floor level slightly, for there is now an uncomfortable step down to the passage which gives access to the staircase. We may also attribute to this period the new doorway

The development of the castle

forced through from the entry passage of the keep to the staircase. The second part of the work of the period involved refenestration of the first and second floors. In part this followed from the insertion of the dividing walls which on both floors blocked the central windows in the south wall. On the second floor it involved the insertion of two new windows in the south wall, on either side of the division, with the western one slightly displaced and shorter to avoid the latrine stair below it. On the first floor a window was also driven through the western half of the southern wall, again displaced to avoid the latrine stair, and the original eastern window was widened rather crudely, at the wall-face and in the splay. The abutment of the dividing wall as well as blocking the central window on this floor also put a strain on the latrine passage in the south wall. This was therefore filled and its eastern termination remodelled as a window recess, the inner jambs being built up in brick.

These works (the new windows and third floor arch) are shown in the view of the castle, datable to before 1566, BL Cotton Aug I ii 42 (*frontispiece*), which also shows that this work predates the reconstruction of the gatehouse (period VI, below). The use of brick and the low segmental arch for the windows indicate a 16th-century date, in the case of the brick later rather than earlier in the century. Peers reported that the castle was in a poor state in 1559 yet he had just had 48 men working in the castle and spent nearly £200. This can only be explained, short of fraud, by arguing that the 1556-9 work was done in a restricted part of the castle, leaving the rest in need of repair. It is tempting to link the drawing of the BL Cotton view to this state of affairs and attribute the work of Period V, as outlined above, to the years 1556 to 1559.

Period VI

The work of this period falls into three phases, two in the gatehouse, largely rebuilt at this time, and the general insertion of gunports into the curtain walls of the castle. The first two phases, in the gatehouse, are treated as having taken place before the third, on the grounds that the gatehouse, vulnerable because it was on the direct line of access, would have been given priority. The first phase, VIA, involved the reconstruction of the central part of the building, the gate passage and parts over it. In the side walls of the gate passage the narrow niches built in period IV to support the vault were replaced by wide segmentally-arched recesses. Above the vault, the building was taken down as far as the change in the quoins still visible (at the present second floor level) and rebuilt to make the present portcullis room with its twin two-light windows with chamfered jambs and square lintels. The pitch of the present roof is lower than the original line, still visible above it on the north wall, cut by the inserted fireplace (Pl 22). The original Co Down slates were found during repointing in 1978. The north wall as rebuilt at this time blocked the front portcullis slot of the gate passage but the rear portcullis seems to have been retained, for its slot in the room above is marked on the 1923 plan of the castle. The present round-headed arches at either end of the passage were probably built, or modified to this shape in the case of the rear one, during this phase.

The second phase of this period, VIB, involved the two towers of the gatehouse. The principal part of the work was cutting in half the gatehouse towers, until then circular, by building their present south walls. These walls link up over the portcullis room roof, and were indeed built over its slates. Repointing in 1978 also revealed that the abutments of the arch which makes up most of the east tower wall were built against the west wall of the portcullis room. These dividing walls rest on the filling of the present ground floor of the towers, which produced the present first floor, cutting across the loops of the original one. Above this level, in the east tower the old circular rear wall was in part retained, to provide support for stairs leading up to the second floor doors of the tower and the protcullis room; the present brick platform presumably replaces an earlier one. In the west tower the area outside the south wall has been obscured by the construction of a small room attributable to period IX, the same period which saw the present infill of the arch across the east tower being built. This arch (Pl 22) is hard to explain but it is of one build with the wall above it across the portcullis room roof and it may well have been originally closed with a timber partition. It will be argued below that the gunports on the second floor of the towers were forced through the original loops at this time.

The third phase of this period, VIc, saw the refortification of the curtain walls by the insertion of at least thirteen brick gunports (Fig 6). In the inner curtain these are at ground floor level, but along the west flank north of the keep they are at first floor. The basement level postern and lower parts of the adjacent south-east latrine tower were filled to ground floor level behind the gunport inserted above the postern. In the inner ward this insertion must have been straightforward enough, cutting through a simple wall for the most part. On the south side of the inner ward the gunports cut through the base of two original windows as noted above (Pl 7), while at the north-west angle of the ward the gunport was sited to take advantage of, and largely destroy, a pre-existing arch. On the west flank of the outer curtain there was more to be done. A secondary inner thickening was added to the curtain, bonded to the inner splays of the gunports. Also in bond with this internal thickening of the curtain wall is a thinner wall presumably running off to meet the wall (later truncated but rebuilt in period IX) running north from the south-east angle of the west tower; its existence at this time is implied by the brick patching at the angle. The relationship of the thickening to the blocking of the north-west tower is unclear but it may well be attributed to this phase. The presence of the guns would imply that the present platform was made at this time but how it would have been retained and how it would have related to the walls just noted is unknown. The new east-west wall just north of the west tower is quite thin and looks more like a partition wall.

Before an absolute date for this period can be suggested, the relationship between the phases must be discussed. The rebuilding of the towers clearly post-dates, at least structurally, the reconstruction of the gate passage. On the other hand it is difficult to believe that it did so by any length of time. Both seem to be responses to the state of the gatehouse in c 1560, as depicted in BL Cotton Aug I ii 42, which shows the gate towers ruinous at the rear, but clearly still circular, and the gate passage unreconstructed (*frontispiece*). The rebuilding of the gate passage left the gate less well defended than before, for the new north wall blocked the front portcullis. The portcullis room as rebuilt anticipated that the rear of the east tower at least should remain open as at present, for it was given new angle quoins and an unbroken east wall. The new south tower walls contain loose reused mediaeval dressings, as they would if they were built with material derived from the demolition of the upper parts of the original circular walls. The gunports would have been an essential part of the reconstruction scheme for as well as blocking a portcullis in the gate passage the new works also blocked two ground floor arrow-slits. The gunports probably caused the ground floor blocking to be inserted; they would also have required the rear walls of the towers to have been sounder than the condition shown in BL Cotton Aug I ii 42. The shape of these gunports and the coincidence of levels between the inserted first floors of the gatehouse and the gunports along the west curtain, link the work attributed here to phases VIB and VIC.

It is the question of when the gunports were inserted which offers the best chance of giving a date to this work. Peers received money for mounting ordnance in 1561; in 1565 he had 100 men at work in the castle and was sent lead for roofing and in 1568 he built a kitchen. In the year before Sidney was said to have 'built' the castle but after this the building effort shifted to the town walls and the 'palace'. BL Cotton Aug I ii 42 shows that first priority was given to the works on the keep, here attributed to period V. It seems very difficult not to conclude that the defences of the castle were considered adequate by 1568 and that these defences after 1561 included the systematic deployment of cannon. The gunports along the curtain walls can thus be dated to 1561-7, and the rebuilding of the gatehouse should be attributed to the same years, which would fit well with the style of the square-headed mullioned window of the portcullis room. The main evidence against this reasoning is that the gate towers are shown as round in Phillips's plans of 1676-1685 (Pl 1). It should however be remembered that the east tower still has substantial remains of its circular rear wall visible at first floor level, while the first floor of the west tower was rebuilt in period IX. The present staircases up to the first floors, which now obscure the rear walls of the towers, likewise post-date Phillips's plans. If circular walls at the rear of the towers still existed at first floor level, Phillips might well have drawn the towers as round. The alternative is to attribute to Peers a plan of work which defended all the sides of the castle except the gatehouse and the line of approach by land. The date of the building of the gunports may also be taken as the date of deposition of the pottery excavated behind the postern in 1962.

This leaves us with the question of whether the present storehouses along the east curtain of the outer ward should also be attributed to period VI. In favour of putting them later is the evidence of Clarkson, dated by McSkimin to 1567, which describes the 'Lord's lodgings' on this site, but the chronology would have to be very precise to preclude the buildings on these grounds. Even if McSkimin's date is right, Clarkson might be writing a year or two *post facto* (compare the use of the 1662 survey for a report in 1676), or the buildings might date to later 1567 or 1568. The storehouses are not shown on the plans accompanying Phillips's survey of 1677-85, but then neither are other subdivisions, such as the cross walls of the keep, nor does he show gunports on the outside, but his detail on this point varies. In favour of their being built before the time of Phillips is the reference by Dobbs to the arched vaults within the castle in 1683; the storehouses of the 1662 report might of course be anywhere. It seems unlikely, however, that the keep, which had only a spiral stair, would have been much use for storage, yet that is clearly the major function of the castle from the mid 16th century onwards. Plans, such as those of Phillips, show few buildings other than the keep except for one in this position. It seems unlikely that Peers would have put no guns along this flank, when for example one considers the effort put into the one over the postern, and yet if the vaults were not built for them they would have been mounted on the floor of a building apparently in poor shape in 1477. On balance, therefore, it would seem more reasonable to propose that these vaulted storehouses were built in the 1560s when the pressure for storage space was at a premium (before the 'palace' was brought into commission) than at any other date. If this reasoning be rejected, however, they could have been built at any time as late as, and including, 1715, when barracks were put above them.

The development of the castle

Period VII

This period is largely concerned with the results of the 1955 excavations. These found that the northern section of the middle curtain had been destroyed and a small building put over the remains, followed soon after by the laying of the present cobbled yard. The pottery would date both these contexts to about 1700 assuming assemblage and deposition dates to be close. The Phillips plans date the destruction of the curtain to after 1677-84, for all versions show the middle curtain in existence, and this precludes identifying the demolition with any of the expediture of the 1660s or 1670s. Goubet's plan if correctly dated would extend this range to the 1690s. In 1714 a barrack was built at considerable cost, presumably the barrack McSkimin recorded as being demolished in 1802; it ran over the storehouses on the east side of the outer ward. It is tempting to link the laying of the cobbling, levelling the whole outer ward, with the establishment of a new infantry barrack in the castle. The demolition of the curtain was not a major job, nor was the erection of the small building over it. The demolished curtain might have provided the materials for the buildings or, indeed, financed the operation, leaving little trace in the documents. This work could well have happened as a preliminary to the barrack building and date from about 1714 too. The only time which seems unlikely is the 1690s when there were serious doubts over the castle's future.

Period VIII

In 1754, according to a tradition preserved by McSkimin (1823, *164*) about fifty feet of the curtain wall on the south collapsed and it had not been repaired by 1760 when Thurot's men attacked, for the resulting breach (and the defenders' lack of ammunition) forced the castle's surrender (McSkimin 1811, *141*). Repairs to the castle were carried out in 1761, making good defects in the gatehouse exposed by the French attack, and it is very likely that this breach would have been built up too. The 18 m of the east curtain wall south of the grand battery is of different build from the rest, better coursed rubble and with many brick pinnings. This stretch is later than a stub of curtain wall at the southern end but earlier than the hammer-dressed granite of the northern two gun embrasures of the east battery of the late 19th century. Eighteen metres is approximately sixty feet in length and if allowance is made for rebuilding the two ends of the actual breach, this stretch equates well with the description of 'about fifty feet'. No other part of the curtain wall shows such an extensive breach. At a similar period, in the 1760s, other repairs to the gatehouse were made as a result of the French attack but none of the work can now be identified.

Period IX

We have seen how a number of buildings were recorded by McSkimin as being built or rebuilt in the castle between 1793 and the winding-down of the castle as an active base between 1816, when it ceased to be an infantry barrack, to the 1830s when almost all the garrison was withdrawn. These can be linked with the plans of 1811 and 1821 (Pl 29). In 1793 the keep was converted for use as a barrack and the outer walls repaired and fitted with guns. Other buildings which McSkimin says were built in this period were, to recapitulate, officers' quarters above the vaulted storehouses and a barrack and guard room opposite, on the west side of the outer ward, a small magazine in the inner ward, and a tower 'on the south' (rebuilt). The work in the keep he tells us involved the insertion of stairs against the south wall and probably the provision of a fourth floor at approximately the level of the original one; there was certainly one there in 1823 (McSkimin, *219*). Later, in 1815, the keep was vaulted in brick, causing some damage. Little remains of any of this work after the 1930s restoration except two windows in the south wall. The officers' quarters can be easily identified with the present custodian's house, above the storehouses of period VI. This building is of coursed dolerite rubble with granite quoins and flat brick arches to its sash windows. The new barracks were largely demolished in the 1930s; the west wall and foundations of the east are there against the west battery but no dressings survive, and there is not enough evidence to tell whether the building was completely new or a reconstruction of a 16th-century building revetting the platform. The reconstruction of the outer walls that McSkimin records must have involved a number of elements. The guns now lining the grand battery bear dates around 1800 and the present embrasures and height of the curtain probably date from this period, as does presumably the ramp up to the battery at the south end. The same work seems to have resulted in the musket loops and parapet along the western flank of outer, middle and inner curtains shown in 1811 and 1821. The loops, narrow, splaying outwards and often angled, are typical of Napoleonic work. The arches carrying the steps up to the parapets, on the west platform of the outer ward and by the keep in the inner ward, are butted against work of period VI, as is the arch now carrying the parapet walk over the gorge of the west tower, and all the arches are of similar style and stone. The new artillery demanded the building of the magazine which now fills the southern end of the inner ward.

This defensive overhaul culminated in the gatehouse. We have seen that the description of work done in 1761, recorded in the *Belfast News Letter*, seems to make it clear that the present vaults were not built then. The loops along the parapet, in particular the double and angled ones over the gate passage, are again typical of this period. They are very evenly distributed between the larger gun embrasures and do not seem to be inserted. The idea of vaulted towers carrying cannon is of course that of the Martello towers of the Napoleonic wars. It seems very reasonable to attribute the present vaults, parapets and the lowering of the towers to this period. This work meant other alterations to the gatehouse: the blocking of the arch at first and second floor levels in the east tower to carry the weight of the vault and the diversion of the spiral stair above the second floor in the west tower. To judge by its sash windows this was the period when the room outside the main second floor room of the west tower was added, and presumably also the arch below and the present platform outside it were built or rebuilt then. Outside the gate the similarity of the loops to the others noted would suggest that this period was also when the earliest of the present walls defending the access ramp was built.

This leaves two areas of work to be discussed. The blocking wall of the arch in the eastern tower of the gatehouse is built of hammer-dressed dolerite and the windows have flat lintels with heavy key blocks. This same workmanship is to be seen on the east side of the inner curtain in the first floor door through the curtain at the south end of the site of the hall of period I (Fig 5). This cut through a triple-arched recess of period II, as we have seen, and was surely related to the two-storey building represented by the three gables in the curtain wall above the hall windows and the south wall at their end (Pl 12). The brick arch through the curtain at ground level here cuts both. The building with the three gables may be the 'small magazine' of McSkimin's account; the link between the door and the east wall of the gatehouse seems clear. The only problems that arise with these equations is that McSkimin's account of 1823 described the magazine as 'built a few years since', yet implied that the triple arched recess was still in existence. The second is the difference in the bricks used in the two pieces of work, which will be discussed later. The implication is that while the doorway was probably built for use with the three-gabled building it may well be later, perhaps nearer 1830 than 1820, while the building may have been constructed in the 1810s.

The last field of activity to be discussed under this period is at the east tower. Here the parapets with musket loops certainly belong to the period (they are shown on the plans of 1811 and 1821), and the irregularity of the first floor windows would imply that they have been rebuilt and enlarged, possibly at the same time. The parapet is of one build with the flight of steps leading to it from the first floor platform in front and south of the tower. Work of the next period abuts against these steps, and it seems safe to attribute them to period IX as well. The west wall of the first floor platform at least for half its height is, to judge from photographs taken in 1955 before repointing and conservation, largely of period II (Pl 23). Its continuation south from the door to the small ground floor room is butted against it and looks to be of one build with the brick jambs of that door. Work of period X abuts against the steps which this continuation supports and so it may reasonably be attributed to period IX. It is tempting to include in this same period the small building with the sunken floor (wall 2), discovered in 1955, post-dating wall 1 which was itself built over the destroyed middle curtain, but pre-dating wall 3 which abuts against the ground floor doorway just noted. It should then be identified as the armourer's shop of 1811 and 1821.

The work of this period, like that of period VI, employs much brick for quoins and dressings and this brick is worth some attention. During the period two sizes were used, 3 and 2-2½ inches thick. The thinner bricks are found in the three gables above the original hall, the vaults and battlements of the gatehouse, the loops of the western curtain parapets, the loops of the wall in front of the gatehouse, and in some of the windows of present custodian's house. In the rest of these windows, the housing of the stair to the gatehouse battlements and the ground floor door south of the east tower the bricks are thicker but also hand-moulded. The only work of period IX using machine-pressed three-inch bricks is the rear arch of the first floor door in the inner ward, which could be the last work of the period. It may well be that it was during this time, between the 1790s and the later 1820s that the bricks used at Carrickfergus underwent two successive changes. The first was to the present standard three-inch width, while the second was from hand-moulded to machine-pressed manufacture.

Period X

As we have already noted the castle was put back into commission as the headquarters of the Antrim Artillery in 1855, which caused a programme of rebuilding to take place, normally using hammer-dressed granite and modern three-inch pressed bricks. The most considerable change was the construction of the east battery for 64-pounder rifled guns mounted on swivel carriages. The wide embrasures for these required the rebuilding of the top of the south-eastern part of the outer curtain and the middle curtain from the east tower to the postern in hammer-dressed granite. It also involved the addition of an outer face to the curtain for the 6 m immediately south of the east tower to align it with the rest of the wall, all this work abutting against the steps and walls of period IX, and being finished off in a curve at the bottom of the lower flight of steps to preserve access to them. This work led to the building of a platform to raise the south gun higher than the rest and this platform blocked the archway through to the inner ward. This caused the construction of the present inner entrance of pressed brick with granite dressings. A further fortification was the addition of a sloping granite and dolerite plinth along the whole eastern curtain from gatehouse to postern, from the base of the wall down to below high tide level, as a protection against naval gunfire.

Within the castle the conversion involved a number of new buildings to serve the new needs. In the inner ward it meant a new magazine, or armourer's shop, built against the south side of the keep, and defended against blast by the arch over its door. To judge by their similarity to the east battery, the two embrasures reached by the long stair at the west side of the ward, all in hammer-dressed granite, were built over the magazine at the south at this time. In front of the magazine was a low building, now removed except for its north wall whose foundations survive; in 1923 this was the armourer's shop. The 'long store', abutting against the north jamb of the brick arch through the curtain, and the latest of the buildings to occupy the site of the original castle hall, must date from the same period. The conversion of the keep once again to a storehouse involved the erection of a hoist on the north wall and openings were pushed through at each floor as a result. This is probably the time when a chamber and door were made in the north wall of the eastern ground floor room. Against the east tower during period X as well as the reconstruction of the curtain wall, already noted, a larger rectangular building was constructed against the west wall (the wall 3 of the 1955 excavations), abutting against the jamb of the ground floor door below the flight of steps, and involving the demolition of wall 2. Just north of this a lavatory was built over an arch of pressed bricks between the outer curtain and east tower; its doorway is of one build with the embrasures of the east battery and butted against the canting wall across the stump of the middle curtain. This lavatory (in 1923 for officers) involved the driving of a sewer below the canted wall, at the level of the internal floor of wall 2, and across the junction of walls 1 and 2, as well as the destruction of a forge and furnace for heating shot dating from at least 1811.

Finally mention should be made of the tramway, installed in 1889 and leading from the pier into the castle. It was entered by a tunnel five feet in diameter at the south-west corner of the inner ward and ended at a crane in the middle of the inner ward, which hoisted the munitions and other materials up to ground level. From here the tramway led through the present entrance to the storehouses on the east side of the outer ward, and perhaps along the north wall of the keep to the hoist. The last section of its tracks was covered in July 1978.

CHAPTER 4

Discussion

A mediaeval castle was a complex building, which we must judge on a number of criteria, but primarily for its defensive capacity and the standard of accommodation it provides as a place of residence for its lord and as a centre for his administration. These aspects should be compared with those of other castles, not so much in pursuit of the archaeological parallel for its own sake, but because a lord's castle and the display of fashionable ideas he makes with it give us a view of the thoughts he entertained of his own lordship. In the exercise of this lordship, the barons of Ireland belonged to an international class; we must not confine our horizons to Ireland alone. Initially John de Courcy relied for his defences on a polygonal stone wall as he did at Dundrum (Waterman 1952) and as did later generations in Ulster at such sites as Doonbought or Seafin (McNeill 1980, chap 4). The real strength of the castle, however, was in the square keep which he built to confront the line of approach along the rock. The entrance he seems to have tried to mask by placing it to the south of the eastern side, hoping to force attackers making for it to expose their right flanks; the result, however, was simply to put the gate in dead ground. The building of the keep meant that the castle courtyard must have been cramped but to have included much more space would probably have stretched his garrison too far.

We know of most of the buildings of the castle under John de Courcy and can reasonably speculate as to their use. The Pipe Roll of 1211-12 (above p 3) records the existence of a kitchen and a barn while the presence of a chaplain implies a chapel. The blocked Cultra stone windows in the south wall demonstrate the presence of a first floor room of some pretensions there and the windows with window seats indicate a similar room against the east curtain at first floor level. Apart from the ground floor, presumably used for storage, and the possible fourth floor, the keep provides three floors of accommodation as well as those buildings just noted. The uses of these three floors are the best starting points for considering the use of the whole castle and to deduce this we must look at the features provided on each floor. The first floor is the entry floor, with access to the well and a double latrine, but only two narrow windows and no fireplace; it must have been a public room with few pretensions to domestic comfort. The second floor has a fireplace and a single latrine but windows in only two walls; it must have been a more private chamber than the floor below. The windows of the third floor and its fireplace indicate that of the three this was the chamber with the highest status: the single latrine shows that it was not a public room, unlike the first, whilst its importance is also shown by the private stair to the battlements. These arrangements are surely to be interpreted as the private chamber of John de Courcy being on the third floor, separated from the public access to the entry floor (and the well) by the chamber on the second floor which would have been for his household officials. The hall of the castle cannot have been in the keep, for the room with the status symbols for this role, the third floor, is both too remote from the courtyard (and the kitchen) and too clearly private. The hall must be identified as the first floor building against the east curtain north of the original entrance, marked by the fine Cultra stone windows with window seats. The building against the south curtain was presumably the chapel. Figure 14 presents a reconstruction of the castle at this time with keep, hall and chapel as indicated; the kitchen is placed across the entranceway from the hall and a barn (or stable) in the only other available space; it is beside the arch which may have been a postern leading down to the quay.

The castle as thus outlined was a remarkable one in comparison with its contemporaries. While the square keep was a conservative feature (Dover of the 1180s was the last of such royal keeps in England), the standard of accommodation was not. In England castles provided with a hall as well as a keep in the 12th century are few. The hall at royal Chilham (Clapham 1928) was probably replaced by the keep; the hall at Newcastle-on-Tyne (also royal) was later (Clapham 1926), while the contemporaneity of hall and keep at Hedingham, built by the de Vere Earls of Oxford, is unclear (RCHM Essex, 51-7). The best parallel in England is to be found at Scarborough, where Henry II put up a keep of similar

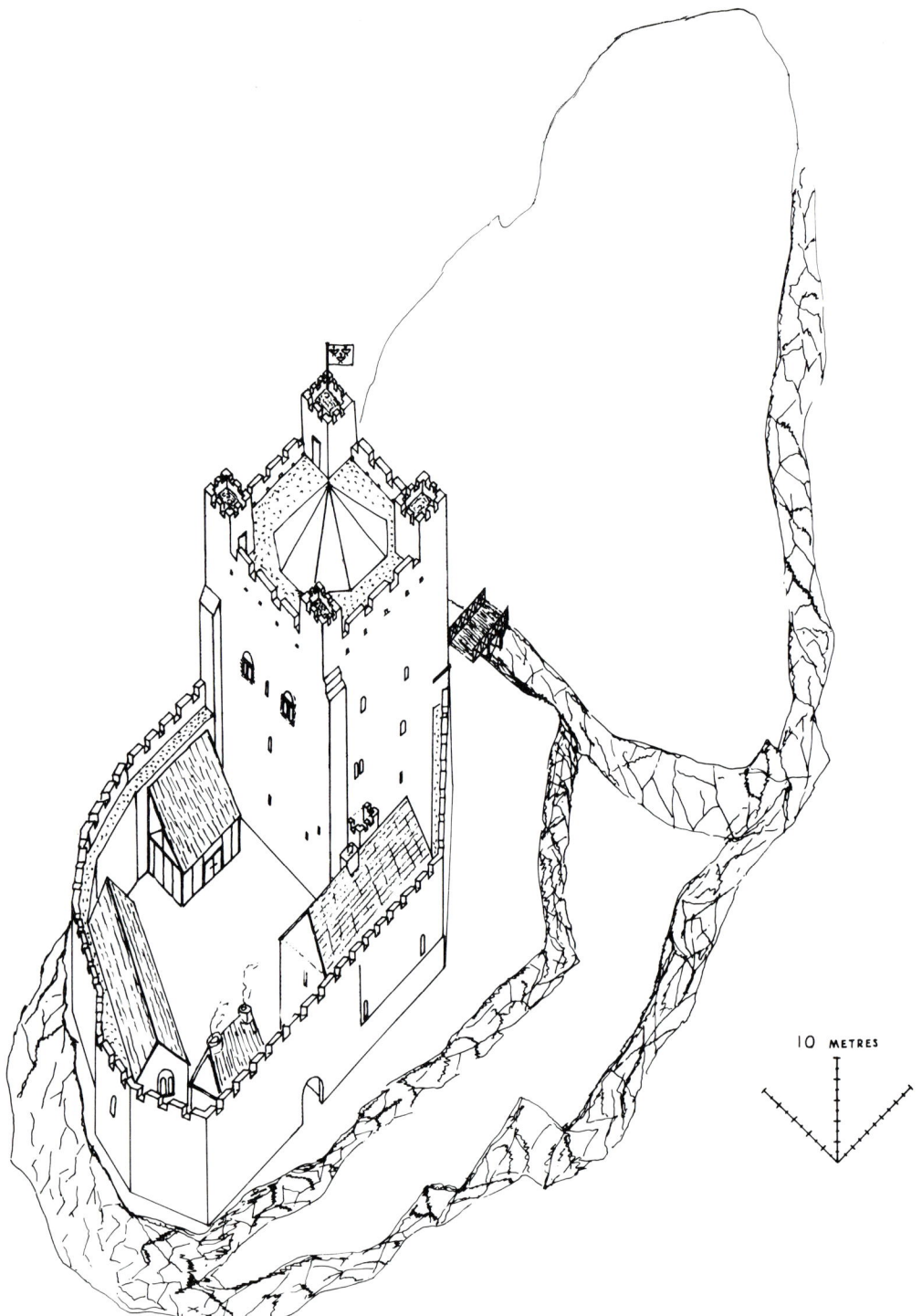

Fig 14 Reconstruction of the castle as it might have appeared in 1200

size to that at Carrickfergus and which in 1260 had an 'old hall' in the inner bailey as well as another hall in the outer bailey (VCH Yorkshire, II, *541-9*; Colvin *et al.* 1963, II, *829-32*). The keep at Scarborough is also marked by double windows in its upper floors. These castles are either royal or, as in the case of Hedingham, built by barons of the first rank; the accommodation which John de Courcy built was not such as might

Discussion

demean him. It was not unparalleled in Ireland, for at Adare there is a fine hall of *c* 1200 beside the keep which presumably provided a more private chamber; unfortunately its builder is unknown (Orpen, Normans, II, *169*). It was only under Henry III that English royal castles can be seen to separate systematically the great hall from the block which contained great and privy chambers. This privacy and accommodation

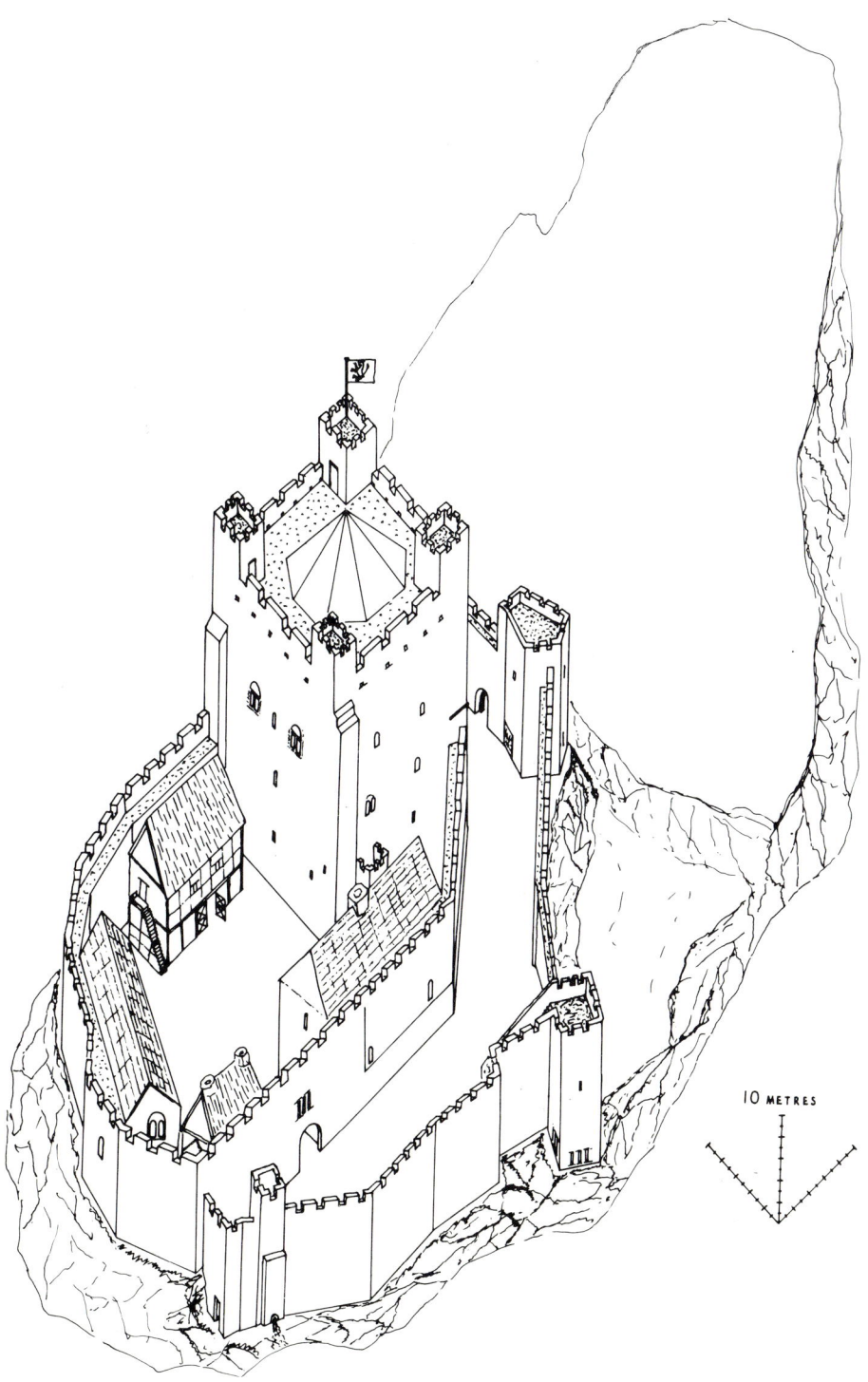

Fig 15   Reconstruction of the castle as it might have appeared in 1225

which John de Courcy provided for himself might explain the length of King John's stay in Carrickfergus in 1210.

The second period at the castle is of interest as one of the earliest royal works in Ireland still substantially extant (it is seen reconstructed in Fig 15). The whole intention was to strengthen the castle's defences, not to add to its comfort. The weak point of the first castle must have been the eastern flank and north-eastern approach during low tide, neither being adequately controlled from the keep. The work of 1216-23 remedied this by providing a new line of defence on the north and east with flanking towers and turrets culminating in the strong point of the east tower. The basement of this tower provides complex loops for archers to control most of the threatened flank (Fig 9). These loops are set low in the wall and the slits themselves are not very high. It is difficult for a standing man to see far out from them, but a kneeling man can. It is also difficult to traverse through the field of fire they offer from the three slits with a long-bow, and the lowness of the embrasures of the south-east loops makes their use with a long-bow very awkward. A long-bow cannot be drawn and fired by a kneeling man but a cross-bow can; it is easy to traverse across the three slits with a cross-bow when down on one knee, pivoting on the front foot with the bow supported on the front knee, like a rifle. Cross-bowmen are specifically noted (uniquely for Ulster) in the Carrickfergus garrison of 1211-12 (Davies and Quinn 1941, 60). The recesses mean that the north-east and north-west archers can kneel far enough into the wall not to be in each other's way, so that four men may fire from the restricted space of the tower basement at a time, as well as those from the upper floors and battlements. The one weakness in the design is the lack of overlap in the fields of fire. A polygonal tower might have offered this but it would have taken up more space which on this rocky site is at a premium. Moreover the area it commands could only be rushed: digging approach works to it would have meant trenches below high tide.

This scheme of a strong point for missile fire sited at the weakest point on the perimeter is very much in line with other later Angevin castle defences. It was employed at the Tower of London with the Bell Tower of 1190-1 (Colvin *et al.* 1963, II, *709-10*), Dover with Avranches Tower of the same date (Renn 1969, *86-89*), Corfe with the west bailey of 1202-4 (RCHM Dorset, II, *60*), and Kenilworth with Lunn's tower probably built under King John (Thompson 1977, *24*). King John kept in close touch with Carrickfergus after 1210 as witness William de Serlande's visits to him in 1212 (above p 3). During the work William was to consult with the Justiciar in Dublin where John had ordered major work on the castle in 1204 (CDI, I, no 226). A further link between John's works in England and Carrickfergus is provided by the master miner Osbert Pinel, in charge of further strengthening of Corfe's defences in 1207 and present at Carrickfergus with John in 1210 (RCHM Dorset, II (i), *61*; Hardy 1844, *206*). Avranches Tower, Dover and Bell's Tower, London both employ grouped cross-bow slits (Renn 1969, *84-5*) but their grouping into arched recesses is best seen at Framlingham, built under Roger Bigod, Earl of Norfolk in the 1190s; these particular loops are for long-bows and point up, by contrast, the design of the Carrickfergus ones (Renn 1973). All these are works of the two or three decades before the building of the middle curtain at Carrickfergus but it would be rash to invoke a time-lag here. The succeeding developments in castle defences, using round towers and strong double-towered gatehouses, are not found at all frequently before the 1220s and the advantages of round towers in resisting mining attacks were of little weight on a tidal rock such as Carrickfergus. Finally it would seem unlikely that the royal works provided more than a master-mason or a design for the new work. The systematic use of Cultra stone, dressed with narrow diagonal tooling, and the shouldered lintels which are found in work of the first three periods of construction in the castle, argue for a continuity of craftsmen between them, working successively for John de Courcy, the King and Hugh de Lacy.

It was Hugh who took the logical step of defending the castle by building the outer ward and so including the whole peninsula within its walls (period III, Fig 16). The western flank was protected by the west and north-west towers, while the eastern flank was covered by the re-entrant angle south of the present grand battery. The whole culminated in the new double-towered gatehouse (Fig 17). This last followed the examples of the Earl of Chester's castles, such as Beeston or Bolingbroke or royal castles, such as London or New Montgomery, all built in the 1220s and 1230s. In Ireland we have Castle Roche of the same date, a close parallel to Beeston. The practice was not universal: Skenfrith, built by Hubert de Burgh in the 1220s (Knight 1977, *152*), lacked a strong gatehouse. The normal pattern for these gatehouses was to have D-shaped towers, unlike the circular towers at Carrickfergus. These are only to be seen elsewhere at Chepstow in the great gatehouse built during the 1230s or 1240s under the sons of William Marshal. They were, as well as earls of Striguil and Pembroke, successively earls of Leinster, while Chepstow was not far from the de Lacy barony further up the river Wye, so that personal links between the two builders of these gatehouses are easy to envisage. Unlike the earlier middle curtain, however, the tall embrasures and loops of the gatehouse seem designed for use by long-bowmen. The buildings within this outer ward are harder to envisage. The probability that the opportunity was taken to use the space provided in the gatehouse to make the first floor of the east tower into a chapel has been discussed

Discussion

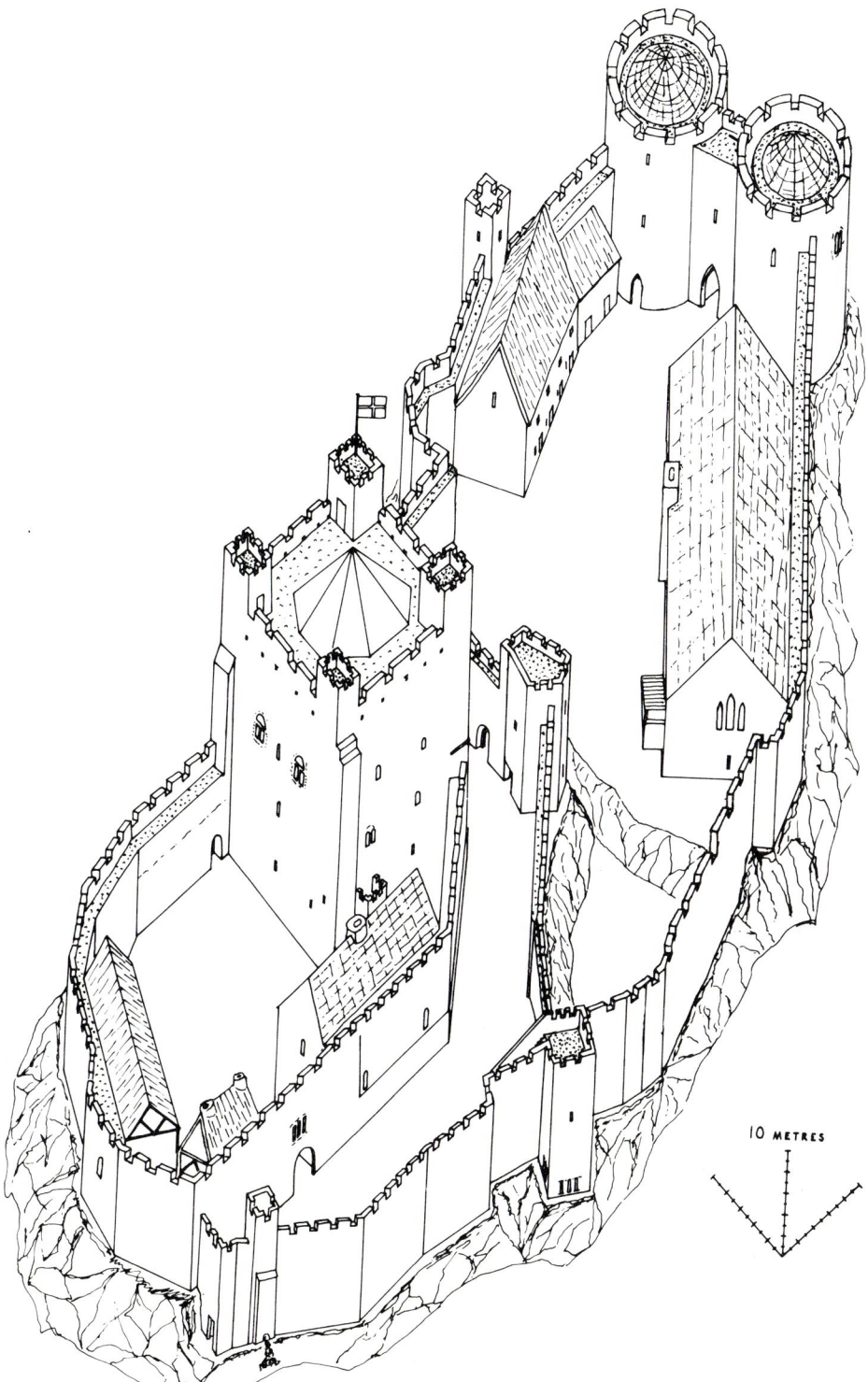

Fig 16 Reconstruction of the castle as it might have appeared in 1250

above, as has the siting of a new hall against the east curtain, and the possible lodging on the west. Whether this all dates from the original building is not susceptible of proof but the gatehouse chapel must do, and the hall walls as preserved for the later storehouses seem to be in bond. They have all been shown as dating to c 1250 in Figs 16 and 17.

The only work which can be seen to have been

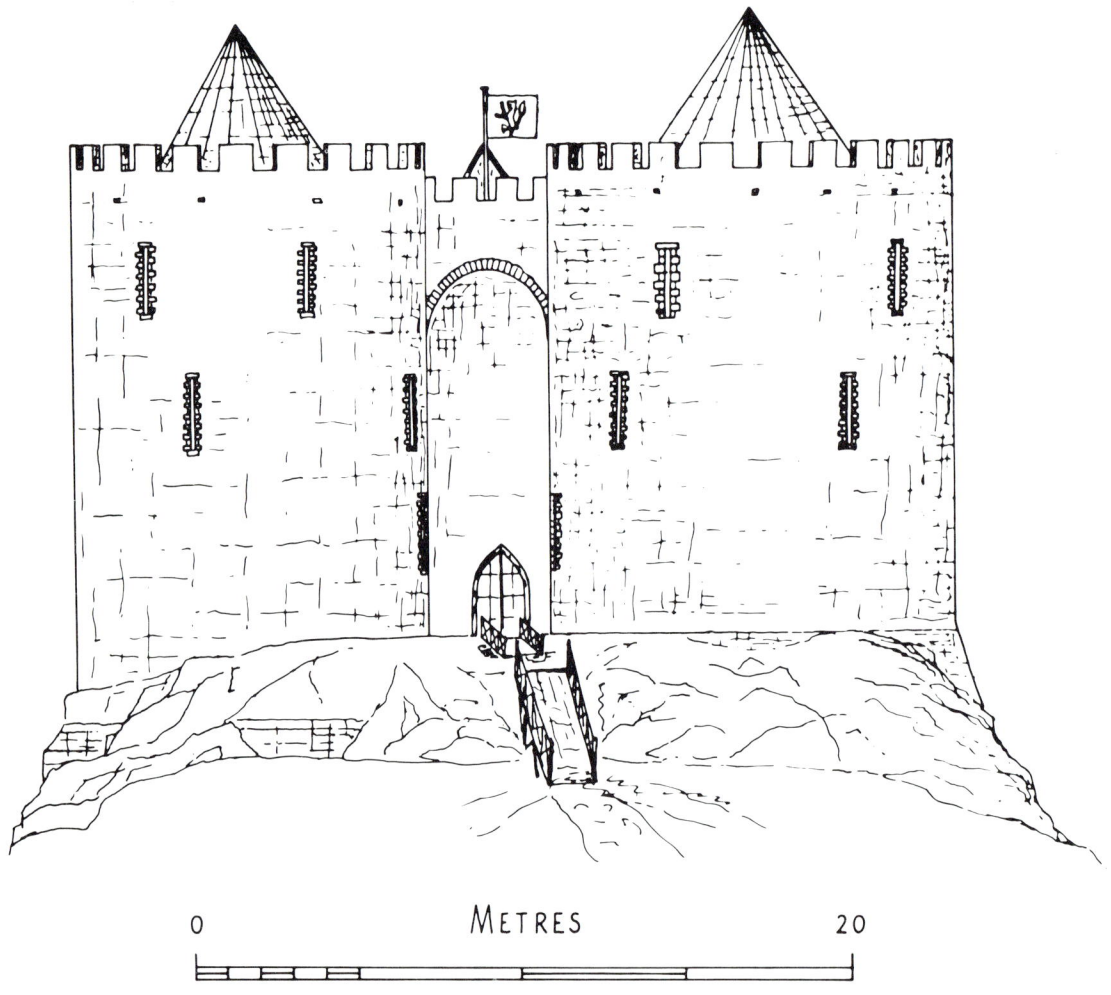

Fig 17 Reconstruction of the original exterior elevation of the gatehouse

carried out between 1250 and 1550 apart from routine repairs was the strengthening of the gatehouse, probably before the Bruce siege. Richard de Burgh was a great castle builder, at Greencastle, Co Donegal, or Ballymote, Co Sligo, but would have found little room or need at Carrickfergus. There are clear indications that he considered it important, the centre of his Earldom's administration, but unless we attribute the building of the hall, as proposed above, to him we have little to record. That the royal administration did not undertake much work in the castle after 1333 need occasion no surprise. In the tale of the diminishing resources of the constables of the castle and their consequent demands on the Dublin government the history of the castle is typical of the period. The 15th century, in spite of such notable achievements as the great hall of Askeaton castle, saw the building of tower houses rather than large castles in Ireland. Even great lords do not seem to have had the same need for the large social and administrative centres of the 13th century, or certainly not enough to spend money on new ones.

Neither the advent of the Tudors in England, in spite of the brief flurry of garrison activity in the 1490s, nor Henry VIII's resumption of the direct lordship of Ireland in 1534, had much immediate effect on Carrickfergus. A change came with the increasing government pressure on the Ulster Irish, facing the twin problems (as seen from Dublin) of Shane O'Neill and the growing MacDonnell power, and with the appointment of the able and energetic William Peers as constable. The nature of his first work, the conversion of the keep, was in line with a continuation of the mediaeval role of the castle. While the division of the lower keep floors may have been to overcome the problem of replacing John de Courcy's massive floor beams, the provision of more windows and the effort to preserve the large third floor room, by means of the massive cross arch rather than a wall, were aimed at the improvement of comfort. Sensibly enough, Peers looked first to providing the const-

Discussion

able with good lodgings. These lodgings were in effect (with the ground floor now vaulted and an upper hall or great chamber) a fine tower house; he put no new windows on the outer facing walls. The reasoning may have been cost but what he started with was a late mediaeval Irish tower house and bawn.

This bawn he proceeded in the 1560s to make defensible by the new weapon of cannon. It is notable that in his reconstruction of the gatehouse, where he might have made provision for domestic accommodation, he made none. There were no fireplaces added; the new first floor is cramped and dark; after the installation of guns in the second floor there can have been little room for anything else; the east tower had apparently only a lightly infilled arch as a south wall. Any other buildings that he installed in the 1560s seem to have been for storage not for living: barracks not lodgings. The use of the guns mounted at this time is not in accordance with the new ideas of fortification, current in northern Europe since the 1540s at least, involving low-mounted cannon, bastions and the provision of systematic enfilading fire. Of course, the conditions of Irish warfare in the 16th century hardly called for the latest ideas to counter sieges by fully professional Continental armies, but the guns in Carrickfergus are still not effectively used. The wide external splay and height above the platforms of the gunports show that they are designed for cannon not hand-guns. They are mounted very high in the gatehouse, presumably because the ports could be made easily by adapting the original long-bow slits. Along the west flank, the enfilading potentials of the west and north-west towers are not exploited, with no north-facing ports; the south-facing port in the tower is the smallest of the series and is angled to face out from the castle not to rake the flank. It is quite possible that no real provision was made for guns along the eastern flank. What Peers did in his second campaign was to use the cannon he mounted, as cheaply as he could (as we can see in the gatehouse), to protect his castle stores from a disorganised rush. In his own defence, he would presumably have said that this was all that he could do with the money he was given, and that the result was successful, for the castle was not taken in 1573 when the town was burned by Brian O'Neill.

This role worked out in the 1560s, a limited accommodation in the keep for a constable and a defensible wall around a stores depot, was the basis of the castle's role for some 150 years. In view of the troop levels of the later Elizabethan wars and the second storehouse at the former Friary site, the castle alone could not be considered as the base to be fortified. Accordingly for fifty years the effort for defence went into the town wall; when eventually built it looked good with its regularity and spear-shaped bastions, but these last had only wall-walks for hand-guns, not solid platforms for cannon. The 17th century and the Scottish settlement of eastern Ulster devalued the castle further. The role of the constable as the prime agent of the government in the region became an anachronism and the last great political magnate, Arthur Chichester, exercised his lordship from his new houses at Joymount and Belfast. The security of the area became dependent largely on the political will of the townspeople and the garrison, as seen in the 1640s and in the Williamite wars; any fortification would be to the town walls. The opening up of the Lagan valley gave Belfast the better communications with inland Ulster and so increasingly it replaced Carrickfergus as the strategic and commercial centre of the region. The consequences of this were summed up in Phillips's report of 1685 which, in line with 17th-century practice and experience, looked not only at individual forts but also at the general strategic position and thus at Belfast Lough as a unit. It was a combination, however, of government parsimony and inertia which saved the castle from abandonment and, given its urban site, almost certain demolition as a quarry. The army needed a depot in the area and it did not matter that Carrickfergus was neither well sited nor adequately fortified when the problems and costs of building an up-to-date fort were considered. As a result, in 1715 an infantry barrack was built inside it and the castle was again something more than a storehouse. The rebuilding of the Napoleonic war period perpetuated this approach with its provision of stores and barracks and its defences. These are based on two 'Martello towers' made out of the gatehouse, and the grand battery commanding the north-eastern flank, backed by the muskets of men on the parapets, which on the gatehouse and east towers are angled to direct fire against a land assault, whether from a repeat of Thurot's raid or local disaffection as threatened in 1798. It is only in the later 19th century that the east battery and its guns facing south and east use the castle to control shipping in Belfast Lough.

The study of the castle can contribute some information on the economic history of the area. Obviously, of course, the castle and the harbour provide the *raisons d'être* for the town of Carrickfergus. In the middle ages, the apparent continuity of mason craft that we can see in the first three periods reminds us of the castle's role as a source of direct employment. Its use of Cultra stone from across the Belfast Lough must have done much to open up the quarry there, while the apparent lack of this stone for use after period III may well tell us that the quarry was exhausted by 1300. In the later period instead of a quarry opened up by the Anglo-Normans, the castle provides evidence of a new industry, brickmaking. The bricks used in Peers's rebuilding of the keep in 1556-9 and the gunports of 1561-7 must be some of the first used in Ulster and probably in Ireland. This was the start of a local industry which continued down to modern times. A point worthy of note, and perhaps linked to this introduction of a new building medium, is the employment of soldiers on the building works, which we find in 1565 and 1615. It is perhaps probable that the men were used as labourers under direction, but it is also possible that the army introduced new skills directly to Ireland. The pottery excavated in 1955 and 1962 came from a variety of sources. In the mid 16th-century deposit we see a number of pieces imported from Spain, south-west France, northern France, the Rhineland, the Netherlands, south-west England, the English Midlands and Scotland, with some local wares. In this we can see a continuation of the weakness of the Irish pottery industry which led to a strong tendency to import wares from a variety of sources (McNeill 1980, chap 3). The pattern of the late 17th-century deposits is quite different: the material is either local, or from south-west England or Staffordshire, the result of the economic stability and growth of the region, and the greatly strengthened ties with Britain, which followed the 17th-century settlements.

Finally something should be said about the general lessons of this exercise. First there is the question of evidence. In the mediaeval period it is often held that there is little evidence for Ireland. Yet Ireland has many castles, often not as well preserved as Carrickfergus, but equally often less confused by later additions and rebuildings. Mediaeval society was an aristocratic one, in which building display was important to the aristocracy. To use this evidence, however, we must have the dates and social context of the buildings, which only documents can provide. In the case of Carrickfergus, as in the case of most castles in Ulster at least, the documentary evidence does exist to form at least reasonable hypotheses on these points, and to give a quarter-century bracket at most to the building periods. Study of the buildings can show us the standards to which the Anglo-Norman aristocracy built, and we find here as elsewhere that these were in line with their peers' in Britain or Europe. Politically a man like John de Courcy or Hugh de Lacy may have tried to emphasise his independence from royal government but culturally he did not. Ironically the only time we can see a possible 'timelag' operating is in the royal works at the castle.

The examination of a post-mediaeval building is in some respects more difficult. While the bulk of documentation increases during the 16th and 17th centuries in particular, it tends to be preserved from the top echelons of the government machine. Instead of the detail that a mediaeval reference may give, if it is preserved at all, we too often encounter items such as '£500 for works at . . .'. The role a building serves is more likely than a mediaeval castle to be specialised, and so it is perhaps easier to judge its efficiency. However, as we can see at Carrickfergus, if that building is a government one it is to be seen against an increasingly complex picture of overall policies. The details we may derive from looking at one building need to be more and more linked to others, as, for example, the role of the fortifications of Carrickfergus from 1790 to 1820 or from 1860 to 1918 in the coastal defence system of Ireland. It is customary to end studies with pleas for more work to be done and in this case we may make the plea again, either for the general work as outlined above or for more detailed examination of the castle itself, for example excavation on a larger scale of the western gun platform of the outer ward or the gatehouse towers, or at precise points such as the forework of the keep or a trench to verify the existence of an inner ditch proposed above.

APPENDIX 1

EXCAVATIONS IN THE CASTLE IN 1955 AND 1962

1955 Excavation: Stratigraphy

The aim of this excavation was to examine the stump of the middle curtain, then visible north-west of the keep, and to see where it led. The work took place between February and mid-June 1955 under the direction of B C S Wilson of the Archaeology Department, Queen's University, Belfast, in two stages. The initial work, from early February to mid-March, involved tracing the line of the wall by means of trenches across its line (Fig 18). Seven (A-G) were laid out at first which traced the wall as far as, and including, the middle tower. Trenches A and B were sited on the assumption that the wall was straight, but found no trace of it. Trench A was excavated some 14 m east of the north-west angle of the middle curtain; trench B lay mid-way between the middle tower and the north gun embrasure of the east battery. Both were excavated to a considerable depth through an apparently homogeneous dark brown soil, rather soft and wet, without finding the curtain wall, A to a depth of 7 ft, B to 9 ft, with a boring a further 2 ft deep before hitting stone. Trench A was later extended southwards to pick up the wall after it had been found to bend southwards nearer the north-west angle. After the outline of the middle tower had been clarified a further five trenches (H-M) traced the line of the curtain to the middle tower. After the trenches had established the line, the whole wall was exposed along with a strip 4 ft wide on the inner (south and west) side. The stratigraphy uncovered in this work appears to have been fairly uniform with the present cobbled courtyard overlying rubble fill laid over or around the middle curtain and other walls, but details of relationships were not noted and the cobbles could have been patched many times. The excavation at this stage removed the cobbles as far as the wall-top and in the deeper trenches dug later, the cobbles are often missing from the sections over the wall for this reason. Two recent walls were discovered in these initial works. In trench B one extended along the east side with a cross wall to the west. In trench J, mid-way between the two towers, the corner of a building lying east-west/north-south was found. Its relationship to the general cobbling of the courtyard is unknown but it certainly post-dated the destruction of the curtain which it overlay: it was cracked as a result of subsidence of the foundations where they were not supported by the curtain. It is possible that the walls in trenches B and J belong to the same building, as they would meet at right angles. A store is shown on the plan of 1923 at this approximate position but the walls do not seem to belong to it: it appears to have been a light structure, quite possibly of timber, and it would have been a little over a metre to the west. Another possibility, particularly for the wall in trench J, is that it is part of the shot furnace marked on the 1811 and 1821 plans.

The second stage of the excavation involved four groups of deeper trenches excavated to bedrock at points on either side of the curtain wall. These were just south of the middle tower (prefixed B), south and west of the east tower (prefixed T), and at two points along the curtain between, centred on the junction between the broad and narrow sections (prefixed W) (Fig 18). The trenches in each group were very small but, although frequently contiguous, had their layers recorded separately. Starting from the north-west corner and going along the curtain wall, trenches were sited at the angle of the wall between the corner and the middle tower; excavated last, in June, these were named W8, on the outer side of the curtain, and W9, on the inner (Fig 20). Both had been sealed by the layer of cobbles set in sand (1), removed in the initial clearance of the area to expose the curtain wall. These cobbles ran over the curtain and on the outside of it a dump of sandy soil (1a) had been used to level the area up for them; within

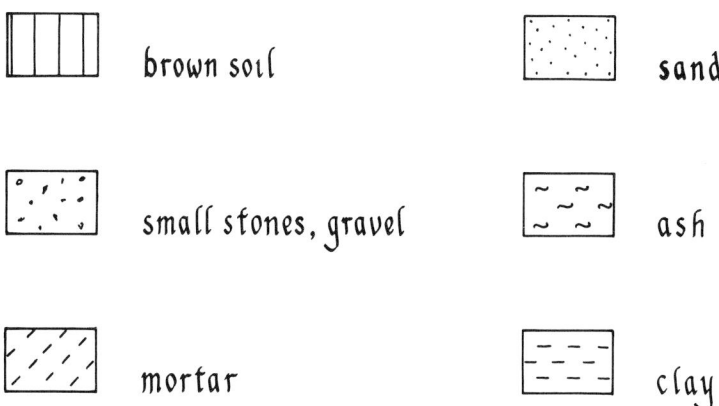

Fig 18 Key to conventions used in the excavation sections

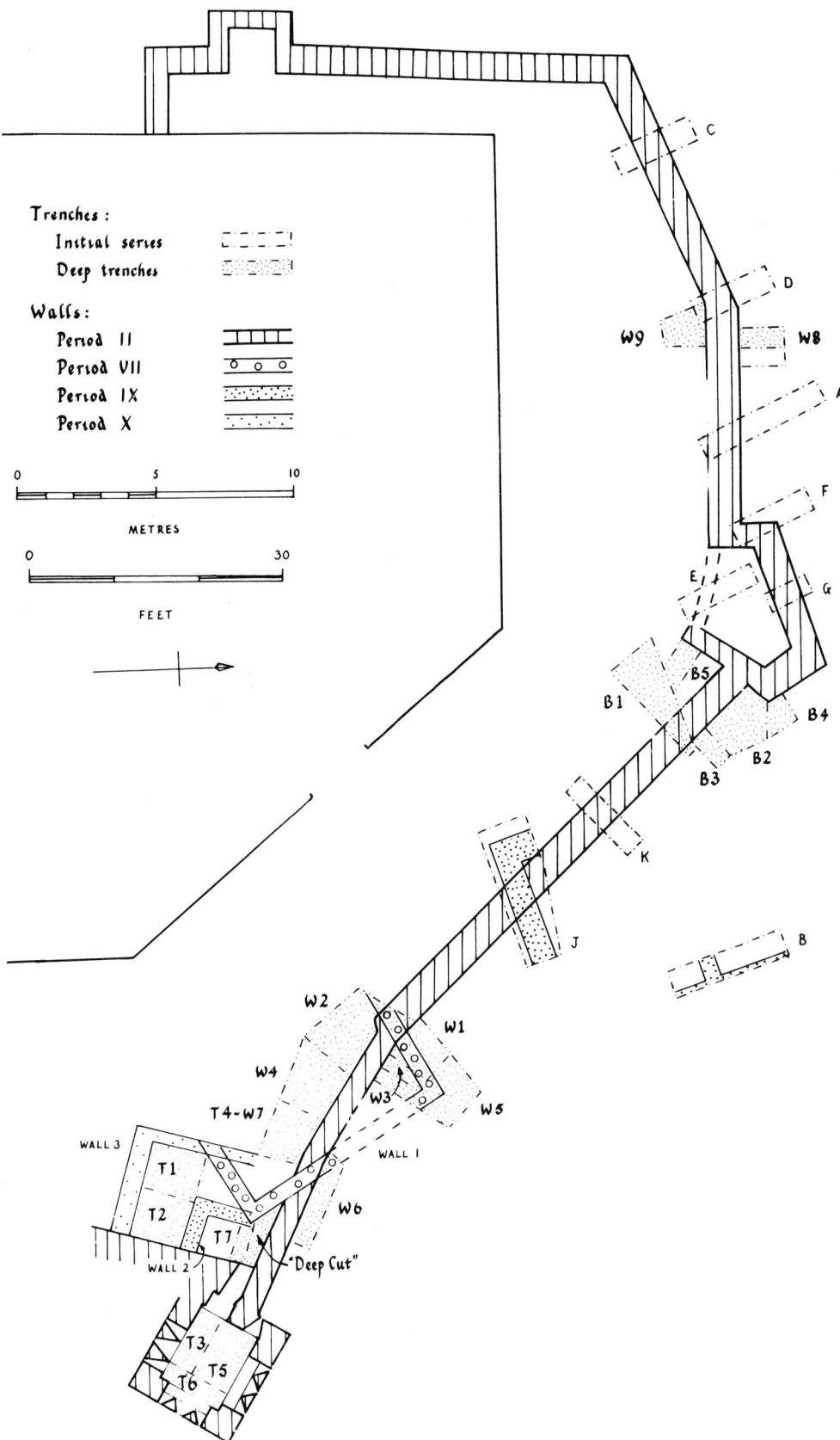

Fig 19 1955 excavations: general plan of the trenches

Excavations in the castle in 1955 and 1962

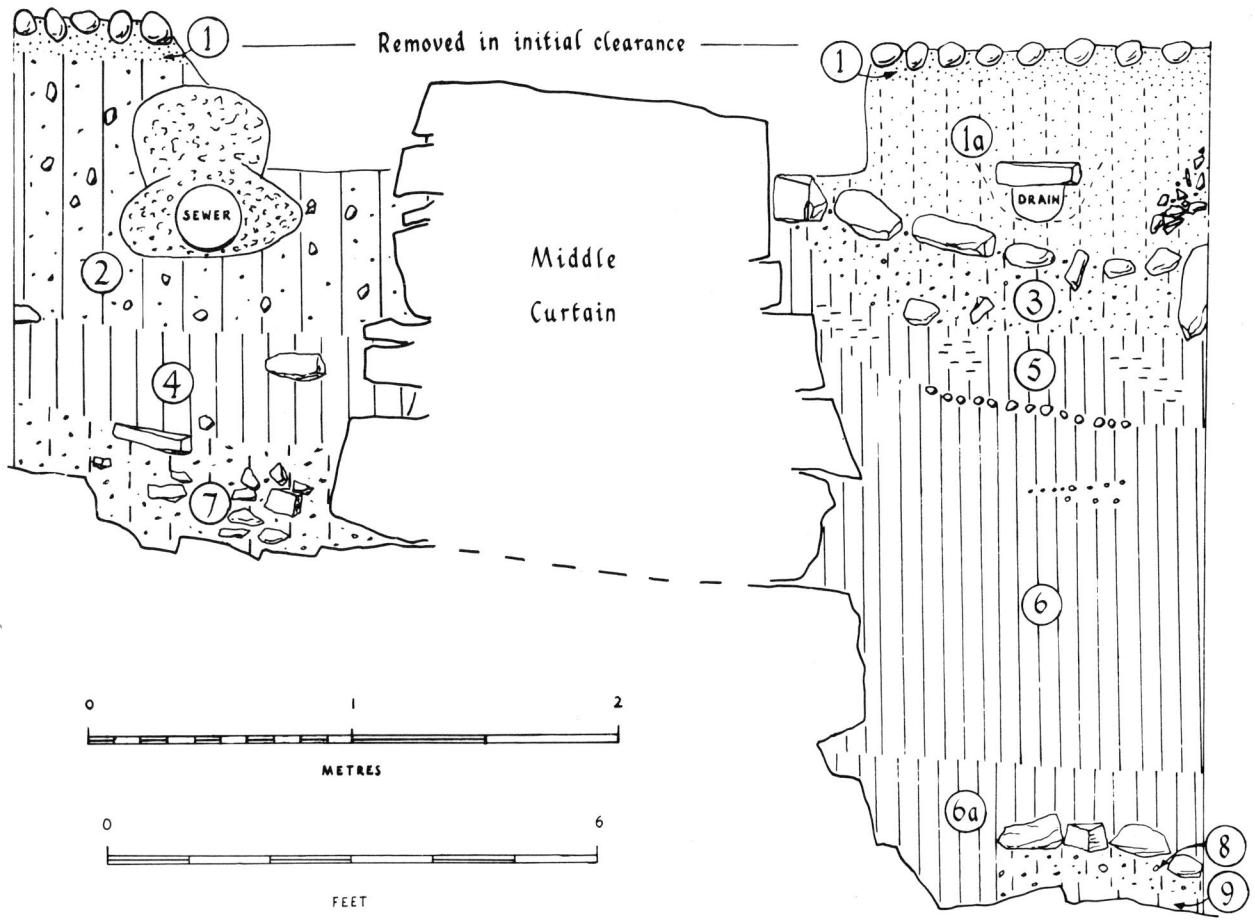

Fig 20 1955 excavations: section of trenches W8 and W9

this sandy soil was laid a drain. This soil had been dumped over a second surface of cobbles set in stony earth (3), and laid over a layer of red clay mixed with dark earth (5). This last, which covered the upper of three offsets of the curtain wall, sealed a 5 ft deep deposit of black fill (6) which produced no finds except small pieces of wood. At its base the soil did not change but now produced pottery, bones, shell, leather, etc. and for finds recording purposes this was divided off from (6) as (6a). At this depth the wall was resting at the edge of a rock cut, against which lay (6) and (6a), which filled the base of the cut and lay against its face. In the northern part of the trench (6a) covered a small patch of stones in black soil (8), which lay over some decomposed rock (9), presumably derived from erosion of the base of the cut. On the inner side of the curtain, the stratigraphy of trench W8 was even simpler. Below (1) a layer of brown soil (2), containing a sewer, had been laid against the wall. This lay at the level of the uppermost of three offsets of the curtain wall foundations, on a layer of dark brown earth (4), which covered a layer of brown gravel (7), probably derived from the bedrock on which it lay. The wall had been built directly on the rock some 5 ft above the base of the rock cut on whose lip it stood.

Five trenches, B1-5, were excavated south-east of the middle tower in the angles between it and the curtain wall, B1 and B5 against the inner face of the wall, and B2, B3 and B4 against the outer. The main trench inside was B1 which may be taken as the starting point for a description of the stratigraphy (Fig 21). The whole was sealed by a uniform layer of cobbles set in sand (1), below which was a layer of mortar with patches of brick debris (3), thick over the curtain wall but tailing off away from it and towards the middle tower; where it was thinner it was levelled up with (2), black, ashy soil. A sewer, or drain, was laid in (3), over the curtain wall, deeper to the north-west and running more nearly on a north-south line than the curtain wall. Directly beneath (3) was a second layer of dark fill, black towards the bastion but at the other side of the trench dividing into brown soil over the curtain (9), with a mortar lens (7), and black ashy soil containing bones, pottery and brick fragments on the inner side of the wall. This latter black fill was divided into two layers, (5) and (8), by a thick streak of brown gravel (6), which faded out near the wall and divided into two away from it. At the south-eastern side of the trench there was a local patch of pebbles (4), between (3) and (9) but it did not stretch more than 4 ft north of the edge of the trench. Below (8) was a layer of brown gravel (11), with patches of mortar (10) on or some-

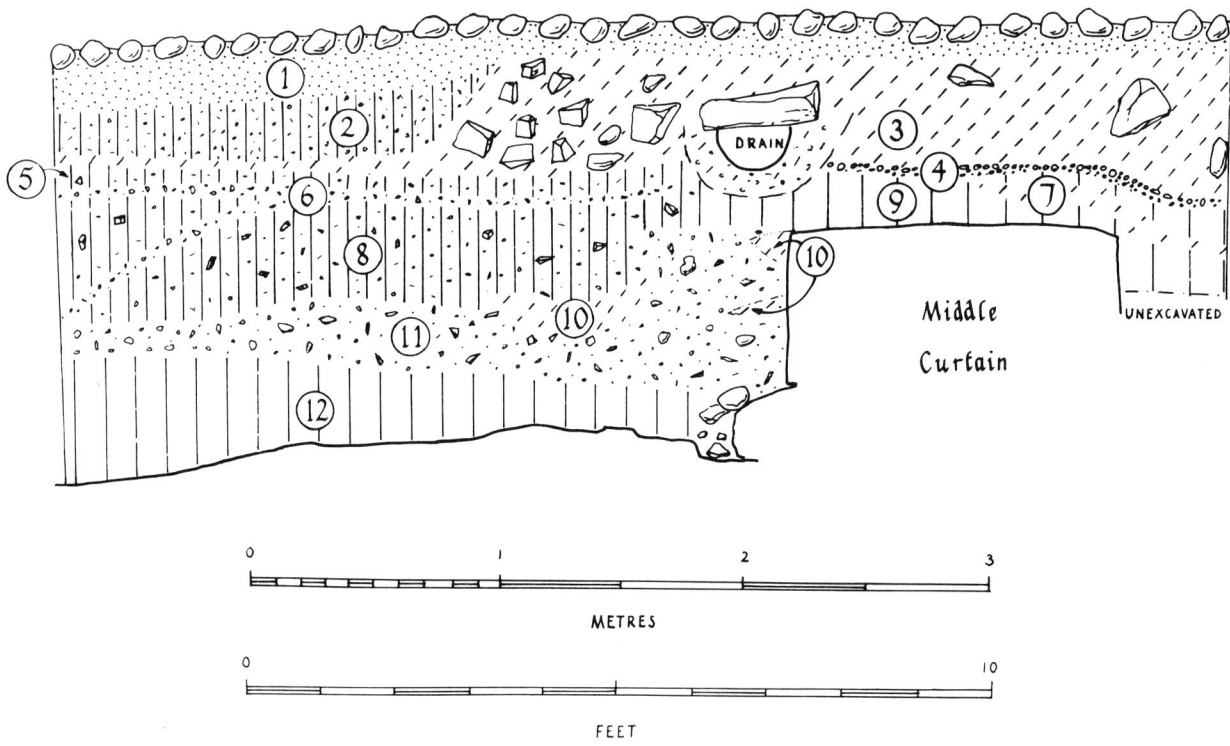

Fig 21 1955 excavations: section of trench B1

times in it, especially near the curtain wall. Here (11) was thicker and (8) seemed to level it up. At the base of the trench a thick layer of brown soil (12), largely sterile, ran over the rock and the footings of the curtain wall.

A 3 ft wide trench, B5, linked B1 with the south-east return wall of the middle tower and the stratigraphy of B1 was largely repeated in it (Fig 22). The succession of cobbles, black ashy fill with mortar and debris over more black fill was the same (B5 (1), (2), (3) and (4)) with the mortar thicker on the side of the curtain wall. The gravel streak, (6) in trench B1 and (5) in B5, did not extend far back from the side nearest the curtain wall; on the south-west, the layers (5) and (8) in B1, ((4) and (6) in B5), were amalgamated. Again the mortar of layer (10) in B1 was confined to the north-east side nearer the curtain wall, the brown gravel (B5 (7), B1 (11)) being unmixed to the south-west. It also ran over the lower courses of the footings of the south-east wall of the tower on the south-west: on the north-east the rock on which the wall was built rose a little higher and both it and the single course of footings projected through (7) at that side of the trench. A layer of dark brown soil (9), covered by a mortar layer (8), tailing away to the north-east towards the curtain wall, covered the rock. The lowest footings of the tower wall were cut through (9), but (8) ran up to them.

The first trench against the outer face was B2, in the outer angle of the middle tower and curtain wall, but also extending back over the latter to link with the north-west side of trench B1 (Fig 23). The upper layers presented a similar sequence to both B1 and B5, over the top of the curtain, with mortar and black soil (B2 (1), (2), (3)) and the drain also buried in the mortar of (3). Below this a thin layer of clay (4) (with a coal ash streak (4a)), over brown earth (6), intercalated with a mortar layer (7), brings us to the level of the top of the curtain wall. On the inner side (3) rested on black soil (5), over brown earth (8), with a wedge of the mortar layer (7), level with the wall-top; this reflects closely the B1 stratigraphy. The trench went much deeper on the outside of the curtain wall however, 12 ft as opposed to 5 ft. The wall had three offsets, the upper of which came at approximately the level of the top course of the footings on the inner side. These offsets were built over a nearly vertical face of rock, going down some 4 ft lower than the bottom of the lowest course. This scarp swung round to avoid the middle tower, in a quarter circle within the angle of the walls. This depth was filled with a largely homogeneous brown soil, lighter brown at the top (10), and stoneless down to a wedge of mortar and stone chips (12), at the level of the upper offset. Below this it contained some large stones but was then again simply dark brown earth as far as the bedrock at the base of the trench (11) and (13). For the purposes of recording finds, which were few, this was divided at the depth of 10 ft 3 in below the level of the cobbles at the surface, but there was no stratigraphical reason for the change. Two other trenches were dug adjacent to B2. B3 was an extension of the trench, 2 ft 6 in to the south-east, excavated apparently only

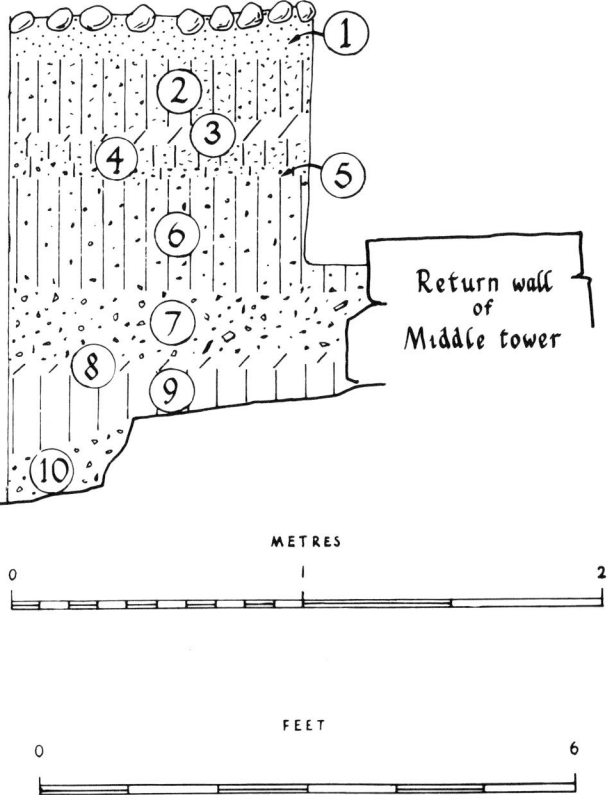

Fig 22 1955 excavations: section of trench B5

to the depth of the upper offset of the curtain wall. B4 was a second extension, also taking only a day to excavate, which exposed the base of the north-east face of the middle curtain. The east angle was found to have been destroyed by a drain, presumably that one which ran over the top of the curtain wall in the other B trenches.

The third group of trenches centred around the junction between the broad and narrow sections of the curtain wall. Initially trench W1 some 5 ft square was laid out on the exterior of the junction, but it was later extended to the south-east in W3 and the area of the two was doubled by the excavation of trench W5 (Pl 23). Opposite these was W2 against the inner face of the curtain wall, giving a combined section across the walls on the south-east sides of the two areas. The stratigraphy can thus be described together (Fig 24). The whole was originally sealed by cobbles set in sand or sandy soil, (1) and (2), which lay on a layer of mortar (3), all disturbed by the trench dug for the lightning conductor from the keep. On the inner side (3) lay over a sequence of brown earth (4), red and grey clay (5), and dark earth (6), with a wedge of mortar (7) in it. To the north-west, across the trench, (5) diminished to become a lens within (4) and (6) which combined into one layer. Outside the curtain (3) lay directly on (6), while the mortar (7) intruded between it and the layer below. At this level two walls crossed the trench (Fig 18), one of stone with a little brick running north-west from mid-way along the south-eastern side of trench W5 to approximately the centre of the trench. Against this was butted a brick wall, standing ten courses high which crossed the curtain wall running to the south-west into the north-west side of trench W2. Below this wall (wall 1), on the outside, from the level of the top of the curtain was a great depth of homogeneous brown smelly soil fill which continued down against a cut in the natural rock 4 ft below the base of the curtain. It contained two localised lenses of slightly different material: 'manure' three-quarters of the way down over the north-eastern part of trench W5, and a softer sticky patch against the rock face and the lower part of the curtain wall. This last may be the result of seepage down the two faces. Again for finds recording purposes this fill was divided arbitrarily, in W1 and W5 at the base of the curtain wall footings. Below this dark fill there were several layers or patches of material: sand (16), red clay (17), mortar (18), brown soil with lumps of red clay (19), and small stones (20). The last two sealed a row of stones running north from the rock scarp. Behind the face which was on the north-west side there were a number of wooden stakes and horizontal planks, but unfortunately the black soil on which these lay could not be excavated owing to pressures of time.

On the inner side of the curtain, in trench W2, layer (6) at the level of the top of the curtain lay over a thin mortar spread (8). Below this, layer (9) of brown earth with stones and brick fragments lay over (13), a fill of dark stony earth which sealed a drain of heavy stones set in mortar. This drain had been built on a base of sand (14), which lay on and disturbed a spread of charcoal (15), which lay up to 6 in thick at the south-eastern side of the trench, extending 3 ft 1 in back from that section along the south-western side. A layer of gravel, or decomposed rock, (22), covered the footings of the curtain wall below (13) and (15) but where the charcoal was absent the drain had been built on this gravel. There was a heterogeneous collection of layers below with flints in blue clay (23), levelling up to the south-east side a dip in a layer of blue-brown clay (24), which could be separated into blue over brown clay on the north-western section. The clay layer or layers were cut by the trench-built footings of the curtain wall. These footings on the inner face could be divided like the wall above into broad and narrow sections: the footings of the latter were laid first and then the broad section's footing laid against and over them (Pl 24). On the outside the footings, because they were built on the edge of the rock scarp, were not buried originally and so were not distinguishable from the wall face. The actual junction of the two sections, meeting at a shallow re-entrant angle, was marked with several courses of Cultra stone. The rock scarp reflected this re-entrant angle, or vice versa, and the rock surface stepped down at the junction, being some 3 ft lower beneath the narrow section.

South-east of these trenches, W1-3 and W5, were cut three others. On the outer face of the curtain trench W6 was excavated against the shallow re-entrant angle in the narrow section of the wall. It was quite small and was only dug to a depth of 3 ft 6 in below the cobbling, through dark brown fill, disturbed by the lightning conductor trench, and to be equated with (6) in trench W5. The angle itself was not well built, with no stones actually forming the angle. Trench W4 was excavated south-east of W2 to relieve its section which was in danger of collapsing but like W6 it was not dug to

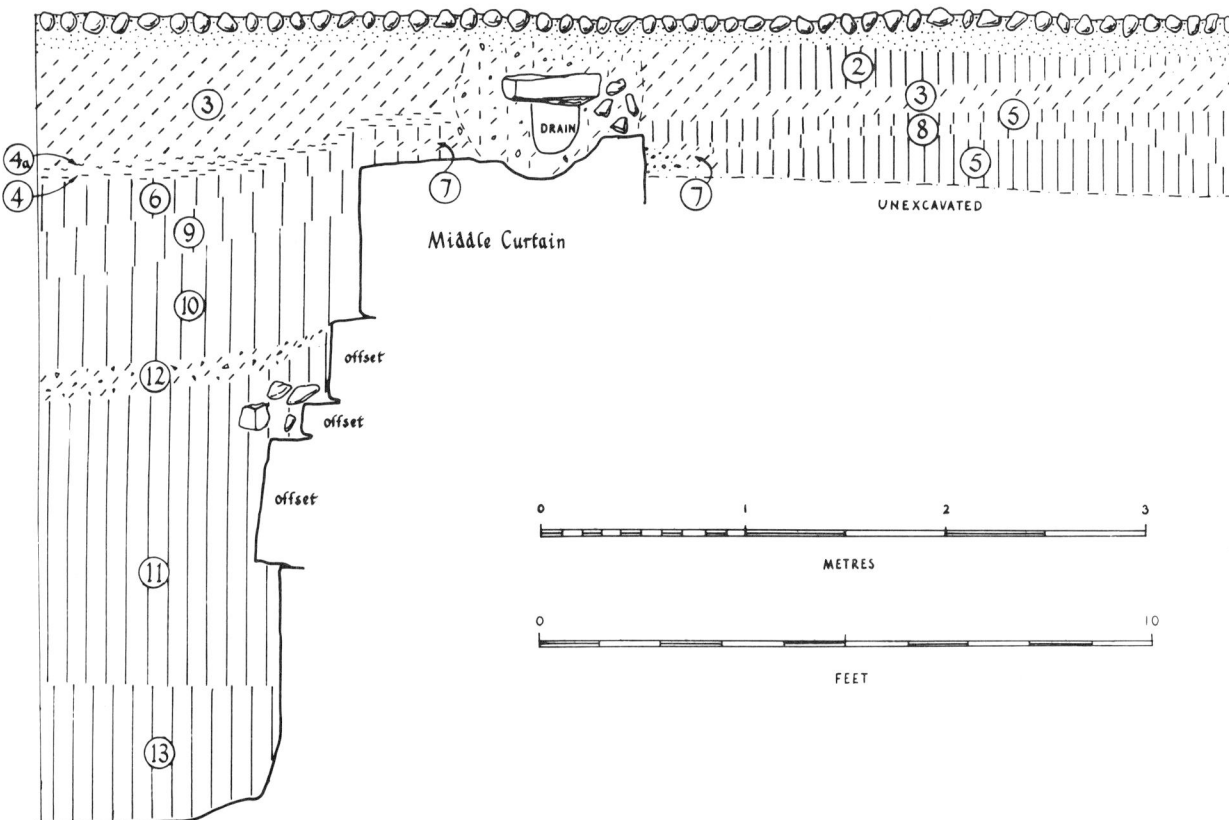

Fig 23   1955 excavations: section of trench B2

bedrock level. It was in fact only taken down to the level of the mortar layer (8) in W2, level with the top of the curtain wall and no layers were distinguished. South-east of this again was a trench some 6 ft square between W4 and the north-west wall of a late 19th-century rectangular building built against the east tower (wall 3). This seems to have been first opened in March when it was referred to as T4 and pottery is recorded as having been found in dark soil over a layer of rubble. In May it was re-opened as trench W7. At the surface was a layer of cobbles and mortar. Below this was brown soil, covering the foundations of the late 19th-century building (wall 3) and a sewer which ran under them to the tower. Below this was a thick layer of small stones and mortar which was thought to be a floor, or a base for one, to go with a wall running diagonally across the middle curtain wall in this trench. This wall aligned with the one (wall 1) noted in trench W5 to the south-east, and a few feet from the east tower it returned at a right angle, parallel to the brick wall in trenches W2 and W5.

This last wall, continuing below wall 3, leads us to the area within the late 19th-century building against the east tower (Pl 26). The whole of its floor was excavated to a greater or lesser depth in 1955 in a series of trenches prefixed by the letter T. The initial clearance work had here exposed the wall (wall 2) of a smaller building, only 4 ft 6 in wide, against the east tower. This clearance had also cut down deeply in a trench 1 ft 6 in wide to expose the door to the basement of the tower. The clearance of the floor generally exposed three features: a sewer noted already in T4/W7, probably serving the lavatories inserted into and built against the east tower in the late 19th century, a small room 4 ft wide built against the tower (wall 2), and the return wall (wall 1) of the building already noted as found running over the middle curtain wall in trenches T4/W7, W5 and W2 (Pl 25). The north-west wall of the small building lay over the angle of this other building and both were cut by the sewer. The cobbled floor of the small building was 2 ft 2 in lower than the top of the outer footings of its wall on the outer side; it was low enough to block the top of the door to the tower basement just below the lintel but the exact relationship was lost with the sewer disturbance and in the deep cut. The walls of the building were of fairly small stones with some sandstone, Cultra stone and brick; the footings carried down on the outside to about the same level as the interior floor.

The part of the later building (wall 3) south of this smaller one was excavated in two trenches, T1 and T2. In T1, against the tower wall, the first layer encountered was a black ashy soil (1), apparently disturbed by the late 19th-century wall. Below this was a layer of mortar (2) with no finds, and then a

Excavations in the castle in 1955 and 1962

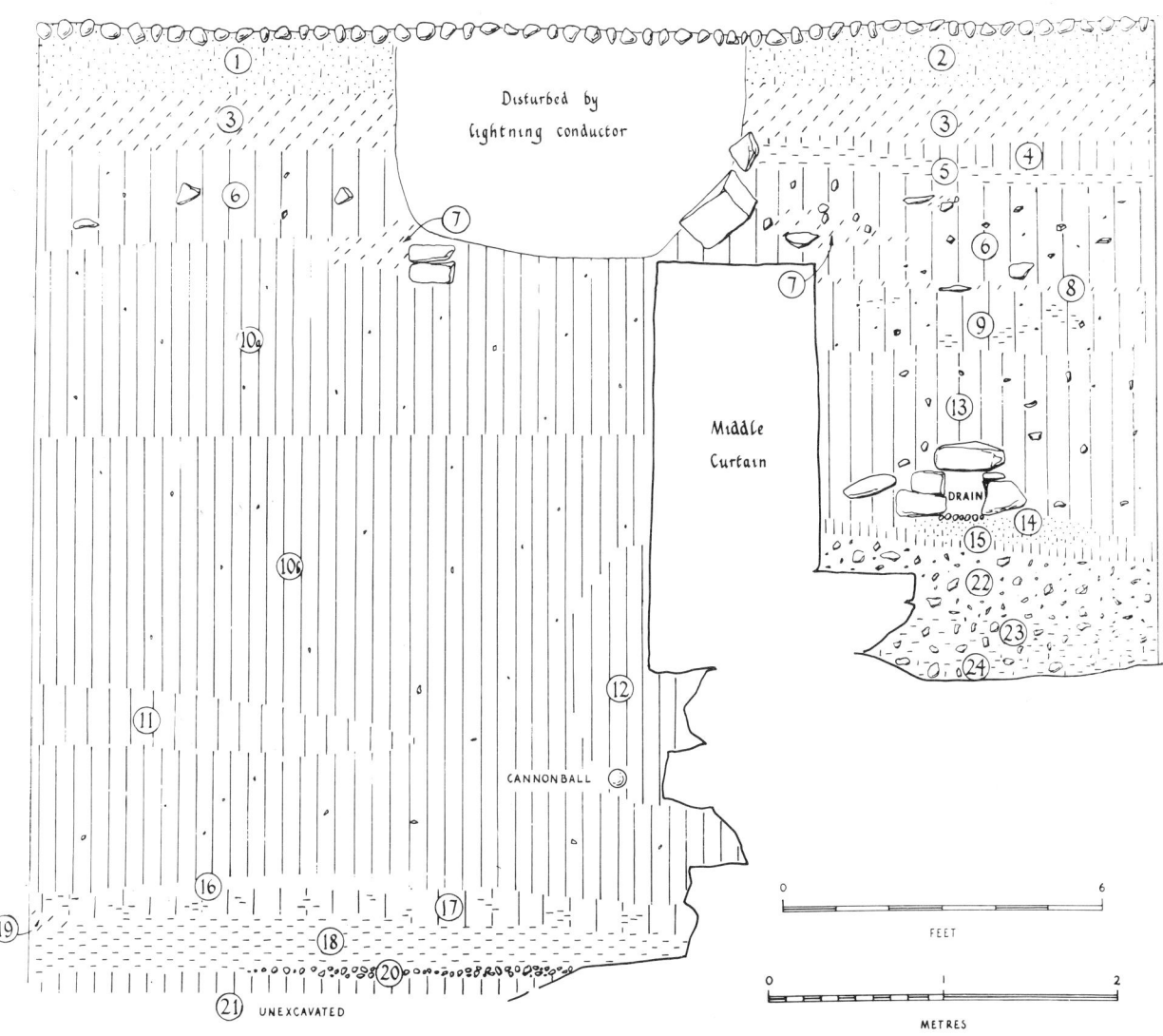

Fig 24 1955 excavations: sections of trenches W2 and W5

layer of black soil (3). T2, to the west, was only excavated as far as the mortar layer (2). The deep cut exposing the door to the tower basement, and its later extension 2 ft southwards, T7, provide our knowledge of the stratigraphy below these levels and the sunken floor of the small building. There seems to have been only dark brown earth (2), wetter at the top, where it was level with the base of the sewer cutting across the area. This carried on down to a floor of sandstone chips and powder. The cutting was then extended to the north-west along the inner face of the curtain wall, to link up with trench T4/W7. At the base of the fill the sandstone floor rose to the north-west: it was 2 ft 6 in lower at the wall of the east tower than it was at a point along the curtain below wall 3. At a point some 4 ft 6 in along the curtain from the tower wall the end of a wall was discovered running off to the south. Time and resources prevented further exploration of the area, but a small trial excavation showed the floor lying over a layer of brown earth levelling up the surface of the rock about 2 ft below.

The interior of the tower presented few problems of excavation, which was initially carried out in several trenches, T3, T5 and T6, later dug as one unit, named T8. The stratification in each was similar, a layer of earth and rubble (1), on which was built the blocking of the basement door and arrow-slits. Below this was a layer of earth with stones and patches of red clay (2), which lay directly on the floor of chippings of Cultra stone (4). This was not level but sloped down to the south-east, being levelled up with a spread of dark brown earth and stones (3A), and red sandy earth (3B). The floor proper, (4), had been laid over brown earth (5), which levelled up the surface of the bedrock beneath. There were no finds of pottery or other artefacts in layers (3) to (5), and few in (1) and (2).

Interpretation of these excavations must start with two

prominent features to which everything can relate. The first of these is the middle curtain wall with the middle and east towers, the uncovering of which was the principal aim of the excavation. The second is the bedrock, its levels and how these have been produced. In trenches W8, B2-4 and W5, there was found a scarp or cut in the rock, on the lip of which the middle curtain was built. The cut into the rock itself was not in fact very deep, for most of the depth of the trenches was produced by the deposits over the rock, but the base was about 5 ft below the level within the curtain. None of the trenches extended more than 12 ft out from the curtain wall and so none could be expected to pick up an outer edge but it is difficult not to equate this scarp with the cut visible in the rock outside the castle below the north-west angle of the middle curtain (Pl 15). This is about 5 m wide and deeper, over 2 m, below the rock surface than the cut we have described, and it is also below the middle curtain in part. This is however easily explained if this is the ditch of the earliest castle, fronting the keep and inner ward. It would have tended to wrap around the keep and might well be deeper at the edge of the peninsula where the rock dropped down to the harbour. The rock topography is not, however, entirely the work of man. On the inner side of the curtain wall it is noticeable that the rock surface is deeper, at the east tower about 13 ft and in trench W2 about 10 ft 6 in below the cobbled surface, than at B2 where it is about 5 ft or in trench W8, much the same. The rock clearly sloped originally, probably in steps, from the west down to the east. In the early trenches rock was not reached in trench B until at least 11 ft down, and again on the outside of the castle the rock below the outer curtain south of the grand battery is visible markedly lower than below the battery. This level continues from the basement of the east tower to the postern gate on the south, as already noted. It is unlikely that such a large volume of rock was dug away by the builders of the first castle. The stones in the inner ward and keep or the middle ward appear weathered, not freshly quarried before use, and the small scale of the rock cutting on the west would be out of place especially as it would have guarded the keep. The rock is a dolerite sill and joints in it can be seen trending north-west to south-east at low tide. It seems likely that there was originally a natural cleft in the rock, to judge from the outside of the castle about 3 m above high tide level along the east side of the peninsula. Its northern face would have met the main rock edge at the south end of the present grand battery. The top of its southern and western face would have followed the present line of the east side of the inner curtain but continued on to meet the northern face, somewhere between trenches B5 and W2. The base of this face presumably runs between the face in trench W5 and somewhere under wall 3 outside the east tower, which is built on the floor of the cleft.

This cutting, ditch or cleft seems to have been kept remarkably free of silt for a long time. At the base of W5 was found an enigmatic but hardly substantial feature of stone and wood but elsewhere the filling seems to have been of a largely homogeneous wet brown or black earth. This does not seem explicable as the product of any natural process of the silting of a rock-cut feature. Nor does it seem to have been the result of gradual filling of a ditch with rubbish thrown in haphazardly over a long period of time. It was uniform throughout its depth, and from W8 to the east tower, and must be considered the result of a deliberate single filling of the ditch. This filling seems to have been left undisturbed in W5 and by the east tower (or any upper fill removed), but in W8 was capped by red clay and cobbles set in sand, and in B2 by a layer of mortar and stone chips. Significantly, in view of the softness of the filling, both of these sealing layers slope markedly down from the curtain wall. This filling of the ditch in all cases rests against the curtain wall which was presumably left standing at the time.

The destruction of the curtain is probably marked by the various streaks and deposits of mortar lying on the ditch fill (B1 (7), B2 (10), W2/W5 (7)). In W2/W5 this seems to be associated with the building of the wall which aligns with wall 1 in trench W7/T4, and which was built directly over the curtain wall. Presumably at the same time on the inner side of the curtain the ground was levelled up to the top of the truncated curtain with brown earth (W2 (9) and (13)), sealed by the floor (8). In trenches B1 and B2 these levels were covered by a rough surface of clay (B2 (4) and (8)) or stones (B1 (4) and (6)) which covered the middle tower wall. West of the middle tower, W9 (4) seems to be the only product of this levelling up apart from the destruction of the curtain, but the surface over the ditch was good. East and south of wall 1, the position at this stage is unclear. Later the wall 1 building was demolished and over the whole area a good cobbled courtyard was laid down over a levelling layer of mortar, stone and brick produced by the demolition of at least one building. A small building (wall 2) was built against the east tower with a sunken floor of cobbles, possibly at the same time. This was demolished to make way for another building (wall 3) on the same site and this stood until the 1930s.

The sequence is therefore clear. The filling of the ditch and the blocking of the east tower basement was followed after an interval of time by the destruction of the inner curtain and the construction of wall 1. The levelling of this wall appears to have been followed by the laying of the cobbles which now cover the whole outer ward. The relationship of these cobbles to wall 2 and the walls found below the general level of the courtyard in the initial clearance trenches is unclear, for the cobbles could well have been repaired over them. There is no reason to doubt that the building of wall 3 came at the end of the sequence: it at least appears to have definitely post-dated the cobbles. There are no absolute dates from the excavation but the general character of the pottery found, discussed in detail later, would place the filling of the ditch in the mid 16th century, and in so far as one can separate the finds associated with the destruction of the middle curtain and the laying of the cobbles, they would indicate that these were close in date.

1962 Excavation: Stratigraphy

The aim of the limited excavation done by S G Rees-Jones of Queen's University, Belfast, in 1962 was to expose the blocked postern gate at the south-eastern end of the middle curtain and to make it accessible for public inspection Fig. 25). The method used was to excavate down from the existing surface against the postern and then to clear the area northwards, from time to time cleaning up the face to produce four successive sections (Fig 25). These all showed a very similar stratigraphy. The original floor was layer (7), a grey-brown sandy clay with flecks of mortar, which sealed a drain running out beneath the level of the lowest course of the postern gate, which curiously seems to have had no sill stone. The drain was cut into or lined with a layer of mortar with

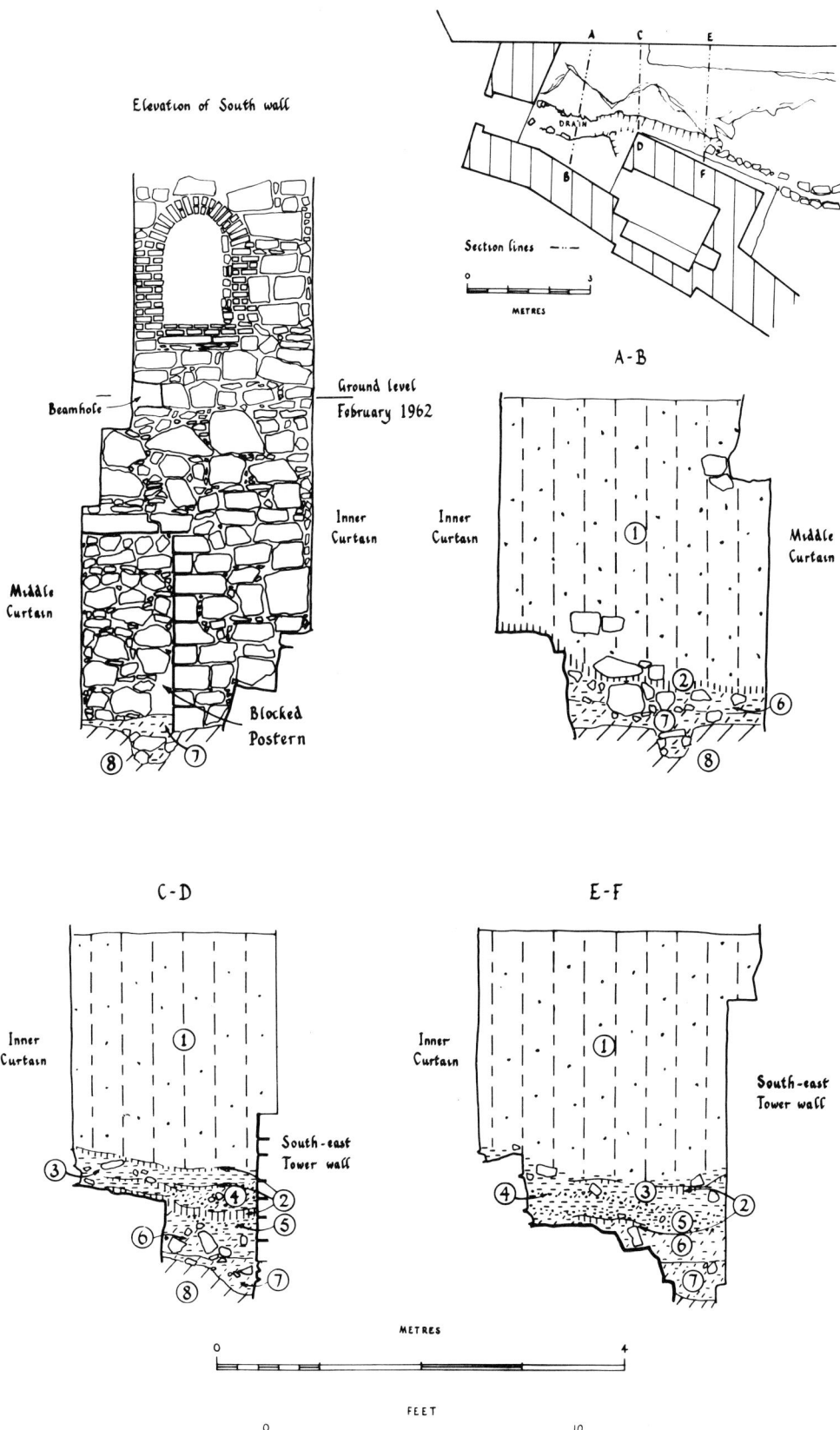

Fig 25   1962 excavations: plan, sections and interior elevation of the postern gate

sandstone chips (8), which apparently lay on the bedrock although, as it was not removed, this cannot be certain; it may be the builders' debris from the construction of the middle curtain. The bedrock itself dropped in steps eastwards from under the inner curtain; at the northern end the upper step was used for extensive footings for the inner curtain. The clearance quite soon revealed the south-east latrine tower built with the middle curtain and already described (above p 31). The floor (7) ran over the footings of this tower. Over this floor lay layer (6), similar but with more mortar and large stones, which rose west of the latrine tower to the height of the rock shelf. It was absent below the blocking of the postern gate but not from the other sections. In the southernmost of these sections, (6) was covered by a layer of dark organic sludge (2) and then a uniform fill (1), but in the others by several layers. The lowest of these, on (6) directly, or in one case also covering some black organic material lying on (6), was (5), a layer of gravel in grey clay usually covering the full width of (6). Over it lay red and yellow clay (3), containing deposits of mortar and pebbles (4), and black organic sludge (2). The area was then filled, to a depth of 8 to 10 ft, with a uniform fill (1). The blocking of the postern was built directly on layer (7).

It is possible that the two layers (5) and (6) may have been renewals of the original floor (7), and they may have been absent to the south because they were designed to make a slope down to the postern gate. This would have been sensible for drainage as well as for not interfering with the clearance of the postern gate itself. It is not clear at what stage the blocking of the latrine tower took place: certainly after layer (7), like the postern, but possibly after (3) or (2) had been laid. The work was done thoroughly. The latrine chute was blocked with paving slabs, presumably from the tower floor. A mass of stones and mortar was then thrown in to fill the chamber to the height of the seat of the latrine, after which the recess was filled with a rough wall, thickening the outer curtain, which was originally only 1 ft 6 in wide at this point. The entrance was then nearly walled up and rubble and earth thrown in to fill the chamber to roof level. The quantity of rubble may be the result of the demolition of the upper parts of the latrine tower but this may not have been done until the later 19th century. The general filling (1), however, is almost certainly to be attributed to the need created by the insertion of the gunport over the postern (above p 47).

The finds from the 1955 and 1962 excavations

The contexts from which these finds were derived have been described above but some further discussion is required to clarify those of the 1955 excavations and their relationship to the finds. The discussion has been related to the layers as they were recorded in the various trench sections but these did not necessarily correspond to the layers as they were dug. The trench areas were restricted and layers distinguishable in sections were often excavated together as one, while some layers, such as the uniform ditch fill, were divided into arbitrary spits. The finds were bagged directly from the ground and the bags marked with the date and a verbal description of the layer excavated. In order that individual sherds might be taken from the groups and studied, when the pottery was washed in 1970 the sherds were marked with a layer number according to a system derived from the notebooks, which were recorded on a day to day system, not one related to the sections as redrawn for publication. As a result the numbers on the sherds need to be correlated to the sections published, which has been done in a table. The layers have been grouped in this table into four main contexts based on the interpretation of the sequence as outlined above: context 1, layers built up against the inner face of the middle curtain; context 2, the fill of the ditch outside it; context 3, the destruction level of the middle curtain and the building of wall 1; context 4, the laying of cobbles over both wall 1 and the middle curtain. Against the east tower there were two other contexts in a purely local sequence: 5 associated with wall 2, and 6 with wall 3. To these may be added the general filling behind the postern, excavated in 1962.

The excavations in 1955 were conducted in small trenches often in poor weather conditions. As a result distinctions of layers may not have been completely rigorously observed and may not necessarily apply in the case of every individual sherd. For example, in trenches W1 and W2 layer (1) includes all material 'down to the level of the top of the middle curtain'. This, combined with problems of some sherds possibly filtering down from upper parts of the sides of narrow

TRENCH B1			
	Figure 21	Notebook/ Sherds	Pottery groups
Context 4	(1) (2) (3) (5) ?	(1) (2)	16, 21
Context 3	(4) (5) ? (6)-(10)	(3)-(5)	5B, 7B, 8, 9C, 12, 14, 15, 16, 17, 19, 21
Context 2			
Context 1	(11) (12)	(6)	

Excavations in the castle in 1955 and 1962

trenches, in particular apply to the boundary between contexts 2 and 3 or 4. A further problem is that of the history of the finds between 1955 and 1970. The paper bags of pottery did not last well and in numbers of cases sherds fell out of broken bags. One such group is derived from a box containing bags of pottery from trench W5, almost entirely layers (3) to (8). This group of sherds, marked u/s α, came from these bags but from which is unknown; sherds so marked may, however, be assumed to derive from trench W5 and from the fill of the ditch, context 2. These problems do not apply to finds from the 1962 excavation, where there are no doubts as to the provenance of individual items. The layer numbers marked on the sherds in 1970 refer to the same numbers on the drawn sections.

TRENCH B2			
	Figure 23	Notebook/Sherds	Pottery groups
Context 4	(1)–(3)	(1)	10, 13, 15, 17
Context 3	(4)–(8) (10) (11)	(2)	1, 8, 9A, 12, 15, 21
Context 2	(12) (13)	(3) (4)	3, 7A, 9A, 9C
Context 1			

	TRENCH B3		TRENCH B4		TRENCH B6	
	Notebook/sherds	Pottery groups	Notebook/sherds	Pottery groups	Notebook/sherds	Pottery groups
Context 4	(1)		(1)–(3)	9B, 21	(1)	9A, 11, 15, 18, 21
Context 3	(2)	8				
Context 2	(3)					
Context 1						

TRENCH B5			
	Notebook/sherds	Figure 22	Pottery groups
Context 4	(1)–(3) (4) ?	(1)–(3) (4) ?	7B, 9A, 13, 14, 15, 16, 17, 18, 19, 21
Context 3	(4) ? (5) (6)	(4) ? (5) (6)	8, 15, 17, 21
Context 2			
Context 1	(7)–(9)	(7)–(9)	

	W1			W2	
	Figure 24	Notebook/ sherds	Pottery groups	Notebook/ sherds	Pottery groups
Context 4	(1)-(6)	(1)	9C, 15, 18, 21	(1)	8, 15, 16, 17, 21
Context 3	(7)-(9) (13) (14)			(2)	4, 5B, 9A, 9B, 9C, 15, 16, 17
Context 2	(10)-(12) (16)-(19) (20) (21)	(2)-(4)	1, 3, 4, 7B, 8, 9A, 9C, 11, 13, 14, 15, 17, 18, 21		
Context 1	(15) (22)-(24)			(3)-(6)	9C

	W3			
	Notebook/ sherds	Pottery groups	Notebook/ sherds	Pottery groups
Context 4	(1)		(1) (2)	1, 14, 15, 17, 18
Context 3				
Context 2	(2)-(5)	3, 8, 9A, 9C, 14, 15		
Context 1			(3)	

	W5		W6	
	Notebook/ sherds	Pottery groups	Notebook/ sherds	Pottery groups
Context 4	(1) (2)	4, 5A, 8, 9A, 9B, 9C, 11, 12, 13, 21	(1)	
Context 3				
Context 2	(3)-(8) (9)	1, 2, 3, 4, 5A, 6, 7A, 8, 9A, 9B, 9C, 10, 12, 13, 14, 15, 17, 20	(2)-(4)	8, 9C
Context 1				

Excavations in the castle in 1955 and 1962

	W8			W9	
	Figure 20	Notebook/sherds	Pottery groups	Notebook/sherds	Pottery groups
Context 4	(1) (2)	(1)	7, 8, 9C, 11, 14, 15, 16, 21	(1) (2)	
Context 3	(4)				
Context 2	(3) (5) (6) (8) (9)	(2)-(7)	1, 9C		
Context 1	(7)			(3) (4)	

The finds from these various contexts must be considered as assemblages before proceeding further. The finds from context 1, layers accumulating against the middle curtain, were few and undiagnostic. Context 2, the fill of the ditch in front of the curtain, produced more, especially from trench W5. The groups of pottery found in the layers of this context are listed by trench below, and compared with those found in 1962.

Pottery groups	B2	W1	W3	W5	W8	1962
1	X	X		X	X	X
2				X		X
3		X	X	X		
4		X		X		X
5A				X		X
6				X		
7A	X	X		X		X
8	X	X	X	X		
9A	X	X	X	X		X
9B				X		
9C		X	X	X	X	
10				X		X
11		X		X		
12	X			X		
13		X		X		
14		X	X	X		X

Pottery of groups 5A, 7A, 8, 10 and 14 would indicate a 16th-century date at the earliest for the assemblage, after the first quarter of it according to pot no 32. On the other hand pottery in a basically mediaeval tradition such as groups 1-4 and especially group 9 may be taken as precluding a 17th-century date. A very similar assemblage to this was found in 1962, where almost all the pottery came from the upper fill, layer (1). The only difference of note is the absence from the 1962 finds of North Devon pottery, group 8. The reason for this may be chronological (ie that context 2 is later), for in the 1540s these wares were apparently not to be found in Scilly (Miles and Saunders 1970, 19). In view of the jugs in context 2, however, this postulated chronological distinction may not be pressed far. It is also possible that the material used to fill the ditch and behind the postern respectively came from different sources. The castle being on a rock, the source of all the earth and filling material must have been in the town, and so there is no way of taking this argument further, but as well as pots of group 8 other coarser wares, such as groups 11 or 13, are also absent from the 1962 deposits. The overall impression is rather of table ware than the more general household pottery of context 2.

The pottery found in contexts 3 and 4 (individually not distinctive) obviously contains much material remanent from the earlier context 2. The pottery is, however, dominated by the large quantities of material of groups 15 and 21. The dating of the first, as a local product, still lacks a frame, but the second is a type well known from later 17th-century contexts onwards (Watkins 1960, 27). The wares from Cheshire and the English Midlands, groups 17-20, in particular the slipwares (especially the combed examples) of groups 18 and 19, would indicate a date of the half century centred on 1700 for the assemblage. The latest contexts, 5 and 6, were unfortunately too mixed and explored too little for much useful analysis: they must also be very late in date. Finally it must be emphasied that these dates apply to the formation of the assemblage, not its deposition in the castle where it was found and with material having to be brought in this might well be a significant distinction.

The Pottery

For the purpose of publication the material has been divided into twenty-one groups based on their fabric and origin. A rough analysis of the distribution of pottery found is provided in the table which lists each group found in each context. Closer analysis, estimating the number of pots concerned, has not been attempted because of the problems of context outlined above and also because it cannot be claimed that the excavations in 1955, with the small trenches, recovered a reasonable sample of the total pottery in any of the deposits.

Group 1 — Spain Fig 26
1 Twelve sherds (seven illustrated) of a costrel from

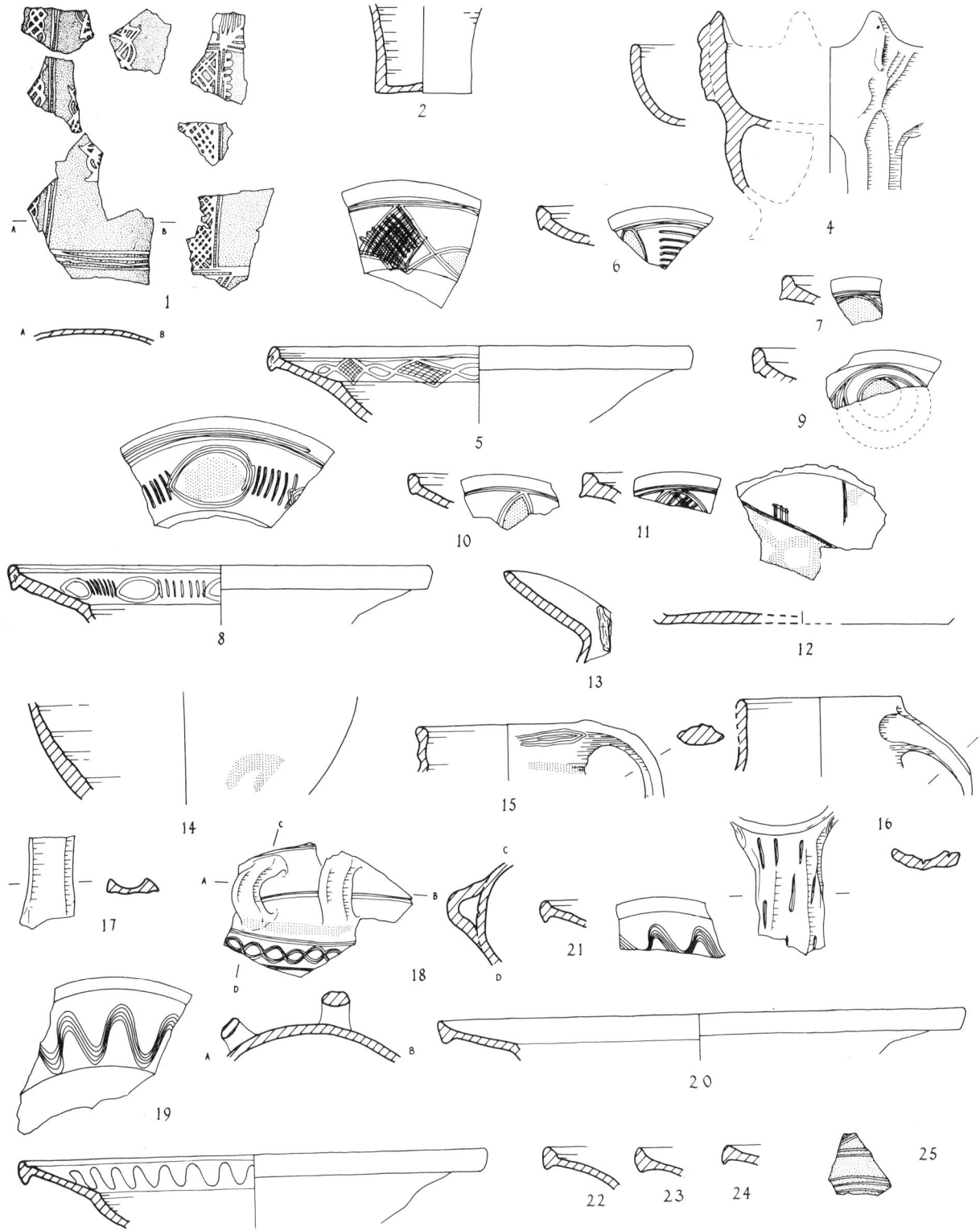

Fig 26 1955 and 1962 excavations: pots, nos 1–25 (x¼)

Merida. Open-textured micaceous orange-red fabric, burnished on the outer surface, painted over with white slip. Two designs are present (either from two vessels or two sides of the same vessel): one is a knot within a rectangular border of parallel lines and interlace, and the other has a complex border of diagonal and criss-cross lines to at least two conjoined rectangles. Cf Hurst 1977, fig 32, no 52. 1955, W8 (3), W1 (3).

2 Plain bottle base in fabric similar to no 1 but wiped rather than burnished on the exterior. Cf Hurst 1977, fig 32 no 51. 1962 (1).

3 (not illustrated) Two body sherds of micaceous orange-red fabric with a bright green lead and copper glaze. Cf Hurst 1977, 103. 1955 W4 (1), W5 (4a).

Group 2 — South-West France   Fig 26

Fabrics are micaceous and white or off-white, often poorly mixed and showing air vesicles and laminations, often but not always containing black and red inclusions. The glazes are lead, clear or copper-green (often mottled) with painted designs in brown and green. Almost all the plates have a brown line along the inside of the rim.

4 Chafing dish with parts of four stylised heads surviving, decorated alternately with yellow and green glaze; charcoal-stained internally. They show stab marks probably to facilitate the drying process and the escape of steam during firing. Cf Hurst 1974A, 239-43. 1955 W5 (4a) and (5), u/s α.

5 Rim sherd of plate, decorated with painted brown lines, to give a diamond filled in with cross-hatched lines and a lozenge partially filled in with green glaze. 1955 u/s α.

6 Rim sherd of plate with brown lines painted to give a lozenge, filled in with green glaze and six parallel lines beside it. 1955 u/s α.

7 Rim sherd of plate decorated with a lozenge outline in brown and filled in with green glaze. 1955 W5 (5a).

8 Rim sherd of plate decorated with lozenges outlined in brown and partially filled with green glaze; between them six vertical brown lines. 1955 u/s α.

9 Rim sherd of plate decorated apparently with a spiral of brown lines terminating in a circle filled in with green glaze. 1955 W5 (5).

10 Rim sherd of plate with a lozenge outlined in brown and filled in with green glaze. 1955 W5 (3), (4).

11 Rim sherd of plate with a lozenge outlined and cross-hatched with brown lines. 1962 (1).

12 Base of plate with an apparently formless decoration of brown and green lines. 1955 W5 (4a).

13 Spout of large jug showing the stump of a broken bridge across it; exterior covered in a streaky and mottled copper-green glaze. 1955 W5 (3), (5), (7).

14 Body sherd of jug or bowl with a double line of green glaze on the otherwise clear glaze of the exterior. 1955 W5 (5).

15 Rim sherd and part of the handle of a jug: on the exterior of the neck a brown horizontal line above a green one; the rest of the exterior is clear glazed. 1962 (6).

16 Upper part of strip jug handle crudely butted to the rim with heavy thumb impressions at the side. A row of stab marks along the junction with the rim and three lines down the handle, but unglazed. 1955 W5 (8).

17 Jug handle partly covered with a copper-green glaze applied as a powder giving a speckled effect with pitting at the edges. 1962 (1).

18 Costrel decorated with two interlacing lines in brown between two brown and two green ones. A groove runs parallel under the two handles; the whole exterior has a clear glaze. 1962 (1).

Group 3 — North France (Beauvais)   Fig 26

Fabrics are micaceous and white or off-white like group 2 but more evenly mixed and sometimes with dark but few red inclusions. The glazes are yellow or green, the latter clear and even, not mottled like some of group 2, but lighter in colour (except no 25). Also sgraffito using a red slip and clear glaze over this fabric (nos 26 and 27).

19 Rim sherd of green glazed plate, the rim decorated with a zig-zag design incised with a five tooth comb or a brush. 1955 u/s α.

20 Rim sherd of plain yellow glazed plate. 1955 T5 (1).

21 Rim sherd of yellow glazed plate with similar zig-zag decoration to no 19. 1955 u/s α.

22 Rim sherd of plain green glazed plate. 1955 u/s α.

23 Rim sherd of plain green glazed plate. 1955 u/s α.

24 Rim sherd of green glazed plate with a small amount of zig-zag motif like nos 19 and 21 showing. 1955 W5 (5).

25 Body sherd (6 mm thick) with red slip incised with lines cut with a blunt tool c 1 mm wide; clear lead glaze overall. 1955 W5 (4a).

26 Fig 27. Base of plate with olive green glaze with concentric lines incised within a ring of zig-zag motif. 1955 W5 (3), (4), (5).

27 (not illustrated) Small body sherd with a complex sgraffito technique on the outer surface, with a white slip over a red slip over the white body. The design (the sherd is too small to tell what sort) is cut through the outer slip to expose the red below. The whole is glazed partly clear, partly copper green, giving white and green colour over the outer slip, but red and dark brown over the sgraffito lines. 1955 W5 (6).

Group 4—France   Fig 27

28 Rim sherd of a small cup: off-white fabric with mica specks and a few red inclusions. A bright green glaze on the interior, paler on the exterior, partially flaked off from both; a horizontal groove around the exterior at the base of the neck. 1955 u/s.

29 Rim sherd of a jug: fine white fabric with some marks of wreathing internally; prominent horizontal ridge below the rim externally. A good yellow-green glaze on the exterior trickling down from the rim internally. 1962 (1).

30 Base of a bowl: laminated white fabric with some dark grit and some red inclusions; the external foot ring appears to have been turned and the interior

shows wreathing. Pale yellow-green glaze internally; the exterior surface is buff and unglazed. 1962 (1).

31 Base of a jug: grey-white fabric with many quartz grits and mica specks and a few red inclusions, cut from the wheel with a cheese wire. A bright copper green glaze on the exterior, occasionally clear at the base angle. 1962 (1).

Group 5 — Stoneware Fig 27
A COLOGNE OR RAEREN JUGS
Grey stoneware fabric, salt-glazed, and varying in colour from dark brown to light grey-brown depending on the localised proportions of iron and oxygen at the time of glazing.

32 Body sherd of jug waist, decorated with applied clay ornament: two vertical floral motifs with a circular disc bearing a helmeted head between. Below this a horizontal band of floral scroll-work, continued by a floral motif like those above but applied horizontally. From Cologne: Moorhouse 1970, fig 21, nos 262-3; Hurst 1974B; Platt and Coleman-Smith 1975, fig 199, no 1217. 1955 u/s. A smaller very similar sherd from 1955 W5 (3a).

33 Rim sherd, plain except for a horizontal groove on the exterior below the rim; some wreathing visible on the interior. Rust-red surface on the interior, brown and black mottled surface on the exterior. 1955 W5 (2). A very similar sherd from T7 (2). Raeren: Moorhouse 1970, 76.

34 Rim sherd with a horizontal groove on the exterior below the rim and a handle scar just below this. 1955 W5 (3a).

B ENGLISH STONEWARE
Thin grey stoneware fabrics with thin, very glossy glazes, usually light brown but also light grey.

35 Neck sherd of tankard with light grey glaze on the interior but matt white exterior, perhaps slipped. A horizontal ridge on the exterior with a handle scar above. 1955 T1 (1).

36 Rim sherd of tankard, horizontally grooved on the exterior; some signs of wreathing on the interior. 1955 B1 (3).

Group 6 — Malling Ware Fig 27
White fabric, quite rough with some grits. Clear white tin glaze on the interior; on the exterior the glaze is mottled and streaky with colour.

37 Rim and body sherd of a jug. The outer glaze is streaked with purple colour. 1955 u/s α.

38 (not illustrated) Body sherd: exterior glaze mottled blue and brown. 1955 W5 (5).

Group 7 — Tin-glazed Ware Fig 27
A DUTCH(?)
39 Rim sherd of small bowl: white fabric (near-stoneware) with white tin glaze internally and externally. On the exterior three horizontal blue stripes below the rim, one broad above and two narrower ones below. At the bottom two splashes of blue, part of the next zone of ornament. Moorhouse 1970, fig 19. 1955 B2 (3).

40 Cup or bowl sherds, in light grey near-stoneware fabric, somewhat laminated, with some black grits. The white tin glaze is speckled black with manganese dust. 1955 W5 (3a).

41 Rim sherd of plate. Fabric as no 40, with white tin glaze on the under surface. On the upper surface decorated with blue lines and small patch of purple. 1955 u/s α.

42 Rim sherd of small bowl, in off-white near-stoneware fabric. A thick white glaze on the interior, an uneven blue on the exterior. 1955 W5 (5).

43 (not illustrated) Small body sherd in uneven white fabric. White glaze internally; external surface with two broad bands of blue between two thin ones, all below a design in green now mostly lost. 1955 B5 u/s.

B ENGLISH (?)
44 Base sherd of bowl, with a pronounced foot-ring, in a white fabric. White glaze on interior and foot-ring; above this on the exterior, three concentric narrow blue lines with an interlinked blue design above. 1955 W1 (2).

45 Rim sherd of a tall bowl, c 21 cm in diameter. White glaze on exterior and interior, the latter with a horizontal blue line above interlinked scalloped blue lines within the rim. 1955 B1 (3).

Group 8 — North Devon (gravel-tempered or gravel-free) Fig 27
These have been recently discussed more fully by Miles (Miles and Saunders 1970, *16-19*). The basic fabric is hard with few inclusions and well-mixed with only rare air vesicles. The gravel temper was added to this, rounded quartz inclusions usually above 1 mm across, often quite densely. It was fired to a pinkish-red when oxidised but often below glaze remained partly reduced and light grey. The lead glazes vary in colour from green to brown, sometimes being perished.

46 Fig 30 (gravel-tempered) Handled bowl, reconstructed from the profile to have two handles. The handle is attached below a prominent ridge beneath the plain turned-over rim. Perished internal glaze. 1955 W5 (3a), (3-4).

47 Fig 30 (gravel-tempered) Rim sherd of bowl with prominent ridge below plain rim. Light brown internal glaze. 1955 W1 (2).

48 (gravel tempered) Rim sherd of bowl like no 47. Good glossy dark green internal glaze. 1955 u/s α.

49 (gravel-free) Rim sherd of small bowl with a similar profile to nos 47-8. Patchy light green external glaze, a good olive green internal glaze. 1955 T7 (3).

50 (gravel-free) Rim sherd of small bowl: internal brown glaze. 1955 W2 (2).

51 (gravel-free) Even grey fabric with all dark green glaze both internally and externally. 1955 W2 (2).

52 (gravel-free) Small bowl with dark brown internal glaze; fired upside down, the glaze has trickled down onto the rim. 1955 u/s.

53 (gravel-free) Rim sherd of bowl with red-brown internal glaze. 1955 W6 (2).

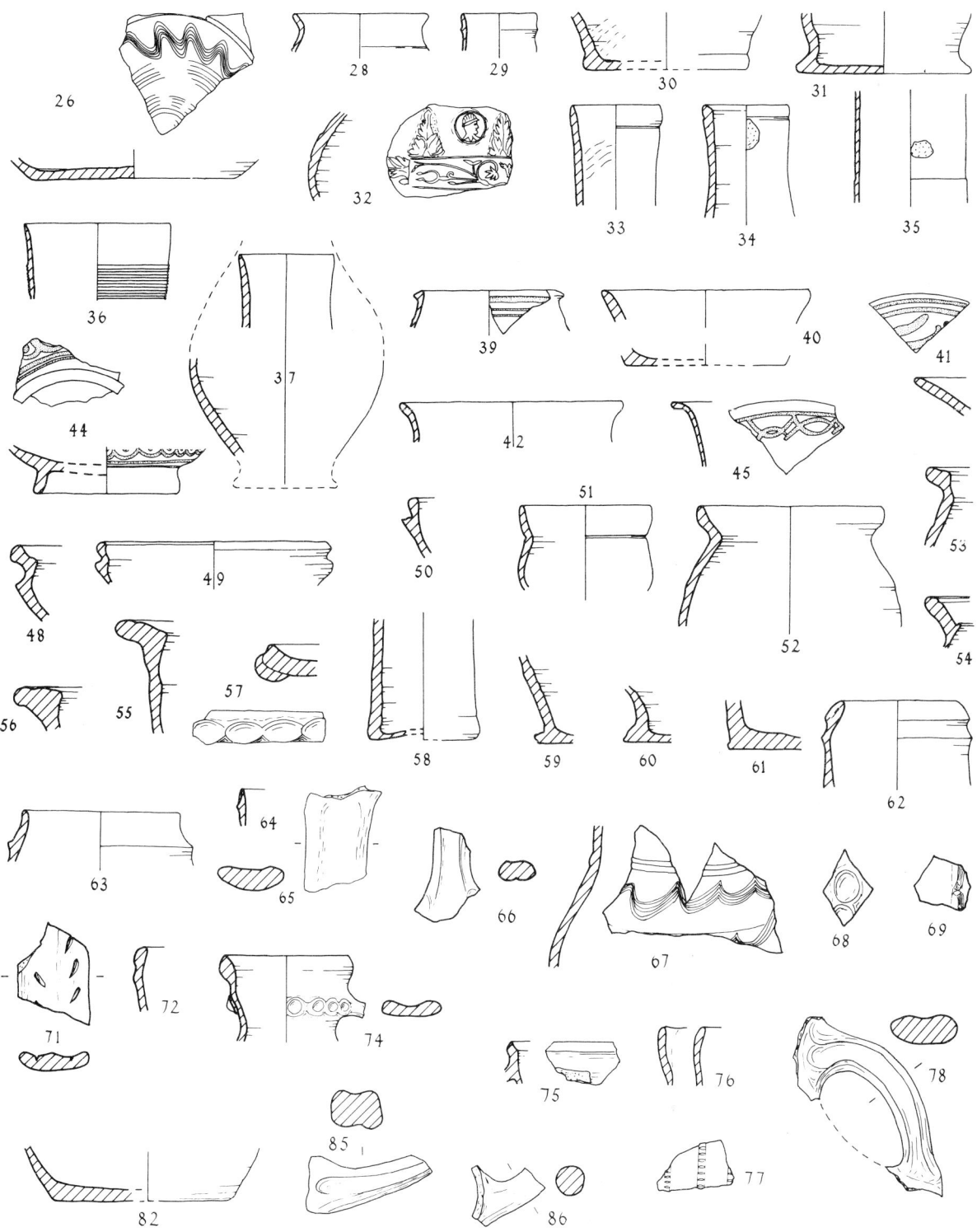

Fig 27   1955 and 1962 excavations: pots, nos 26–86 (x¼)

54 (gravel-free) Rim sherd of bowl with wide flanged rim: thick olive green internal glaze. 1955 W6 (2).
55 (gravel-tempered) Rim sherd of heavy pancheon: olive green glaze internally. 1955 u/s.
56 (gravel-tempered) Rim sherd of pancheon: olive internal glaze. 1955 W5 (3a).
57 (gravel-tempered) Rim sherd of flat dish with heavy thumbed strip along the exterior. 1955 W2 (2c).
58 (gravel-free) Base of a small jar: light green internal glaze. 1955 W1 (2).
59 (gravel-free) Base of a bowl with pronounced foot ring very roughly finished: thick brown glaze internally. 1955 W5 (3a).
60 (gravel-free) Base of bowl similar to no 59. 1955 u/s.
61 (gravel-free) Base of heavy bowl: internal glaze perished. 1955 W2 (2).

Group 9 — Jugs   Fig 27

A DARK GREY OR BLACK FABRICS, GREEN GLAZE

The clay is well-mixed with little grit added. Occasionally the surfaces are lighter than the rest of the fabric but the pots were clearly fired mostly in a heavily reducing atmosphere. The body sherds show incised and applied clay decoration; the exteriors are covered with a glossy dark green glaze. Probably of Scottish manufacture.

62 Rim sherd with a horizontal ridge below the folded-over rim. 1955 B2 (2).
63 Rim sherd with horizontal ridge below the plain rim. 1955 T7 (2).
64 Small rim sherd. Above the horizontal ridge a flake has blown off in firing as shown by glaze on the scar. 1955 W5 (3a).
65 Pulled strap handle. 1955 W5 (2).
66 Pulled strap handle, compressed and folded when luted to the body. 1955 B5 (1)-(4).
67 Neck sherds decorated with incised scalloped lines (made with a five-tooth comb) below three horizontal grooves and above a second scalloped line. 1962 (1).
68 Body sherd with an applied strip broadly thumbed. 1955 W1 (3).
69 Body sherd with applied pieces of clay probably part of a vertical row, glazed black, presumably by the addition of iron. 1955 W5 (4a).
70 (not illustrated) Body sherd with the base of a handle luted on, and a small piece of scalloped decoration like no 67. 1962 (1).

B ROUGH WHITE FABRICS

Clays poorly mixed with laminations and some fine white grits. Yellow lead glazes, sometimes with glaze-painted stripes. These jugs are in a mediaeval tradition found in both the English Midlands and eastern Scotland (e.g. Colstoun kiln): both the date and fabric with rather sparse grits would match the latter area better.

71 Strap handle decorated with two rows of diagonal stab marks and yellow glaze. 1955 T8 (1).
72 Rim sherd with thin yellow-green glaze. 1955 W5 (3a).
73 (not illustrated) Body sherd decorated with two crossed diagonal brown glaze lines. 1955 T7 (2), (3).

C LOCAL PRODUCTS?

More or less well mixed clays usually with fine grit and some fine mica specks. Fired in a mixed atmosphere producing oxidised surfaces, usually red or buff, but a grey, more or less reduced core. Usually a yellow, red or brown glaze on the exterior. The apparently barrel-shaped forms with pulled handles, largely undecorated, are in the local mediaeval tradition.

74 Rim with strap handle springing from a horizontal applied pinched strip. The exterior patchily covered by a bright green (copper?) glaze. Poorly made with a roughly finished rim and poorly luted handle and applied strip. 1962 (1).
75 Rim sherd with the stump of a strap handle: brown glaze. 1955 W2 (2).
76 Rim sherd with plain pulled out spout: shiny purple-brown glaze. 1955 T7 (2).
77 Body sherd with three applied, vertical strips of clay, nicked transversely. 1955 W6 (2).
78 Pulled strap handle: patchy dull green glaze. 1955 u/s α.
79-81 (not illustrated) Plain pulled strap handles: dull green glazes. 1962 (1) and (8).
82 Base sherd: patchy green or brown glaze. 1955 u/s.
83-4 (not illustrated) Base sherds, similar to no 82. 1955 u/s α.
85 Very abraded pipkin handle: pulled, with grooves on both sides. 1955 W5 (3)-(6).
86 Pipkin handle (?): glossy brown glaze. 1955 W5 (3a).

Group 10 — Surrey Wares   Fig 28

Off-white fabrics, well-mixed with little grit. Bright copper green glazes. For a further discussion see Matthews and Green 1969 and Holling 1969 and 1977.

87 Rim sherd of a small jug with plain pinched spout. 1955 W5 (6).
88 Small bowl. A bright green glaze covers the interior to the rim; there are occasional splashes on the exterior. 1962 (1) and (6).

Group 11 — Internally-glazed Bowls   Fig 28

Hard fabrics with some grit added. Fired in a mildly oxidising atmosphere, producing red or buff surfaces with grey cores. Usually glazed a dull green internally.

89 Small bowl with rough dark green glaze. 1955 W7 u/s.
90 Rim sherd, dark green glaze on the interior and patchily on the exterior. 1955 W1 (2).
91 Rim sherd: two horizontal grooves at the base of the sherd. 1955 B6 (1).
92 Rim of heavy bowl with a heavy rod handle. 1955 u/s.

Group 12 — South Devon   Fig 28

More or less laminated fabric with fine black grits, fired red in an oxidising atmosphere and double glazed.

93 Strongly ridged bowl rim sherd: orange glaze. 1955 W5 (2).
94 Rim sherd of small bowl with a simple pinched spout: orange glaze. 1955 W5 (3a).
95 Rim sherd of small bowl with a simple rim: glossy brown glaze. 1955 B2 (2).

Excavations in the castle in 1955 and 1962

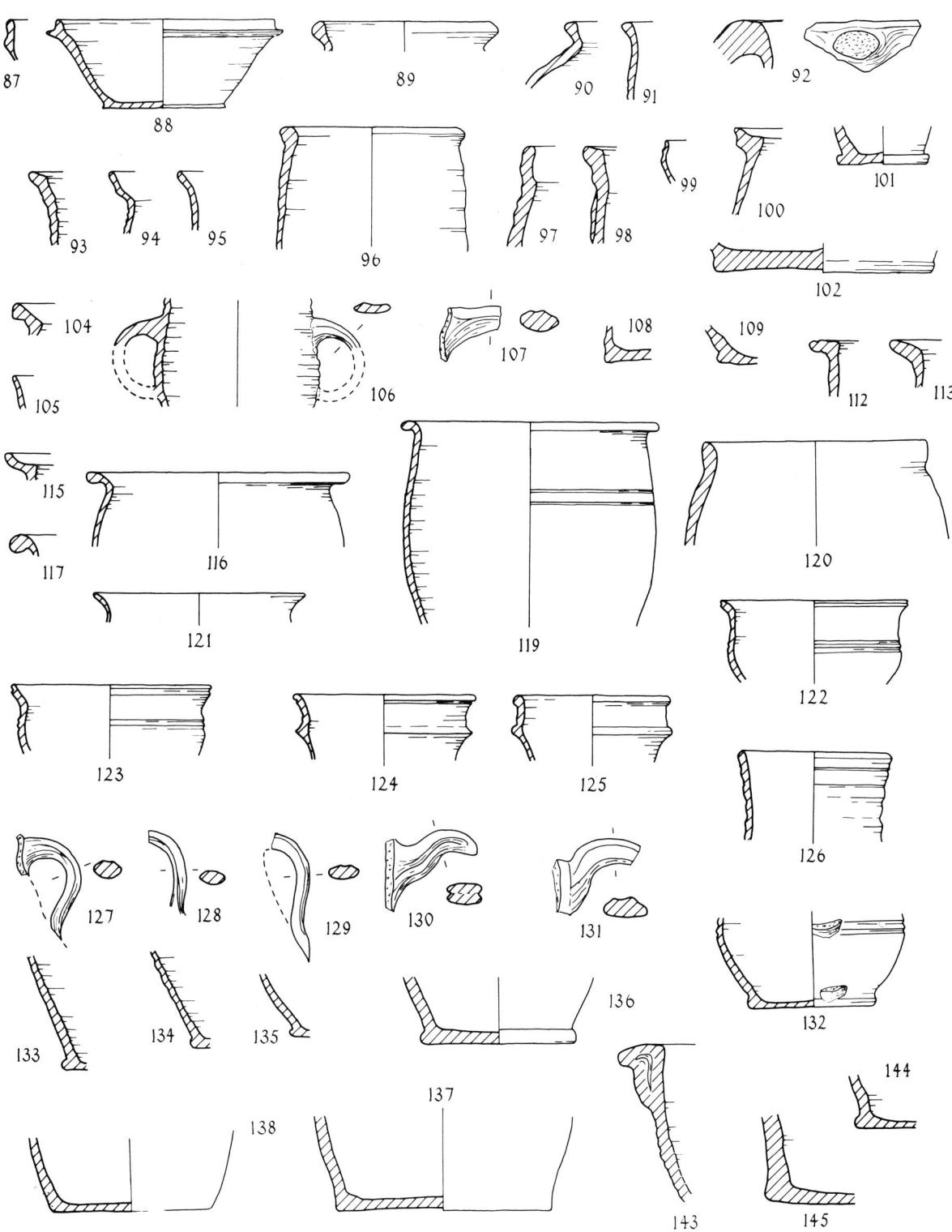

Fig 28 1955 and 1962 excavations: pots, nos 87–145 (x¼)

Group 13 — Midland Purple Fig 28

Dense dark red or purple fabric, often with fine white grit, fired to a near-stoneware temperature. Glazed with an iron-enriched lead glaze varying in colour from black to purple; when thin it can be reduced to a purple surface sheen. The ware is the result of a continuous history from the 14th century of over-firing the refractory clays of the Midlands Coal Measures, with glazes derived ultimately from the Cistercian ware tradition.

- 96 Upright butter pot: 1955 u/s α.
- 97 Rim sherd of a vertical-sided jar with a possible lid seating on the interior; exterior heavily ridged. Good glossy purple glaze. 1955 W5 (3a).
- 98 Rim sherd of a vertical-sided pot: below the heavy rim there is an applied pad of clay, perhaps part of a handle attachment. 1955 W5 (3)-(4).
- 99 Rim sherd of a small cup or bowl with a good dark brown glaze inside and out. 1955 W5 (3a).
- 100 Rim sherd of a small bowl. 1955 W5 (3a).
- 101 Base of a small bowl glazed internally, and in part externally, with a glossy purple-brown glaze. 1955 W5 (3)-(6).
- 102 Base of a bowl: stacking ring of a vessel of similar diameter visible on the underside. 1955 W3 (4), W5 (5).
- 103 (not illustrated) Body sherd of a cylindrical vessel c 18 cm internal diameter and c 1 cm thick: glazed internally and partially externally. One end of the sherd has been cut across while wet at an angle of slightly more than 90° to the lines of wheel-throwing. 1955 W5 (3a).

Group 14 — Black Wares Fig 28

The fabric is brick red, usually gritless, well prepared, fired to earthenware temperatures. This fabric is often similar to that of Group 15 pots but the glazes are hard, glossy and black, often speckled with white inclusions. Probably English imports, from the Midlands or Yorkshire (Le Patourel 1955, Brears 1967 and 1971, 37-9, Drewett 1976).

- 104 Rim sherd of small bowl. 1955 W5 (3a).
- 105 Rim sherd of cup. 1955 W5 (3a).
- 106 Body sherd, with one handle surviving, of a cup or tankard. 1955 W5 (3a).
- 107 Pipkin-type handle of a bowl glazed internally and externally. 1955 B1 (3).
- 108 Base sherd of double-glazed bowl. 1955 W7 (1).
- 109 Base sherd of a small shallow bowl. 1955 T9 (1).

Group 15 — Brown Wares Fig 28

Brick red fabric with little grit but often laminated. The glaze is usually brown, applied more thickly to the inside; like the Midland Purple glaze when thin it runs off to a purple sheen. A large variety of shapes are found in it which bear a general resemblance to those of the coarse wares of the English Midlands, especially Staffordshire, but there are few precise parallels and the glazes are not the same (the relevant material is the Black wares). This group is apparently the product of a local potter working in a tradition derived from the English Midlands, presumably Staffordshire. The wasters, nos 139 and 140, also point to local production.

- 110 Fig 30. Plate or dish with glossy brown glaze internally; smoke blackened on the base. 1955 B5 (1)-(4).
- 111 Fig 30. Heavy-rimmed bowl with worn yellow brown glaze. 1955 B6 (1).
- 112 Rim sherd of a heavy-rimmed bowl. 1955 W7 (1).
- 113 1955 B6 (1).
- 114 Fig 30. Moulded rim sherd of bowl. 1955 B1 (3).
- 115 Rim sherd of a small flange-rimmed bowl. 1955 B5 (6).
- 116 Bowl with rolled-over rim. 1955, surface clearance.
- 117 1955 B6 (1).
- 118 Fig 30. Bowl with rolled-over rim; exterior surface partly smoke-blackened. 1955, surface clearance of middle tower.
- 119 Tall bowl with rolled rim; two horizontal grooves on the exterior. Outer surface much blackened. 1955 B1 (1) and (3).
- 120 Butter pot, only patchily glazed on the interior and exterior. 1955 W5 (5) and (6).
- 121 Rim sherd of small bowl; purple sheen rather than a glaze. 1955 W1 (2), T4 (1).
- 122 Small bowl or posset cup; horizontal grooves on the exterior. 1955 B1 (3), T1 (1).
- 123 As 122. 1955 B6 (1).
- 124 Small cup with prominent horizontal ridge. 1955 u/s.
- 125 1955 B5 (1)-(4).
- 126 Yellowish glaze, especially internally. 1955 W1 (2).
- 127-9 Handles of small bowls. 1955 u/s, W4 (1), B6 (1).
- 130 Pipkin handle, formed by folding over a strip of clay longitudinally. 1955 B1 (3).
- 131 Handle of pipkin or large bowl. 1955 u/s α.
- 132 Small handled bowl or posset cup with horizontal grooves: cf no 122 or 123. 1955 B1 (3).
- 133-6 Bowl base sherds with foot rings. 1955 B1 (1), (3), W2 (1), u/s.
- 137 Bowl base sherd. B1 (1) and (3).
- 138 Bowl base with internal olive green glaze; smoke blackened on the base. 1955 B6 (1).
- 139-140 (not illustrated) Two clear wasters of Group 15 pots, both a pair of body sherds stuck together by the glaze. 1955 B1 (3), W5 (1).

Group 16 — Creamers Fig 28

The predominant colour in the fabrics varies in colour from buff to dark red but all are marked with white or light yellow streaks in the clay. The glazes (usually only internal) are glossy and black, similar to those of Group 14, except for no 141. The streaky clay is very similar to that from Buckley (cf Mesham and Barton 1956, 71) and these pots may have been made there.

- 141 Fig 30. Light fabric with more grit than others. The glaze is a streaky light brown. 1955 T9 (1).
- 142 Fig 30. 1955 B1 (1)-(4), (3), u/s.
- 143 Heavy folded rim. 1955 T1 (3).
- 144 1955 T7 (2).
- 145 Bubbly (over-fired?) glaze. 1955 B1 (3).

Group 17 — Tankards and Bowls Fig 29

The clay is well-mixed and free of iron giving an even white, or off-white fabric. The glaze is a lead one with iron added either evenly to give an even glassy dark brown, or unevenly to give a light brown with dark streaks. It was applied thickly, collecting in grooves on the body or at the base, and as much

Excavations in the castle in 1955 and 1962

as 4 mm thick in the angle between the two. There are either tall, vertical-sided tankards, often decorated with horizontal ridges at the base and on the body, or bowls with flaring rims and foot-rings. One of the latter (no 151) is slip-decorated. Pots like this were produced in Staffordshire, and by emigrant Staffordshire potters (using very similar clays) at Buckley in Flintshire. The two industries' products cannot be distinguished but geographically Buckley seems the likelier source.

146 Tankard, with nine glaze-filled ridges below the rim. 1955 B1 (3), B5 (1)-(4), T4 (1).
147 Rim sherd, slightly flared; broad shallow ridges on the exterior. 1955 B6 (1).
148 Tankard base with horizontal ridges. The interior glaze has pooled in the base angle; the exterior is glazed down to the ridges. 1955 B1 (3), B5 (6).
149 Tankard base; part of the four horizontal ridges smudged when the clay was wet, presumably while taking it from the wheel. 1955 u/s.
150 Plain tankard base. 1955 B1 (4).
151 Rim sherd of a bowl, decorated with a dark brown slip reserved or cut away to show a simple floral design in the white body clay below the light yellow overall glaze. 1955 B1 (1).
152 Three small rim sherds of the same bowl. 1955, B2 (1), W1 (2), T4 (1).
153 Handled bowl or cup. 1955 T4 (1).
154 Base of small bowl. 1955 W1 (2).
155 Base of bowl with glaze pooled in the angle. 1955 W2 (1).
156 As no 155. 1955 B1 (3).

Group 18 — Yellow Wares   Fig 29

The fabric is even and white with little grit, very similar to that of Group 17. The vessels are glazed with a clear yellow lead glaze, sometimes decorated with painted dark brown slip under the glaze. The products of Midlands England or Bristol, more probably the former (Barton 1961, Woodfield 1966, Brears 1971, *31-6*, Pearson 1979, *201-6*).

157 Plain bowl with lid seating; crackled glaze on exterior, interior unglazed below the lid seating. 1955 W1 (2).
158 Small bowl or posset cup with one handle scar. Slip decoration consists of a line of dark brown blobs below the rim and at least three combed lines below the handle. Cf Addyman and Marjoram 1972, fig 40, no 66, Barton 1961, fig 2, and Pearson 1979, fig 7, no 45. 1955 B5 (1)-(4), T4 (1).
159 Small bowl with frilled rim. Internally decorated overall with lines of brown and yellow combed slip. Cf Pearson 1979, fig 7, no 50. 1955 B5 (6).
160 Base sherd of small bowl, with a possible handle scar at the top of the sherd; the base is smoke blackened. 1955 W1 (2).

Group 19 — Slip-trailed Ware   Fig 29

The clay is usually poorly mixed with some grit, fired in an atmosphere not fully oxidising, to give red surfaces but a grey core. Decorated with trailed white slip, and then sometimes glazed with a light glaze. A common type of 17th-century coarse ware, it is difficult to provenance and with its rather poorly controlled fabric it could be local.

161 Rim sherd of a plate with two lines of applied swags and dots, covered with a light green glaze. 1955 T4 (1).
162 Rim sherd of pot 24 cm in diameter with irregular slip design and thin brown glaze. 1955 u/s.
163 Body sherd of flat vessel: pink fabric and good light brown glaze. 1955 u/s.
164 Base of small jar: exterior slip painted but unglazed, interior with dark olive green glaze. 1955 u/s.

Group 20 — Buckley Ware   Fig 29

165 Rim sherd of cup or bowl. Red fabric with yellow streaks and inclusions. Orange internal and external glaze. 1955 T9 (1) and surface clearance of middle tower. Cf Chester Museum, unglazed cup from Prescott's pottery for shape.

Group 21 — Sgraffito Ware   Fig 29

The clay is well mixed and normally without grit, usually fired a dull orange-red in an oxidising atmosphere but occasionally it is partially reduced, usually under the glaze. All the vessels have a white slip on the interior (except no 187): the decoration is cut through this to reveal the body colour below. Glazes are usually a clear yellow, but where the firing has not been fully oxidising it can be green. The forms are either dishes or bowls not always to be distinguished. The decoration (Pl 27) is on the flatter wares (except no 166), either along the rim or on the base. Three designs prevail among the decorated rims: chevrons (*c* 10 examples), spirals (*c* 8 examples) and a wave pattern of horizontal S-S (5 examples). As well as this there are single examples of abstract or floral designs, the latter in one case having an area of slip removed as well as lines. The basal ornament appears to be normally freely drawn floral designs, except for no 166 and one sherd with a spiral motif (possibly, of course part of a larger floral design). At least one of these designs is a relatively naturalistic tulip motif, while at least two plates show designs with large areas of slip in the 'petals' removed as well as the outlines. One sherd (Pl 27) may show part of an inscription. The exception to all the foregoing is no 186 which is a double glazed bowl with decoration on the exterior. This group is clearly either from the North Devon or Donyatt (less likely) kilns or related to it: the rouletting of no 186 is a feature of the Barnstaple industry (Watkins, 1960, fig 11). The presence of no 187, a waster, could well point to local production however, while the decoration involving areas of slip removed rather than lines (Pl 27) is not a feature of the English industry.

166 Fig 30. Dish or bowl. Three zones of scribbled zig-zag lines on the rim and a compass-drawn (the holes of the points are clear) marigold design on the base. The exterior, especially the base, is smoke-blackened. 1955 B1 (1).
167 Small plain dish. 1955 u/s.
168-71 Rim sherds of dishes: 168 has a lime-green glaze; 170 was fired in a reducing atmosphere giving a grey fabric and olive green glaze; it and 169 have wave motifs on the rim. 1955 u/s, W1 (2), W5 (2), B1 (2).

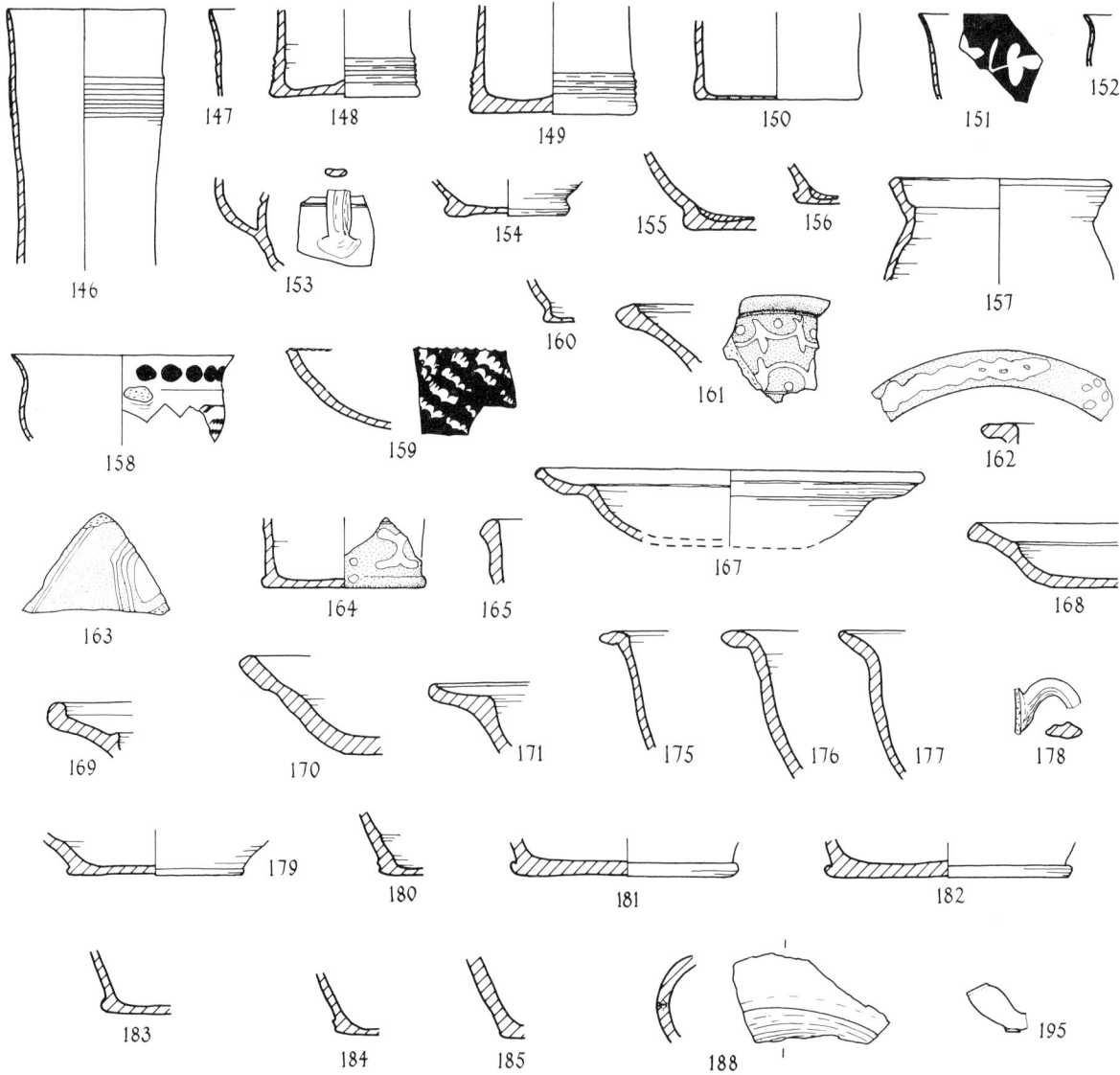

Fig 29 1955 and 1962 excavations: pots, nos 146–188 and clay pipe bowl, no 195 (x¼)

172 Fig 30. Plain bowl with horizontal groove on the exterior, below the rim. 1955 B6 (1), W2 (1), u/s.
173 Fig 30. Tall plain bowl. 1955 B1 (3), (1)-(4).
174-7 Rim sherds of plain bowls. 1955 W2 (1), B6 (1), T4 (1), B6 (1).
178 Small handle of bowl or chamber pot. Slipped on interior but some glaze on the handle as well. 1955 B1 (1).
179 Base of small bowl, with smoke blackened base. 1955 B1 (1).
180 Base sherd of bowl with bubbled glaze. 1955 B1 (3).
181 Base sherds of a bowl; poor greenish glaze. 1955 B1 (3), T4 (1).
182 Base of bowl; glaze as near green as yellow: smoke blackened base. 1955 B1 (3), W1 (2).
183-5 Base sherds of bowls. 1955 T9 (1), W7 (1), T9 (1), B1 (3).

186 (Pl 27). Two body sherds of a bowl with a perished internal glaze, but no slip. The exterior is slipped and decorated with a linear design and rouletted lines. 1955 B6 (1), T4 (1).
187 (not illustrated) Rim sherd (waster) of dish. The clay has blistered nearly to bursting and glaze has trickled into a crack over 2 cm long through the sherd and perpendicular to the rim; it has also gathered into a blob on the rim. 1955 W2 (1).

Pl 27 shows the range of decorative motifs employed in the group.

Sherds of unknown origin

188 Fig 29. Laminated grey-white fabric with sparse black grit and some mica flecks. A mottled red-brown

glaze on the convex surface; the other (unglazed) surface is stained brown or black. In section it looks as though two pieces, both wheel thrown, have been luted together. The fabric and glaze could well be from the English Midlands: the sherd might be part of a ring costrel. 1955 W5 (6).

189 (not illustrated) Fine buff fabric with sparse fine black grit and mica specks. The main part of the sherd is wheel-thrown and, to judge from the curve, part of a globular vessel. At one edge of the sherd it has been cut (at an angle of *c* 45° to the lines of the wheel throwing) when the clay was wet. A strip of clay at least 5 cm wide has been luted to the convex surface of the sherd beside the cut. The fabric of the sherd could well be Mediterranean and it might be part of a costrel. 1955 u/s.

190 (not illustrated) Body sherd of even fabric with little grit, mostly dark grey but white on the inner surface, not a slip but the result apparently of oxygen being present. Double glazed, dark green on the outside and yellow on the inside over the oxidised surface. 1955 T7 (3).

191 (not illustrated) Body sherd of laminated red fabric with an internal white slip. Double glazed, olive green on the outside, light green on the inside over the slip. 1955 W3 (2).

Both these sherds might pass as mis-firings of group 18 but come from layers of context 2, which should be mid 16th-century in date.

Floor and roof tiles   Fig 30

192 Red fabric with an impressed design; the whole top surface was covered in a white slip and clear glaze with green patches. 1955 W5 (6).

193 (not illustrated) Two worn fragments of a second tile with the same design as no 192. 1955 T1 or T2 (1).

194 Red fabric with impressed design; no slip but brown glaze preserved in the hollows of the design. 1955 T1 or T2 (1).

The design of tile no 192 is Eames' design no 191 and 194 is Eames' design no 186, which belong to her Irish/Cheshire/Salop group of line-impressed tiles. There is a very close parallel to no 192, unprovenanced but probably from Chester, in the Grosvenor Museum, Chester (no 192a in fig 30); a similar one in the same museum from Vale Royal abbey, is itself precisely matched by an unprovenanced example in Rowley's Museum, Shrewsbury. The general interlocking double vesica frame is also found, for example at Buildwas Abbey, Shropshire. Mrs Eames suggests a 15th-century date for this group (Eames 1980).

Thirty fragments of roof tiles were also found, 28 in 1955, 2 in 1962. Two fabrics are present. Eighteen fragments are similar to the fabrics of the North Devon gravel-tempered ware (group 8) and are presumably imported from there; all are glazed. Crested ridge tiles occur in this group which is mainly derived from layers of context 2. The second fabric is sandy with some quartz grits and fired brick red; fragments were found from layers of all deposits in similar proportions.

Clay pipes

195 Fig 29. Bowl of late 17th-century type. Together with 5 stem fragments, it is recorded as having been found in 1955, trench W5 (3a), but this is a layer otherwise containing only mid 16th-century material, so that these are probably either out of context or the top of the ditch fill was disturbed in the 17th century. Fig 22.

Metal objects   Fig 30

196 Lead seal box lid (Pl 28), 6.4 cm in diameter, 3.5 mm thick. The upper face bears the impressed design of a shield, having the leopards of England quartered with the six fleurs-de-lis of France ancient, surmounted possibly by the initials RH, and surrounded by the SS collar of the house of Lancaster, which is joined at the base by two square buckles and a trefoil link. The other face has a loop for a hinge and, opposite that, a broken catch. It is bent along a line about 5 mm in from the outer edge, presumably because it was somewhat larger than the box it covered. Found in 1955 (W8 (3)), it was apparently lost in the mid 16th century, but it must date from the reign of Henry IV, the first Lancastrian king but the last king of England to quarter the arms of France ancient. Henry V adopted the three fleurs-de-lis of France modern (*Burke's Peerage*, 1884, LVI-LVII). For the general type of seal or weight box, see Seaby 1958.

197 (not illustrated) Copper alloy tube, 81 mm long, 1 mm thick; the internal diameter is 3-3.5 mm at one end, widening, as the joint expands, to 3.5-5.0 mm at the other. 1955 T3 (1).

198 Iron knife with bone handle. The blade is thin, single-edged and complete with a bluntly pointed tip which may be a re-working after the tip was broken; there is a maker's mark on one side of the blade. The blade widens out to made a stop for the handle, which is joined to a round-sectioned tang running its full length. To judge from an X-ray tang and blade are one piece. The handle is bound at the butt end by a strip of metal to the tang which is visible at the end. 1955 W5 (5) or (6).

199 Small single-edged knife blade broken at one end. W5 (9a).

200 Small square-sectioned iron buckle; the pin is simply looped over the shank. 1955 W1 (2).

201 Iron pin, bent but otherwise complete; the oval head is decorated with a row of indentations. 1955 u/s.

202-3 (not illustrated) Two identical cannon balls, 6.3 cm (2½ ins) in diameter. 1955 W5 (5), and u/s.

Leather objects   Fig 30

Parts of at least five shoes of late mediaeval type from 1955 W8 (5). Delamination, the separation of flesh and grain sides of the leather, is usual, the result of poor tanning. For the terms used see Thornton 1973, or Jones 1975 and 1976.

204 Left-foot sole, pointed toe, narrow waist; edge/flesh stitching holes at 5 mm intervals. A hole in the toe, worn at the heel.

205 Right-hand quarter: lasting margin, except at the extreme front, worn away. Back seam, joining it to the other quarter, with a closed seam, the holes 5 mm

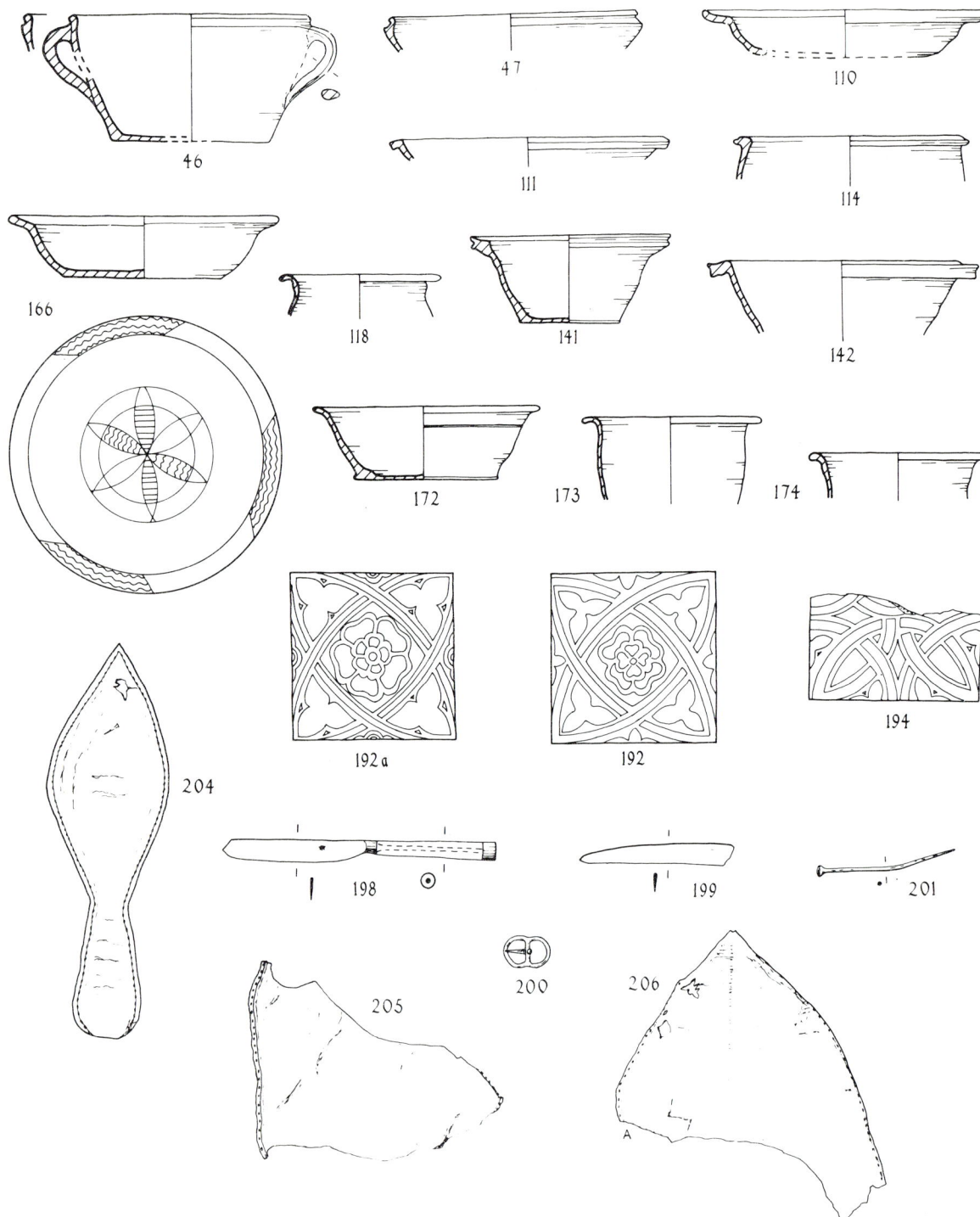

Fig 30   1955 and 1962 excavations: large pots (x⅛), tiles, metal and leather objects (x¼)

apart. Edge/flesh stitching along the front edge: a row of stitching holes 5 mm apart along the top on the inside, possibly to attach a lining.

206 Vamp of a right-foot shoe with pointed toe. Stitching holes on the lasting margins are irregularly spaced 5-6 mm apart. Butted seam with edge/flesh stitching holes along the upper edge (A-B on Fig 30) worn away on the right at the junction with the right-hand quarter. A line of imitation stitching stretches from the toe to the throat.

207-10 (not illustrated) Parts of one left-foot, and three right-foot soles; one extremely pointed.

211 (not illustrated) Binding strip around the ankle along the top of the quarters and the rear of the vamp.

16th- AND 17th-CENTURY PLANS AND VIEWS OF CARRICKFERGUS

APPENDIX 2

1   British Library Cotton Augustus I ii 42 (*frontispiece*): perspective view 26 ins × 21 ins.
    Dunlop 1905, no 84; Camblin 1951, *frontispiece*.
    Dated to before 1566 (the friary is shown unfortified): here (above p 13) argued as *c* 1560. Accurate for the castle (see above, p 47) its distorted perspective limits the use of its detail for the town.

2   Trinity College, Dublin, ms 1209-26: perspective view 13 ins x 9 ins.
    Dunlop 1905, no 87.
    Attributable to Robert Lythe, showing the town as it was in 1567. Concentrates on the town, rather than the castle.

3   Trinity College, Dublin, ms 1209-27: perspective view 15 ins x 12 ins.
    Dunlop 1905, no 86.
    A pair with the preceding, illustrating Sidney's proposed fortification of the town. The castle is shown in ground plan only.

4   Public Record Office SP 64/1/10 (MPF 77): plan and views 21½ ins x 16 ins.
    Dunlop 1905, no 89.
    Dated 1569. Map of the district around Carrickfergus with a view *c* 1 in square of the castle and town.

5   Public Record Office SP 64/1/31 (MPF 98): perspective view 16 ins x 12 ins.
    Dunlop 1905, no 85; Camblin 1951, pl 1 (omits lower part). Inscribed on the back 'Ye platt of Knockfergus/ ... Peter White ... John'.
    Datable to 1574 or soon after (the church is roofless; it was burned in 1573). Rather sketchy on the castle but it seems to be more accurate on the town.

6   British Library Cotton Augustus I ii 54.
    Letters and Papers, Henry VIII, XXI (11), 1546, 454-76, where it is attributed to *c* 1546.
    Dunlop, 1905, no 84: considers it eccentric and of slight value.
    Not seen by the author.

7   British Library Cotton Augustus I ii 41.
    Inscribed 'John Dunstall Pinxit 1612'.
    Copy of Trinity College, Dublin, ms 1209-27.

8   National Library of Ireland, ms 2557: plan with inset view (Pl 1).
    From the Ormonde papers, accompanying a copy of Phillips's report of 1677 x 1685. Includes measurements of the proposed new fort.

9   National Library of Ireland, ms 3137: plan with inset view.
    Rather plainer copy than no 8, with less incidental detail in the view; omits the measurements from the plan of the proposed fort.

10 British Library K TOP 51-42.
    Very similar to no 8 but omits the measurements on the proposed fort. Camblin 1951, pl 16.

11 British Library K TOP 51-44: plan.
    Copy of nos 8-10, careless in some details, eg St Nicholas's church. Omits the proposed fort but gives in addition a detailed plan of the gardens of Joymount House; annotated ('The castle', 'Church', etc).

12 British Library K TOP 51-45: plan.
    Copy of no 11, but covering a slightly smaller area.

13 British Library K TOP 51-46: plan.
    Sketchy copy of nos 8-10, showing the proposed fort. The scale is annotated in French ('500 pieds'), and other details are noted in French ('mer', 'eau', 'bordure d'arbres', 'jardin', etc).

14 British Library K TOP 51-47: plan.
    A small (4¾ ins x 3½ ins) copy of the above series, omitting the proposed fort. See no 16.

15 British Library K TOP 51-48: view.
    A romanticised reworking of the inset views of nos 8-10.

16 British Library K TOP 10920 (i): plan.
    Second copy of no 14, inscribed on the back 'From Mr. Tindal's continuation of Mr. Rapin's History'. Cf Camblin 1951, pl 18.

17 National Library of Ireland, ms 2742: plan.
    An independent survey from the above (nos 8-16) but casual in its detail. A Sotheby's sale catalogue entry, pasted into the cover, describes it as 'Typical product of the period of the Grand Alliance' and attributes it to Goubet as part of a collection of 28 plans and sketches of fortifications.

BIBLIOGRAPHY

Addyman, P V and Marjoram, J (1972): 'An eighteenth century mansion, a fishpond and post-medieval finds from St Neots, Huntingdonshire', in *Post-Medieval Archaeol* 6 (1972), *69-106*.

Annals of the Four Masters: *Annals of the Kingdom of Ireland by the Four Masters*, ed J O'Donovan, 7 vols (Dublin, 1848-51).

Annals of Ulster: *Annals of Ulster*, ed W M Hennessy and B McCarthy, 4 vols (Dublin, 1887-1901).

BL: British Library, formerly British Museum, manuscripts.

Barton, K J (1961): 'Some evidence of two types of pottery manufactured in Bristol in the early eighteenth century', in *Trans Bristol Gloucestershire Archaeol Soc* 80 (1961), *160-68*.

Benn, G (1877): *A history of the town of Belfast* (London, 1877).

Berry, H F, ed (1914): *Statute Rolls (Ireland): Edward IV, part 1* (Dublin, 1914).

Brears, P D C (1967): 'Excavations at Potovens, near Wakefield', in *Post-Medieval Archaeol* 1 (1967), *3-43*.

——— (1971): *The English country pottery, its history and techniques* (Newton Abbot, 1971).

CDI: *Calendar of Documents relating to Ireland*, ed H S Sweetman, 5 vols (London, 1875-86).

Cal Papal Registers: *Calendar of entries in the Papal Registers relating to Great Britain and Ireland: Papal Letters*, vols 1- (London, HMSO, 1893-).

CSP Dom: *Calendar of State Papers, Domestic Series* (London, 1856-).

CSPI: *Calendar of the State Papers relating to Ireland, 1509-1670*, 24 vols (London, HMSO, 1860-1912).

Camblin, G (1951): *The Town in Ulster* (Belfast, 1951).

Chart, D A (1935): *Register of John Swayne, Archbishop of Armagh and Primate of Ireland 1418-39* (Belfast, 1935).

——— (1939): 'Carrickfergus Castle, exploration, repair and other work', in *Minutes of Proc Roy Ir Acad*, session 1938-9, *19-24*.

Clapham, A W (1926): 'The castle at Newcastle-upon-Tyne', in *Archaeol Aeliana* ser 4 2 (1926), *1-15*.

——— (1928): 'An early hall at Chilham castle, Kent', in *Antiq J* 8 (1928), *350-3*.

Close Rolls, England: *Calendar of Close Rolls* (London, HMSO, 1892-).

Cole, H (1844): *Documents illustrative of English history of the 13th and 14th centuries* (London, 1844).

Colvin et al (1963): H M Colvin, R A Brown and A J Taylor, *The history of the King's Works* (London, HMSO, 1963).

Conway, A (1932): *Henry VII's relations with Scotland and Ireland, 1485-98* (Cambridge, 1932).

Davies, O and Quinn, D B (1941): 'The Irish Pipe Roll of 14 John', in *Ulster J Archaeol* 4 (1941), supplement.

De L'Isle and Dudley mss: Historical Manuscripts Commission: *Report on the manuscripts of Lord De L'Isle and Dudley*, 6 vols (London, 1925-66).

Drewett, P (1976): 'The excavation of the great hall at Bolingbroke castle, Lincolnshire', in *Post-Medieval Archaeol* 10 (1976), *1-33*.

Dunlop, A I (1950): *The life and times of James Kennedy, Bishop of St Andrews* (Edinburgh, 1950).

Dunlop, R (1905): 'Sixteenth century maps of Ireland', in *Engl Hist Rev* 20 (1905), *309-37*.

Eames, E S (1980): *Catalogue of medieval lead-glazed earthenware tiles in the Department of Medieval and Later Antiquities, British Museum* (London, 1980).

Exchequer Memoranda Rolls: *Calendar of Memoranda Rolls (Exchequer) 1326-27* (London, HMSO, 1968).

Gilbert, J T (1870): *Historical and Municipal Documents of Ireland, 1172-1320, from the archives of the city of Dublin* (London, Rolls Series, 1870).

Giraldus Cambrensis, *Expugnatio Hibernica*, ed B Scott and F X Martin (Dublin, Roy Ir Acad, 1978).

Hardy, T D (1844): *Rotuli de Liberate et Misis et Praestitis, regnante Johanne* (London, 1844).

Hill, G (1873): *The MacDonnells of Antrim* (Belfast, 1873).

Holling, F W (1969): 'Seventeenth-century pottery from Ash, Surrey', in *Post-Medieval Archaeol* 3 (1969), *18-30*.

——— (1977): 'Reflections on Tudor Green', in *Post-Medieval Archaeol* 11 (1977), *61-66*.

Hurst, J G (1974a): 'Sixteenth- and seventeenth-century pottery imported from the Saintonge', in *Medieval pottery from excavations*, ed V I Evison, H Hodges and J G Hurst (London, 1974).

——— (1974b): 'A sixteenth-century Cologne jug from Newcastle', in *Archaeol Aeliana* ser 5, 2 (1974), *281-83*.

——— (1977): 'Spanish pottery imported into medieval Britain', in *Medieval Archaeol* 21 (1977), *68-105*.

Jones, J (1975): 'Medieval leather', in T Tatton-Brown, 'Excavations at the Customs House site, City of London', in *Trans London Middlesex Archaeol Soc* 26 (1975), *154-67*.

——— (1976): 'The leather', in T G Hassall, 'Excavations at Oxford castle 1965-73', in *Oxoniensia* 41 (1976), *275-84*.

Jope, E M (1962): *Carrickfergus Castle* (Official guide) (Belfast, HMSO, 1966).

Justiciary Rolls, Ireland: *Calendar of Justiciary Rolls, Ireland*, 3 vols (Dublin, 1905-56).

Knight, J K (1977): 'Usk castle and its affinities', in *Ancient monuments and their interpretation*, ed M R Apted, R Gilyard-Beer and A D Saunders (London, 1977).

Laing mss: Historical Manuscripts Commission, *Report of the Laing manuscripts preserved in the University of Edinburgh*, 2 vols (London, 1914).

Laud ms Annals: *Chartularies of St Mary's Abbey, Dublin* (ed J T Gilbert), vol 2 (London, Rolls Series, 1884).

Le Patourel, H E J (1966): 'The pottery', in P Mayes and E J E Pirie, 'A Cistercian ware kiln of the early sixteenth century at Potterton, Yorks', in *Antiq J* 46 (1966), *255-76*.

Letters and Papers, Henry VIII: *Letters and Papers, foreign and domestic, Henry VIII*, 21 vols (London, 1862-1932).

Longfield, A K (1960): *Fitzwilliam Accounts, 1560-65* (Dublin, Irish Manuscripts Commission, 1960).

Matthews, L G and Green, H J M (1969): 'Post-medieval pottery of the Inns of Court', in *Post-Medieval Archaeol* 3 (1969), *1-17*.

McNeill, T E (1980): *Anglo-Norman Ulster* (Edinburgh, 1980).

McSkimin, S (1811): *The history and antiquities of the county of the town of Carrickfergus* (Belfast, 1811).
   2nd Edition (expanded) (Belfast, 1823).
   3rd Edition (continued and revised by E McCrum) (Belfast, 1909).
Mesham, J E and Barton, K (1956): 'The Buckley potteries', in *Flintshire Hist Soc Publ* 16 (1956), *31-87*.
Miles, T J and Saunders, A D (1970): 'King Charles' castle, Tresco, Scilly', in *Post-Medieval Archaeol* 4 (1970), *1-30*.
Moody *et al* (1976): *A new history of Ireland*, ed T W Moody, F X Martin and F J Byrne, vol 3 (Oxford, 1976).
Moorhouse, S (1970): 'Finds from Basing House (*c* 1540-1645), part 1', in *Post-Medieval Archaeol* 4 (1970), *31-91*.
Morrissey, J F (1939): *Statute Rolls, Ireland: Edward IV, part 2* (Dublin, 1939).
NLI National Library of Ireland, manuscripts.
Ormonde mss: Historical Manuscripts Commission, *Calendar of the manuscripts of the Marquis of Ormonde, preserved at Kilkenny castle*, 1st series, 2 vols (London, 1895-99); 2nd series, 8 vols (London, 1902-20).
Orpen, G H: *Ireland under the Normans*, 4 vols (Oxford, 1911-20).
PRO: Public Record Office, London, manuscripts:
   AO – Audit Office.
   SP – State Papers.
   SO – Signet Office.
   T – Treasury documents.
   WO – War Office.
PRONI: Public Record Office of Northern Ireland.
Patent Rolls, England: *Calendar of Patent Rolls* (London, HMSO, 1891-).
Patent and Close Rolls, Ireland: *Calendar of the Patent and Close Rolls of the Chancery in Ireland*, ed J Morrin, 3 vols (Dublin, 1861-63).
Pearson, T (1979): 'The contents of a pit from North Petherton, Somerset', in *Post-Medieval Archaeol* 13 (1979), *183-210*.
Platt, C and Coleman-Smith, R (1975): *Excavations in Medieval Southampton*, 2 vols (Leicester, 1975).

RCHM: Royal Commission on Historical Monuments, county inventories.
Renn, D F (1968): *Norman castles in Britain* (London, 1968).
——— (1969): 'The Avranches traverse at Dover castle', in *Archaeol Cantiana* 84 (1969), *79-92*.
——— (1973): 'Defending Framlingham castle', in *Proc Suffolk Inst Archaeol* 31, part 1 (1973), *58-67*.
Seaby, W A (1958): 'A bronze weight box from Grey Abbey, Co. Down', in *Ulster J Archaeol* 21 (1958), *91-100*.
State Papers, Carew: *Calendar of the Carew Manuscripts, preserved in the archiepiscopal library at Lambeth, 1515-1624*, 6 vols (London, 1867-73).
Story, G (1691): *A true and impartial history of the most material occurrences in the Kingdom of Ireland in the last years* (London, 1691).
Swanston, W (1898): 'Unpublished view of Carrickfergus', in *Ulster J Archaeol ser* 2, 5 (1898), *1-4*.
TCD: Trinity College, Dublin, manuscripts.
Thompson, M W (1977): *Kenilworth castle*, Department of the Environment Official Guide (London, HMSO, 1977).
Thornton, J H (1973): 'The shoes', in J Gould 'Finds from the Minster Pool, Lichfield, Staffs', in *Trans S Staffordshire Archaeol Hist Soc* 14 (1972-3), *53-60*.
Tresham, E (1828): *Rotulorum Patentium et Clausarum cancellariae Hiberniae calendarium* (Irish Record Commission, 1828).
VCH: *The Victoria County History of England*.
Waterman, D M (1952): 'Excavations at the entrance to Carrickfergus castle, 1950', in *Ulster J Archaeol* 15 (1952), *103-18*.
Watkins, C M (1960): 'North Devon pottery and its export to North America in the seventeenth century', in *US National Museum Bulletin* 225 (1960).
Woodfield, P (1966): 'Yellow glazed wares of the seventeenth century', in *Trans Birmingham Archaeol Soc* 81 (1966), *78-87*.

Plate 1 Plan and view of Carrickfergus by Thomas Phillips, 1677–85 (NLI ms 2557)

Plate 2   The castle from the south-west

Plate 3   The castle from the south-east, at high tide

Plate 4 The castle from the south, at low tide

Plate 5 The castle from the north-east, at low tide

Plate 6 The keep, inner and middle wards, from the north

Plate 7 The inner curtain from the south-west, showing the change of stone in the quoins and the original windows cut by gunports

Plate 8 The castle from the north-west

Plate 9 The south-west angle of the keep, showing its junction with the inner and middle wards

Plate 10 The keep and inner ward from the north-east

Plate 11 The keep from the south-east

Plate 12 The east side of the inner ward, showing the site of the first hall and of the original entrance

Plate 13 The east flank of the inner curtain

Plate 14 The third floor of the keep, looking north-west (Photo: B C S Wilson)

Plate 15 The north-west angle of the middle curtain showing infilled rock-cut ditch

Plate 16 The battlements of the keep looking south

Plate 17 The forework of the keep

Plate 18 The east tower at low tide

Plate 19   The west tower and gun platform

Plate 20   The outer ward and the gatehouse from the south

Plate 21 The gatehouse from the north-east

Plate 22 The east tower of the gatehouse from the grand battery

Plate 23 General view of the 1955 excavations (Photo: B C S Wilson)

Plate 24 1955 excavations: the junction of the broad and narrow sections of the middle curtain (Photo: B C S Wilson)

Plate 25 1955 excavations: wall 1 crossing the middle curtain and the outer curtain butted against it. Junction of outer and middle curtains marked by ranging rod (Photo: B C S Wilson)

Plate 26 1955 excavations: tower trenches, showing walls 1, 2 and 3 (Photo: B C S Wilson)

Plate 27 Decorated sgraffito sherds from the 1955 excavations

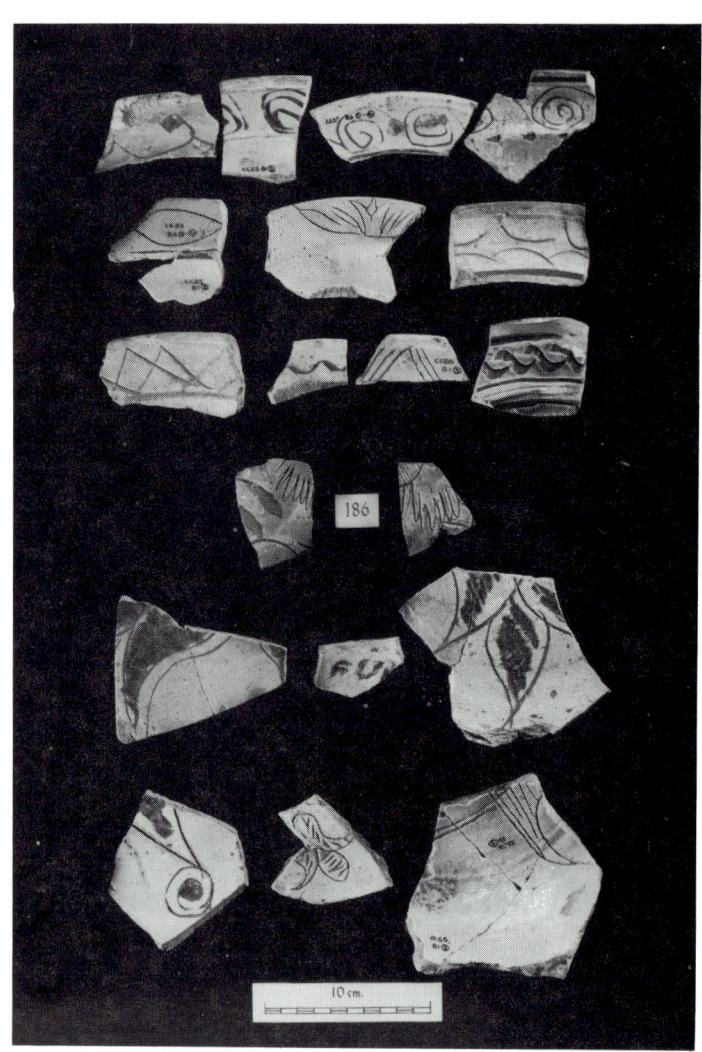

Plate 28 Seal-box lid from the 1955 excavations; lower face to the left, upper face to the right

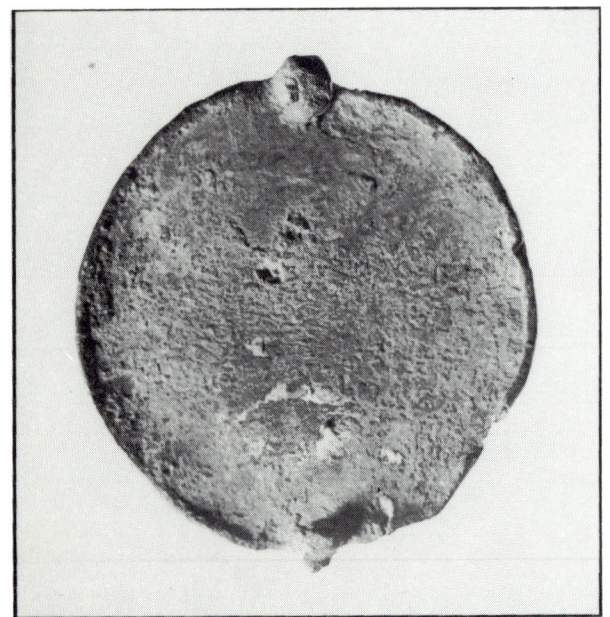

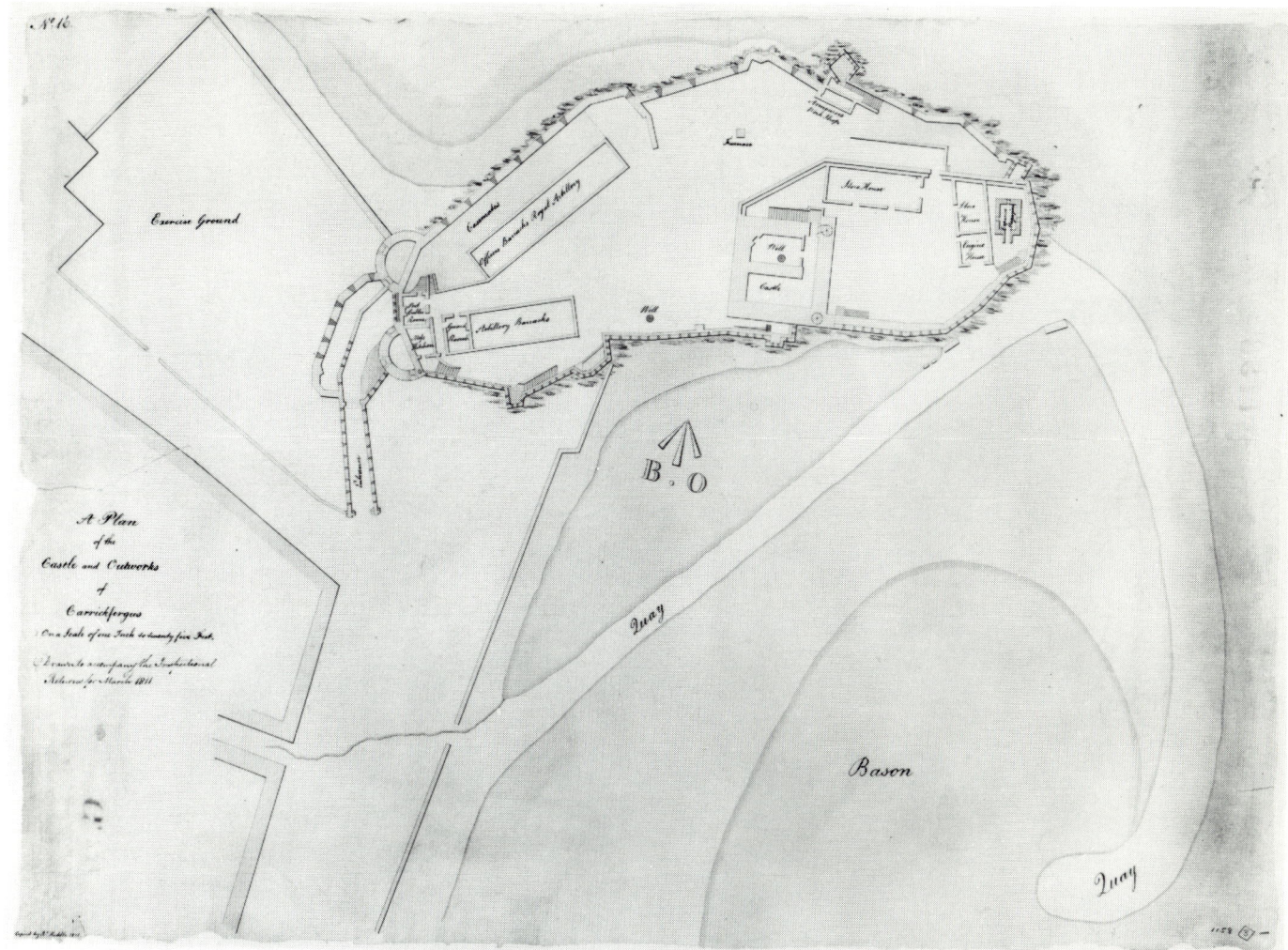

Plate 29 Plan of the castle in 1811 (PRO WO 78/1158)

Printed in Northern Ireland for Her Majesty's Stationery Office by W. & G. Baird Ltd, Antrim
Dd 622243 K12 2/81